revised edition

W9-BMG-089

making a living
in your
Local Music Market

Realizing Your Marketing Potential

by Dick Weissman

ISBN 0-7935-9562-2

HAL•LEONARD®
CORPORATION

7777 W. BLUEMOUND RD. P.O. BOX 13819 MILWAUKEE, WI 53213

Visit Hal Leonard Online at
www.halleonard.com

ISBN 0-7935-9562-2

Dick Weissman is available for seminars on various aspects of the music business. For further information, contact Skye Griffith at Skyline Talent,1424 Larimer St., Ste. 300, Denver, CO 80202, (303) 595-8747.

Contents

Chapter 18

Afterword: The Global Marketplace

Appendix A

Preface

T he main purpose of this book is to provide you with an understanding of the options and choices that make up a career in the contemporary world of music. It may not be the easiest life in the world, but a thorough understanding of your career options should provide you with some practical information about whether it is the life that will fulfill your needs.

Special thanks to Marv Mattis, to my editor, Ronny Schiff, Harry Tuft, Dan Fox, and to Paul Weissman for computerization. This book is dedicated to all the people who are helping the regional music scenes to grow, especially to Ernie Gammage in Austin, Katherine Dines in Denver, and to Larry Littman and Richard Ranta in Memphis. I also wish to express my gratitude to all the artists and managers who submitted promotional materials.

Thanks to John Cerullo at Hal Leonard for getting the revised edition off the ground. Thanks to Paul Weissman for computer fail-safe procedures.

Thanks to Arthur Bernstein at the Liverpool Institute of Performing Arts, for shedding light on European perspectives, Alan Remington of Orange Coast Community College for his night club gig formula, and to Tim Hayes at Elmhurst College and Bruce Ronkin at Northeastern University for their ideas and insights about various issues. Finally, thanks to Ron Sobel for his chapter on the shape of the future and for many stimulating discussions.

Introduction

This is a good book. If you are browsing and haven't bought it yet, buy it. If you own it, congratulations!

The strength of this music do-it-yourself book is that Dick Weissman really knows what he's talking about. He is a savvy music industry professional (a veteran of both the New York and Los Angeles music scenes), who has a finely-honed sensitivity to the problems of "out of towners" who want to make music their living but who, for one reason or another, have decided to do their living outside of the major music centers-Hollywood, New York, Nashville and Toronto. He knows the music of out-of-towners well because, as a long time resident of the Denver area, he is indeed one of them.

Never before in the history of pop music has there been a better time for musicians in regional music centers to seriously pursue music careers with the expectation that their efforts will pay off. The music of the '50s and '60s broke the ground for regional centers. It encouraged people from all areas and walks of life to create music. The wide range of musical "bags"or styles that are currently recorded, presented on stage and aired on radio and television reflect the sheer variety of the creative musical opportunities that exist in today's world. It is crystal clear that music is no longer the private property of an elite group of writers and musicians who work out of the four music mecca cities of North America. Recording equipment has become so inexpensive that basic recording can be done anywhere there is an electrical socket and some talent. Look at the Chart of Music Business Centers on page 3 to get an idea of how decentralized the business has become. In the 1940s, if you wanted to make a record, it was New York, Los Angeles and marginally, Nashville. Period!

The scope of this book is remarkable. Weissman crosses all the "t's" and dots all the "i's" in a way that only someone who has lived his subject matter can do. That kind of attention to detail puts this book in a very special category of self-help music books.

If that were all it did, this book would earn a place on many a bookshelf. Happily, however, the book offers even more. It is not simply a manual on how to get things done—it offers considerable scope and insight into the business of music.

The only negative I feel about *Making a Living in Your Local Music Market* is that I'm green with envy that I did not write it.

Marv Mattis
Hollywood, September, 1989

Author's Note: I guess Marv did take this book seriously. He now lives in Santa Fe, New Mexico.

chapter   1

Can a Musician Make a Living outside the Major Music Centers?

Twenty years ago, I wrote a book about the music industry entitled, *The Music Business: Career Opportunities and Self Defense.* My goal in writing that book was to provide a general outline for musicians about the way the music industry works, how artists get contracts with major record companies, what these contracts commit the artist and the record company to, the functions of agents, managers and music publishers, etc.

The more I used that book in my own teaching, and the more I read about the music industry in the numerous books that have appeared since then, I began to realize that there was a whole area of the business that I had neglected. The music industry in North America is centered in the cities of Los Angeles, Nashville, New York and Toronto. Outside these cities you will not find any major record company headquarters. Chicago is an important center for the production and recording of commercials, but has much less activity in the areas of records and television. Few network radio or television commercials are conceived or produced outside the major music markets, and only a handful of major talent agencies or personal management firms can be found in regional markets. Yet there is a lively music business, with many musicians and singers working in such markets, and there are many others trying to break into the business.

This book is intended to help you explore the options for musicians and singers who want to pursue music business careers, and who are not necessarily concerned about the "big time," but are worried about whether they can make enough money to put bread on the table and gas in their cars. Each chapter of this book covers various aspects of local music markets.

I have done almost all of the things I am writing about, and I continue to do them today. I've sung and played in a touring group that recorded three albums for Capitol, recorded solo albums for major and minor labels, worked as a contract songwriter for two different publishers in New York and Los Angeles, written two feature film scores for low-budget films produced in Colorado, and have done extensive studio work. I have also written songs and instrumental music for several theatrical works and produced records as a staff and independent producer for various large and small record companies on a local, regional and national basis.

Twenty-five years ago, I moved to the Denver-Boulder area, where out of necessity I gained a new perspective on the nature of the music industry. Why did I move to Denver in the first place? After working on and off for more than ten years in the New York market, I realized that as long as I stayed in New York, I would earn the bulk of my income from playing on commercials. Although I don't have anything against doing commercials and was always happy to get the healthy re-use checks for commercials that ran for as long as ten years, I did not make the mistake of confusing this income with the reasons that caused me to choose music as a profession to express my feelings and ideas in the medium with which I am most comfortable. The point that I am making is that after building up a whole network of contacts in New York, I had to start over again in order to learn what life in the music world was like outside the "big city." This book is designed to help you to avoid my somewhat haphazard trial and error process, to steer clear of my mistakes, and to be able to scope out local opportunities while developing an overall understanding of the music industry.

There are four major music markets in North America (See the chart on the following page.) These markets are in Nashville, New York, Los Angeles and Toronto. Although all of these cities provide work in all aspects of music, Los Angeles and Toronto are centers for a tremendous amount of film and television work; Nashville specializes in records; and New York remains the center for recording radio and television commercials.

Music Business Centers

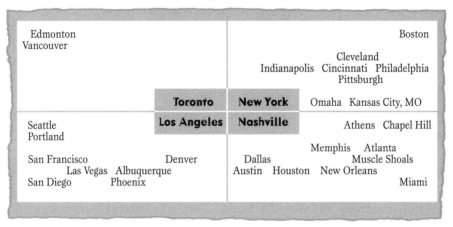

Edmonton Vancouver			Boston
			Cleveland Indianapolis Cincinnati Philadelphia Pittsburgh
	Toronto	**New York**	Omaha Kansas City, MO
Seattle Portland	**Los Angeles**	**Nashville**	Athens Chapel Hill
San Francisco Las Vegas Albuquerque San Diego Phoenix	Denver	Dallas Austin Houston	Memphis Atlanta Muscle Shoals New Orleans Miami

Although most of the major business of music takes place in the four music centers, there is a great deal of regional and some national recording work in what are called the secondary music markets: Atlanta, Austin, Chicago, Dallas, Memphis, Miami, Minneapolis, Montreal, New Orleans, Philadelphia, Portland, San Francisco, Seattle and Vancouver. They are active in different ways, as you'll see later. For example, Austin is an important center for songwriters and records, while the Dallas-Fort Worth area is a very active jingle center. Another group of cities has an even smaller, but still tasty piece of the pie. These are Athens (Georgia), Chapel Hill, Cleveland, Calgary, Denver, Muscle Shoals and Phoenix.

Try to think of the music business as a large circle, with the four major areas in the center, the secondary markets constituting the satellites somewhat removed from the center of the circle, and the less active areas surrounding the far edges of the circle.

The basic assumption governing this book is that for one reason or another you do not wish to, or cannot move to one of the major music business centers. This may be because you are not comfortable in a high-pressure, heavy-hype sort of environment. The major music centers, with the possible exception of Nashville, are congested, overpopulated and share a high cost of living. It may be that you simply like the place where you live, or that you have developed a variety of music contacts in your town that you are reluctant to abandon. It is also possible that family commitments or other business opportunities require you to stay where you are.

Finding the Right Place

Even if you do not wish to relocate to one of the major music business centers, you may wish to live in a city where there is a bit more action than your current location offers. I have a friend named Jerome Gilmer who moved from Macon, Georgia to Denver, where he has established a thriving, although not a gigantic, business doing music for commercials and film and video projects. He consciously chose to move to a larger market, but not to one of the four major cities where he felt that he might be lost in the music business shuffle.

How can you tell whether there is more happening in another town than where you are currently living or working? There are a number of sources that you can turn to for assistance. You can write to one of the many locals of the Musicians' Union (American Federation of Musicians), get in touch with local songwriters' organizations or check out weekly entertainment papers from various towns. Appendix B of this book will tell you how to access these sources. You can also check with music schools in the area, consult the *Yellow Pages* of the phone book, or look for lists of recording studios in the annual *Mix Magazine Directory.*

It is an excellent idea to visit your prospective hometown. Check out how it feels to you, find out what housing and food costs are like, and try to determine whether the skills that you have to offer seem to be in short supply, or if the market is flooded with possible competitors.

Remember, there are many types of work available for musicians. You should also be conscious of the changes that develop over time. Today's regional hotspot may become tomorrow's ghost town, or vice versa. The Seattle music market went from being invisible to being the center of "grunge" music, and subsequently has eased back to a position as an important regional music marketplace.

Developing and Packaging the Product: You!

Can you make a living in music? The first rule of survival is to *have a product to sell.* Whatever your musical skill, package it in a form that is accessible to people who are not musicians, and who may lack interest or knowledge about complex aspects of musical style. When a club owner asks what kind of music you play, don't simply tell him "everything." Hand him a tape, a video or a promo kit that explains who you are and what you do.

Once you have a product to sell, whether it's a Dixieland band, a rhythm and blues combo, or whatever, *package the product.* A promo kit should contain such items as pictures, a group bio, reviews, set lists, lists of places you have played, a recording (if you have one), and a list of significant appearances at clubs or schools that your client will recognize.

Packaging the product includes coming up with a name for your group—one that is attention-getting, but not too bizarre (unless, of course, you plan to build your reputation by emphasizing the bizarre).

For example, "The Monday Night Band" is not a good name for an alternative rock group. On the other hand, "Twisted Methuselah" is not a good name for a cocktail lounge group. Know who you are and design your promo kit to stress the particular style of music you are selling. Then direct it in a way that will be comfortable for the type of client who is to apt to buy your sound. The style in which you write your bio and the sort of pictures that you include should reflect the spirit of your musical focus.

Once you have packaged your presentation, it is time to get that package to local buyers, local agents, and anyone else you can think of who might offer you work. If you don't plan to pursue a career outside of the area where you live, it is probably unnecessary for you to have a personal manager.

Local agents may have access to employment opportunities behind the scenes. I call these jobs "invisible work." Invisible work involves performances that are not open to the general public. Certain cities are popular convention centers for regional meetings or national conventions. Sometimes, a one hour job for such a group pays better than a whole week of working in a club for four or five hours a night. (See the chart on page 6 that breaks down the differences between visible and invisible work.)

One of the reasons that agents have access to conventions is that often there is more talent being booked than simply music. The agent may book typists, models, comedians, and together with a caterer, may even be partly responsible for the physical arrangement of the meeting. Caterers, by the way, are another source of invisible work. They may even recommend you to a client without you knowing about it.

Grants provide another source of invisible work. There are state, federal and city grants for musicians and composers, and there are also grant monies available through private or corporate foundations. Each state has an artist in residence program, which sends artists (including musicians) into schools, nursing homes, prisons and communities in any part of the state. Additional grants are available through state or federal humanities programs. Humanities grants usually involve critical studies about various forms of music. There are also state and federal grant programs in the folk arts.

Visible and Invisible Work

Visible Work	
Type of Work	**Primary Sources of Work**
Night clubs, concerts, resorts, restaurants	Booking agents; occasionally personal managers; auditions
Recording artist career	Personal manager; sometimes music business attorney; rarely audition tape or word of mouth
Songwriting	Music publishers
School performances through Young Audiences or other arts organizations	Auditions
Symphony jobs	Solo performances through personal managers; regular orchestral jobs by audition

Invisible Work	
Type of Work	**Primary Sources of Work**
Conventions	Booking agents; caterers; event planners
Writing Commercials	Personal contacts; a demo
Writing special material (e.g. songs for specific events)	Agents; personal contacts
Freelance musial work (touring shows, pops symphony gigs)	Personal contact with contractors; word of mouth; referral
Grants	Contact state, community or federal arts councils or foundations; research books about grant programs
Weddings, parties, funerals, celebrations, proms, fraternity parties, church work	Agents; union; direct contact
Studio work	Recording studios; contractors; word of mouth
Overseas tours, cruises	Direct contact (see resources)

Other Sources of Work

Ads in Yellow Pages; demo tape or video; union referral books; cards at wedding party supply or music stores; cold calls to prospective clients; auditions for band leaders; referrals from your teacher; sharing leads with others

A key factor in pursuing a lifetime career in music is *developing versatility*. The more instruments that you can play and the more musical styles that you master, the better are your chances of getting freelance work. This work may be in local recording studios, dinner theaters, playing for touring Broadway shows, the circus or for touring ice shows. Besides having the ability to play more than one musical instrument, it is desirable to develop your skills both in reading music at sight and being able to improvise. Usually, there is one relatively short rehearsal before you are expected to go out and do a professional performance, where you sound good and play in tune. If you play rhythm-section instruments such as guitar, keyboard, electric bass or drums, you also need to have instruments and accessories that are used in current musical styles.

There are also some psychological aspects involved in pick-up jobs such as the ability to get along with conductors, contractors and other musicians. You must be able to perform well under what can be intense pressure. It is also important to have a broad grasp of musical styles so that you can understand the nuances of, say, swing vs. Dixieland jazz, or bebop.

Full-time music teachers have a steady source of income, and hopefully enough job security to enable them to survive. Teaching part-time can provide you with a useful source of extra income, and may even prove helpful in improving your own skills. Teaching opportunities can be found at local colleges, community colleges, music studios, private schools, in your own home or music studio, and through grant-funded artist-in-residence programs. Other possibilities are after school programs at local schools, YWCA/YMCA classes, churches, private schools or community organizations.

Another key to your ability to get work is to *use organizations as a source of referrals*. There are some three hundred locals of the American Federation of Musicians in North America. They all receive calls asking for harpists to play at weddings, bluegrass or Dixieland bands to play outdoor concerts, organists to perform at churches, etc. There are pros and cons of union membership, but the union can provide a considerable amount of work for local musicians. Together with record companies, they co-sponsor the Music Performance Trust Fund, which provides matching funds to subsidize concerts in malls, hospitals, and schools all over North America. Some local unions have actually begun to act as booking agencies for their members,

Unions are only one of many possible sources for job referrals. Local recording studios, music stores, and state or community arts councils can also provide you with job leads. One friend of mine got a six-month residency in Saipan through a referral from the Colorado Arts Council.

Tips for Composers & Songwriters

If you feel you have skills as a composer, available local work includes writing words and music for jingles, doing musical arrangements for jingles or theater works, scores for short of feature films, music for slide shows, and writing special material for such venues as planetariums. Celebrations of special events can offer additional opportunities.

If you are a songwriter, the publisher of your music has the legal right to control the first recording of a song. Under copyright law, once that recording is issued, anyone can record a song, provided they pay royalties to the publisher. Songwriting can also provide the writer with entrance into the world of the recording studio. It is quite possible that the songwriter may be used to sing or play background parts on a record. This is a double opportunity—you can contribute musically to the realization of your song and you can also earn good money for performing on the recording session. You should certainly pursue such opportunities, but never push your talents so aggressively that an artist or producer not only refuses to hire you on the session, but also turns against your song. Because the modern world of recording includes the use of synthesizers, drum machines, sequencers and samplers, it may be possible for a composer to "realize" most of the musical score without the aid of other musicians. Another possibility is to use a few other players or singers to provide a specific sound that a machine can't successfully emulate, but to do most of the work with synthesizers.

The opportunity of hearing your own work on tape will undoubtedly lead to further progress in your own musical career. You may find that some of the instruments that you play don't sound good enough for a recording, or that your skills on, say oboe, are considerably less than what you had hoped or fantasized. Recording generally serves to deepen a musician's understanding of what she can do, and perhaps also what's best to avoid. Sometimes, an understanding of your own limitations will lead to collaborations which themselves may bring you more work through the network of contacts your collaborators have developed.

The Multi-Dimensional Musician

As a musician or singer, you may find that you are perfectly able to function in more than one musical group. In one group you may be the leader, hiring the other musicians, taking responsibility for the sound system and musical arrangements, and receiving as much as double the wages of the other musicians. In another group you may simply be a side musician, taking a call from another leader to play a particular date for a given fee. As a side musician you should not be responsible for anything other than playing the date—the headaches are the leader's problem. Some musicians function better as leaders; some prefer less responsibility and willingly (or unwillingly) accept less money. An alternative is a cooperative group, where everyone splits the money evenly and tasks are shared. One person may be responsible for the sound system, one may actually book the job, another may own the van, and so forth.

Sometimes, a group starts out as a cooperative, but various people drop out. The remaining leader actually owns the name and hires new musicians for set (usually lower) wages. This is what happened when Kenny Rogers took over the First Edition, which subsequently became known as Kenny Rogers and the First Edition. Many of the touring '60s and '70s rock bands like The Mamas & The Papas and Kiss have similarly evolved.

There are innovative ways of participating in more than one musical group. In Aspen, Colorado (a small town renowned for its skiing and summer music festival) during the busy ski season, some local musicians work as many as three musical jobs a day playing such events as breakfast meetings; after-ski jobs in clubs or ski lodges; and evening nightclub gigs. Some of the rock groups turn into country groups by adding or subtracting a key player or two.

A bluegrass group based in the Denver-Boulder area came up with an entertaining solution to the problem of wanting to play more than one style of music, and yet having a specific musical identity to sell to the public. As Hot Rize, this four-piece vocal and instrumental group played bluegrass and newgrass music, using the traditional instrumentation of banjo, fiddle or mandolin, guitar and bass. After the first set of their shows, they came back on stage in different outfits and with electric and lap steel guitars. The "second band" was called Red Knuckles and the Trailblazers. The two bands dressed differently—the performers even referred to one another by different names in the second band. They carried this device to such extremes that they even recorded a number of albums under each band's name. Hot Rize stuck to bluegrass and Red Knuckles performed Texas swing and some rock and roll oldies. The band no longer exists on a regular basis, but during occasional reunion tours they retain both identities.

Besides greatly expanding their audience appeal, these musicians found an amusing and innovative way of gaining acceptance in more than one musical genre. This kept their music fresh and vital, while expanding their opportunities to work.

Financing and Marketing CDs and Tapes

Many musicians dream of making their own recordings, setting down on tape their own musical concepts and selling them in the marketplace. For the vast majority of musicians, the dream of finding a national recording contract with a major label is just that, a "dream." More and more musicians are producing their own recordings, usually in relatively modest quantities for their own local markets. These recordings can be financed and marketed in a number of ways. One option is for musicians to finance the recordings themselves. Good studios are now available in almost all local markets with engineers who are conscientious and capable. They may not have the latest multi-track digital machines or automated mixing consoles, but every major city has a number of twenty-four track studios, not to mention the proliferation of one inch sixteen track equipment, semi-pro four and eight-track basement studio operations.

There has also been a major change in the picture since the first edition of this book was published in 1990. Currently, 8-track A-DAT machines are available for about $3,000. The machines can be ganged together, so that three machines give you the capability of 24 tracks for an investment of under $10,000. This does not include the purchase of microphones and a mixing console. The bottom line is that with an investment of $10,000-$15,000 your band can have a 16- 24-track studio at your rehearsal space. Another piece of good news is that the cost of A-DAT tapes is about $15 for a forty-minute tape or $42 if you use 24 tracks. Compare this with tape costs of $600 and up to make an album in the old analog format.

CDR Formats

Many producers are now using the CDR format instead of dealing with mastering studios. A CDR is a CD reference disk and the master can be manufactured directly from it. Since high-end mastering studios charge from $3,000 to $5,000 to master albums, and cutting a CDR at a studio costs less than $100, there is a considerable saving involved.

Some artists are actually manufacturing their own CDs by using CD "burners": machines that duplicate CDs. All the artist needs to do is buy a blank disk to duplicate the album. The price of these machines is continually going down and at this time is around $2,000. During the next few years, it will undoubtedly go down further, as the demand for them increases.

This is an ideal way for artists who intend to sell their albums in performance or on the Internet to cut costs to a minimum. Since most radio stations won't play cassettes, some artists are cutting a minimal number of CDs and giving them to a minimal number of local radio stations.

Superstar artists still use mastering studios because they have a broad range of high-end equipment that can improve the sound of an album; most recordings don't really need this extra level of sound processing.

Many artists are recording their own albums on A-DATS and then taking the master tapes to a well-equipped studio to do the mix. This enables the band to pursue the tracking and vocals at their own pace. Depending upon what city you live in, a 24-track studio rental can cost anything from about $50 an hour to five times that amount. Some major label rock bands are taking their A-DATS on tour with them to use as either songwriting tools or to cut part of their albums on the road.

Let's get back to the subject of financing your project. It is possible to raise money from a specific investor or a group of investors. These may be people who are friends of the artists and have a sincere interest in helping the artist find an outlet for his music. One friend of mine in Denver actually sold shares for his recording project to a group of investors. He was able to raise a considerable amount of money for what was basically a local project.

If you raise money from a group of investors, it is important for you to explain there is a good chance they will either lose most of their investment or that they will end up making little or no income from the project. Many investors have some sort of fantasy of financing a massive supergroup operating out of a city like Terre Haute, Indiana. Of course, anything is possible in the music business, but it is important that you explain the risks inherent in music projects to your investors. Since the investors are often family members, if you don't give them an accurate picture of what is involved, relationships may be irreparably damaged.

Even some artists of national stature, like John Prine or Arlo Guthrie, have begun to release their own recordings. As the record companies become larger and increasingly corporate, the break-even point on a record is so high that even sales of a hundred thousand records are considered unsatisfactory. Through the complicated arithmetic of the record business with its many deductions from royalties for packaging, promotion copies and "breakage" fees, a locally-produced record may actually generate more revenue for an artist than one produced by a major label.

Some artists, like Ani DiFranco and Fugazi, prefer to establish their own record labels because they simply don't want to be marketed or controlled by multi-national conglomerates whose primary interest is often not in the artist's music but in the sales of a "product." Di Franco has even established her own label in Buffalo, New York(!) Instead of receiving a royalty of 10-12% of the retail selling price of her recordings, she is the record company. A few aspects of control that disturb artists are the way an album is advertised; the cover art; the use of outside record producers who do not always share an artist's musical vision; and in general the world of the corporate "suits."

If the artist owns the record label, she must undertake all of the financial risks, but she also gets all of the profits. Since Di Franco is now selling more than fifty thousand copies of her albums, this has been for her something of a financial bonanza.

Remember that the ability to sell a locally-produced recording involves such matters as getting airplay, newspaper publicity, store displays, collecting money from record stores or distributors, and most of all, selling recordings before, during and after performances.

CDs Vs. Cassettes

With the exception of dance music and some alternative or punk rock projects, vinyl is a dead item. Regardless of whether you personally like the medium of vinyl, the fact is that turntables are a dying breed. This leaves you with the question of whether to go with cassettes or CDs for your album.

The main advantage of cassettes is that they can be duplicated in small quantities. They are also extremely portable. If you play regularly in tourist resorts, there is a much greater chance that travelers will have Walkman machines, and cassette players are much more common in cars than are CDs. However most radio stations will not play cassettes, because it is a nuisance to find specific tracks, and the sound quality is not acceptable.

There are a number of advantages of CDs. They last longer than cassettes because they are larger in size, the cover art is more appealing, and in general, presenting a club owner or a prospective record company with a CD package will make a much better impression of your professionalism than a cassette package. There is also more room inside the jewel box for readable album notes if you wish to include lyrics or information about the songs or your band. When cassette J-card inserts contain much printed information, they require the buyer to possess Superman's X-Ray vision to read them.

CDs must be duplicated in quantities of a thousand to be cost effective. There are duplicators that will sell you five hundred copies, though usually the price of a thousand albums is only half as much as a five hundred CD run. In other words, five hundred CDs might cost you $1,000; a thousand albums might come in at $1,400 or $1,500. The final price will depend on such issues as whether you are providing cover art, who is printing the CD booklets, whether you want the company to design the package, etc. Low budget CDs feature two color generic album covers, though they have little individuality or appeal. See the Resources section at the end of this chapter for information about locating duplicators for your album.

Another new development since the first edition of this book is the use of CDRs for mastering. A CDR is a CD reference disk that can be made in many recording studios today. The cost of making this disk is about $50-$100. It is no longer necessary to send records out to a separate mastering facility to be processed. This saves about $500, depending on what studio is used and how much time is spent on the mastering.

One of the keys to selling recordings locally is to develop an extensive mailing list. These people constitute a ready audience for your product. They are interested in an artist on a personal and musical level, as well as provide a ready market for any recordings you may make. On the following page is a chart that illustrates the advantages of recording for a record company as opposed to producing your own album.

Before we leave the subject of independent recording, Eugene Chadbourne presents a dissenting opinion about cassettes in his entertaining book, *I Hate the Man Who Runs This Bar.* Chadbourne has achieved an "underground" reputation as a creative guitarist who spans many musical styles. He prefers to make cassettes, re-recording over old cassettes and actually hand-making creative covers for each unit. This may strike you as being extremely impractical, but consider whether you have the equipment to duplicate cassettes at home. Since Chadbourne has a reputation as an innovative musician in the first place, it could well be that his way of doing things is quite appealing to his fans.

Dealbreakers

Over the years, I have produced many projects for artists who have released their own recordings. I also have many other friends who have produced similar projects, and know many artists who have released their own recordings. Far too many

Record Companies vs. Producing Your Own Album

Advantages	
Self-production	**Record Company Production**
Total creative control of music	Better budget
More money per unit	Better distribution
Control of advertising and imaging	Possible overseas release
Retain all publishing rights	Access to radio and record stores
Control cover art, notes, production	Possible access to major producer

Disadvantages	
Self-production	**Record Company Production**
Bookkeeping, bill collection if albums are consigned	Could be lost in shuffle of a company's other products
Must pay for pressing, recording, graphics, etc.	Company will probably control cover art, imaging of group
Necessity of raising funds	Most records never earn any royalties at all
Paperwork, promotion, constant follow-up calls	Reduced publishing royalties or loss of publishing rights

of these projects went astray because the artist had devoted considerable thought and preparation to the artistic and technical aspects of recording, but very little consideration to the marketing of the recordings. In my opinion, there are two fundamental questions that an artist must answer before pursuing this avenue:

1. How will the record be sold and/or distributed? Will the record be in stores? Will it be available outside of your home town? Will there be any effort. made to get radio play?
2. Who will do follow-up to get paid for records that are consigned? Who will keep appropriate receipts for tax records? Who will obtain a bar code for the record (if it is sold in stores)? Who will work with the graphic artist, etc.? If no one in your band is willing or able to do this boring but important work, do you have a manager or even a family member who can do it for you?

In my opinion, if you are unable to answer any of the preceeding questions, it would be wise to delay making a record until you figure out the business side of your particular story.

Other Opportunities in Local Markets

Even an artist who has no particular desire to tour nationally can maintain and utilize national contacts to advance her career in such areas as songwriting, developing instructional materials for other musicians and obtaining some regional college bookings. Regional college booking conferences provide the opportunity to expand the geographic area an artist covers. Other opportunities are available for high school concerts, performances in public schools, and for specialized audiences such as senior centers and nursing homes. In the Appendix A of this book are resources for contacting the people who can provide this work.

One of the ways to keep a musical career alive and vital is to keep studying new or old forms of music. This can be done at local colleges or through private teachers. Developing new skills is a good way to maintain your interest in music, which may open up new employment opportunities. Classes and seminars are offered in many areas of the country that will enable you to meet successful professionals who are working in fields such as songwriting and arranging.

There is more involved however, other than getting jobs. A musician should strive to keep his level of enthusiasm high. This is a necessity to successful performing, but is also important in terms of maintaining a long-term career in music. The longer one has been playing music, the more exciting it is to find new musical areas to explore. If you are able to continually expand your musical horizons, you will be able to renew your enthusiasm in music as a profession.

It is also possible to work and tour nationally, but live in an area outside the major music centers. By utilizing business help in the form of a personal manager, booking agency or attorney who is knowledgeable about music business procedures, a performer can live anywhere she chooses, as long as her business is being run by skilled professionals. The late-1990s found John Cougar Mellencamp living on an Indiana farm; Gloria Estefan in Miami; Pearl Jam and a number of other artists in Seattle; and other artists spread out all over North America. Some artists maintain more than one residence, sharing their time between idyllic spots like Aspen, Colorado and Los Angeles. All of the artists mentioned above are active in the business and tour on a regular basis.

CHAPTER 1 RESOURCES

In addition to the more detailed information available in the appendices, each chapter will list some useful basic resources that will provide the reader with information that is relevant to the chapter itself.

Working As a Musician

Buttwinick, Marty. *How to Make a Living as a Musician So You Never Have to Work a Day Job Again!* Glendale: Sonata Publications, 1993. This guide is detailed to the point of being irritating, but has many useful tips for freelance musicians. It is particularly valuable if you contemplate leading any sort of band.

Chadbourne, Eugene. *I Hate The Man Who Runs This Bar: The Survival Guide for Real Musicians.* Emoryville, CA: Mix Publications, 1997. Chadbourne definitely has an off-beat approach, but if you are interested in musical styles that are off the beaten track, this book is for you. It is useful to freelancers and members of musical groups.

Levine, Mike. *How to Be a Working Musician.* New York: Billboard Books, 1997. Probably the best guide currently available for those whose goal is to be freelance musicians. The book presupposes that you are living, or want to live in a large city, and offers information about writing and playing on jingles, working in one dance band groups that play for weddings or social functions, theater work, etc. A number of brief but helpful interviews with other musicians are included.

Note: A number of other books on this subject have appeared in the last few years. Many of them are listed in Appendix D, but the three listed above are, in my opinion, the best currently available.

Making & Selling Your Own Records

Rapaport, Diane Sward. *How to Make & Sell Your Own Recording: A Guide for the Nineties.* Englewood Cliffs: Prentice Hall, 1992, Revised Fourth Edition. The best source of information on album design, graphics, consignments, building a mailing list, etc.

Stanfield, Jana. *Making & Selling Your Own CDs & Cassettes.* Cincinnati: Writer's Digest, 1997. Somewhat similar to Rapaport, but the author is herself a writer and performer, and has a somewhat different perspective.

Sweeney, Tom & Mark Geller. *Tim Sweeney's Guide to Releasing Independent Records.* Torrance: TSA Books, 1997. Sweeney has a very realistic perspective on contemporary radio.

Note: The Rapaport and Stanfield books tend to focus on folk, New Age and singer-songwriter sorts of records, and Sweeney's book is almost entirely oriented to rock records. None of these books are very useful with regard to what it takes to make records, as opposed to selling them.

CD Pressing

Two publications feature many advertisements for pressing and album production facilities. They are: *Billboard* and the *Music Connection.* These ads also appear to a lesser degree in other music business periodicals. See Appendix D for addresses.

Getting It Together:

Developing Your Talent

How do people learn to sing and play and what enables them to parlay that early talent into a career in music? There are no single, simple answers to these questions. To a great extent, it's primarily a matter of desire. Watch any three or four year old child. Invariably, kids of that age hum and sing to themselves and make up their own tunes. Sometimes, the words don't make a lot of sense, but are simply a single phrase that the child repeats over and over again. When my son was that age, he became fixated on the phrase "Colorado Railroad Train," and he would sit in the back of the car singing and humming that phrase repeatedly.

The point is that for most people, talent is not necessarily as significant as most people think it is. It's a question of how talent is developed, and in what direction it is taken. Most people probably have some musical talent— they simply don't bother to use or direct it.

Over the years, I have watched some students who I thought had very little natural musical ability mature into excellent musicians. They did it by practicing longer and harder than their more gifted peers. Some of these musical "ugly ducklings" went on to achieve successful careers as professional musicians.

Unfortunately, the young child who likes rock or country music is not apt to get much musical help in school. School music programs are oriented towards band instruments and the performance of existing materials. Vocal music programs tend to stress choral singing, except for occasional forays into musical theater productions.

Studying various kinds of music in school can be a very useful and even exciting experience, but most schools don't allow much flexibility in what the student is allowed to study. Because of this fact, we have the phenomenon of a well-trained teacher who has never heard of the musical artists that his students listen to and appreciate, and whose records they actually "study."

Schools have not adjusted to the notion that pop music, whether country, rock or rap, is essentially a rhythm-section-oriented form. The principal instruments are electric bass, drums, keyboards and guitars. Other instruments perform auxiliary roles. This is not true in middle-of-the-road (MOR) styles of pop music performed by such singers as Barbra Streisand or Celine Dion, nor is it necessarily true in jazz, where horns or saxes often dominate.

Many rock and country stars are self-taught or have taken lessons outside the school music setting. Schools often take the position that everything starts with the study of classical music or swing-style big band jazz. It follows from these assumptions that each student must learn to play band or orchestral instruments and learn these styles of music before attempting any other musical genres.

If you want to play or sing rock or country music, don't expect a lot of help from the academic world. This is not to say that you're left on your own out in the cold. There are good rhythm section players all over North America. The ones you want to seek out for lessons are the ones who not only play the music that you like but also have the ability to teach what they know. A good teacher is not always a "monster" player, but is someone who has the ability to analyze musical styles and to translate that analysis into a form that a student can grasp.

Look for people who have some teaching experience and who enjoy sharing their knowledge of playing or singing. Avoid those with too many outside commitments, who don't seem to remember your name or what assignment they gave you last week. Try to avoid teachers who have such a heavy teaching load that they seem to be unable to concentrate on the lesson.

One of the difficulties in learning pop and rock music is that written music is not necessarily the best vehicle for transmitting this information. Though some of the best pop or country performers read music, many do not. Artists who do know or read music often bypass that skill in their everyday work. It's easier to make a rough tape of a song than to bother writing out the melody in music notation. An interview with Stevie Winwood mentioned that he had played music in church at an early age and had even taken college music classes for a year. He then disclosed that he seldom wrote down any music anymore because he could use the medium of tape or store information on computer-based synthesizers.

Reading music should be viewed as a useful tool rather than a substitute for developing your ear or learning how to "fake" and improvise. You can acquire many musical skills by listening to records and singing or playing along with them. There are series of CDs that are designed for that purpose, with the rhythm section on one channel of the stereo, and the lead part on the opposite speaker. You can play along, or you can shut off the lead singer or player and do the solos yourself.

More and more music instruction videos are coming out. The advantage of video instruction is that it shows you how a player holds an instrument, breathes into it or fingers it. A student with a good ear can benefit from audio or video instruction tapes, even if he is unable to follow the written music. However, the easiest way for a composer to communicate his music is still to write it down and have singers and instrumentalists read it. Being able to read music also makes it easier to move from band to band or to play in more than one band at the same time.

There are a variety of ways to find teachers. Ask for referrals from better-quality music stores. Some of these stores also employ teachers, so they are apt to recommend their own people. Since the store wants to continue doing business with you, they will probably refer you to someone who is at least competent. You should also check with your local Musician's Union. Most of the good, working professional players will be members of the union, although some good teachers may no longer play professionally. You can also call upon the resources of the music departments of local colleges. Many colleges offer music classes or lessons through their continuing education departments.

Be sure that your lessons will cover things that you want to know, rather than a prescribed course of study that has no relevance to your needs. Check on some of the teacher's credits. With whom have they played? What is their musical education? What kind of music do they like? Do they write any music or have any recording experience? A top-quality teacher can prove to be an excellent source of job referrals, sending you on gigs that she either can't make or chooses not to play. A teacher will seldom refer you for a job that could prove too difficult for your skill levels. After all any recommendation is a reflection on the person who makes it, thus the teacher's reputation will be adversely affected if she gets a call complaining about the poor job her student did.

Studying voice presents its own set of challenges. There are many different styles of vocal production. Aretha Franklin, for example, usually doesn't sing like an opera singer. Singers who have had a great deal of operatic training almost invariably sound stiff when they try to sing contemporary popular music. Broadway vocalizing is sort of a halfway point between current pop styles and "legitimate" singing.

The difficulty here is that if you are in the early stages of a musical career, you may not even know what sort of musical style you are striving to achieve. Try consulting the music department of a local college, or check with a singer who performs locally, whose vocal technique you admire. Where did he study and is he happy with his teacher? Perhaps he gives lessons.

A good voice teacher is a rare gem. He or she can save your life by teaching you how to sing through a cold or tiredness, and can show you vocal exercises that will extend both the top and bottom of your vocal range. This is particularly valuable if you are basically an instrumentalist whose vocal goals are to sing passable harmony back-up parts. If you are able to sing, you will become that much more of an asset to your band.

Beware of the voice teachers who are too psychologically oriented. It is true that your voice will show the effects of tension or illness, but if what you really need is psychological help, you shouldn't be getting it from a voice teacher. Be sure your teacher has a good idea of which kind of musical help you are seeking. Don't let him or her transform your musical style into something grotesque or inappropriate.

Getting the Group Together

Let's assume that you have your singing and playing together and have now decided to either put a band together or join an existing group. How do your find people with whom to sing or play, and what are some of the problems that are apt to come up?

You need to identify exactly what kind of music you want to play and how serious you are about it. Most daily newspapers have ads after their "Musical Instruments for Sale" classifieds that are placed by bands looking for new or additional members, or individuals starting to put a band together. If there is a local entertainment weekly or monthly in your town, you will find similar advertisements in it. Other sources of information are the bulletin boards at music stores and the music departments of local college or community college music departments, community centers, record stores or even supermarkets. Your local Musicians' Union may have a newsletter as well as a bulletin board, and if there is a songwriters' organization in your town, attend some of their meetings and try to hook up with someone who shares your musical interests. Recording studios and instrument repair people are another possible vehicle for your search.

Starting a Band

When you start a band, there are some things you will need to work out. First is the question of leadership. Is one person going to lead the band? If this is the case, that person will usually call the rehearsals, work out some way of getting promotional materials together, book the band himself or talk to booking agents about getting work, set up auditions with club owners, and be the contact person for your band. The leader may also provide and transport the group's sound system. In return for accepting all of these responsibilities, the leader may want an extra share of whatever money the group earns. In the big band era of the '30s and '40s, the band leader always made at least twice as much money as the rest of the band. In fact, even today most union contracts specify that the leader of the group must earn double scale, or twice the minimum wages that the other musicians receive. Some groups split this money, but others do not.

In some groups, one person naturally seems to gravitate towards a leadership role. Often, the other people in the band don't mind—in fact they may feel a sense of relief that someone is willing to take most of the responsibility. Trouble can start however, when it comes time to decide how the music you are going to perform will be chosen. Although a musician may be indifferent to what brand of microphone is on the stand, who is booking the group, when are rehearsal hours, or even what the group wears. Most people will show a great deal of concern about whether their own songs or their choice of cover tunes will be performed, and who is going to sing and play the solo parts.

Sometimes, a group will have one person who acts as the music director; another one who handles the sound equipment; a third who owns the van; and a fourth who does the booking. In these groups, the band usually splits the money as well as the responsibilities.

It is also possible, although clumsy, to apportion income to different group members on an uneven basis. One or two people may actually own the group's name and they may simply hire other people to fill the empty slots. This is typically the case with revival rock groups, where it is the original member or two who owns the name. A new band can't readily afford such a course of action because the group rarely has a guaranteed income.

Sooner or later your band will have to make an important choice. Are you going to be a cover band, doing tunes that are already on the charts? Or are you going to use your band as a vehicle for developing the writing skills of those in the group? Sad to say, though a cover band will have quicker access to work in most local markets—if you don't write songs, there is nothing that will set you apart from the hundreds of other bands performing in your region.

Most groups come up with some sort of compromise. They agree to learn a certain number of contemporary hits in order to get work, but they insert their own tunes into the show, especially very early or late in the evening.

One of the first things you will need to do is to find a name for your musical organization (this will be covered in the next chapter). You will also need to figure out a rehearsal schedule and find a place to practice. You will need to decide who is going to be at your rehearsals, how often they should occur, and how long they should be.

The answers relate to what your goals are. It's partly a question of how old you are and whether you are going to be able to work in bars. Like it or not, the bulk of work in most music markets is in the bar scene. In most states, this means that you must be 21 years old in order to work. Chances are that some of the people in your group have other commitments, whether they include school, jobs, sports, boyfriends or girlfriends. Sometimes, the best way to judge the seriousness of a musician's intentions is by measuring their other commitments.

There are several rules that should work for most rehearsals:

- Start at a set time and work for approximately the same amount of time whenever you practice.
- No visitors should be allowed, unless they are there for a specific reason. For example, you might want to ask another musician to come to a rehearsal to see if the vocal balances are correct. Don't allow friends, people you are dating, fathers, mothers or other relatives or friends to visit.
- Never have anyone who is visiting a rehearsal (who, remember, you are not supposed to have invited) take sides in a group dispute. It's not fair to your fellow band members and it puts the visitor in an embarrassing spot.

Where are you going to rehearse? The answer may depend on the instrumentation and size of your musical group. If you are an acoustic guitar duo, you can probably rehearse in a basement or garage without bothering your family or neighbors. If you're a hard rock band though, you need to look for some "industrial" space where you can scream your lungs out without annoying anyone else. A garage that is soundproofed or set away from the house might do the trick. You may need to consider a space that is not in use at night or on weekends. This could be a school, warehouse, loft or something similar.

In larger cities, rehearsal space is available in buildings set up for that purpose. Sometimes they have keyboards or drum sets available with the room. This is a great convenience, but chances are the rental fees will wreck your budget. Some locals of the Musicians' Union allow members to rehearse in their buildings. This is a good solution, but it may obligate you to join the union at an earlier time in your career than you might otherwise choose. This may be a worthwhile move, depending upon your situation.

Develop some practice routines that will help move your rehearsals along smoothly. Try running over a few old favorites to warm-up. Time should be set aside for working out new songs, experimenting with new arrangements, and perhaps learning some of the latest hits. There is a certain psychology to knowing when to keep rehearsing a song, when to put it aside for another rehearsal, and knowing when to "abandon ship." Not every group can do every song.

Common musical goals are an important part of the glue that can bind a group together in tough times. Without these goals, the group can be destroyed by senseless bickering. One of the most divisive aspects of group decisions is the question of whose material is to be performed and how that choice will be made. It seems that 90% of the time when a person in the band writes a song, she is going to sing the lead part. There is no rational reason for this—it's simply a question of ownership. Most groups would be much better off if they dealt with the question of who sounds best on a particular song, rather than assuming that since Jane wrote it, she ought to sing it. The writer needs to accept that she may not be the one with the best vocal quality for a particular song.

Group members need to be able to criticize each other honestly, without any feeling of bitterness or holding back of opinions. This doesn't mean that a person needs to be insulting or hostile, but that ultimately there is no way to disguise bad news.

Try to look at this from a positive point of view: if you have a band member who is not really a singer, but has a true writing talent, the idea that he won't have to sing the song in order to get it performed can be a very liberating feeling. The writer may then open up and start to compose songs with more demanding vocal parts that he could never personally perform. A spirit of cooperation can develop, where band members make suggestions on minor revisions of a lyric, or a new chord change that brings the tune to a whole new musical or emotional level.

The process of auditioning, whether you are the one on the griddle or the one making the decision, is never much fun. If you are looking for people to form a band, think out clearly what you want them to do. If you want someone who can read music, then obviously you are going to need to have some charts ready to test their reading skills. Can they read fluently, slowly or not at all? Remember that auditions usually make people nervous—don't expect a faultless performance from the outset.

What about musical styles? Do you want a guitar player who is fluent in rock and roll, but who can also play an occasional fingerpicking guitar part on ballads? Be sure that you go through the entire range of music you expect the person to be able to play. Don't just set up a group jam session where everyone plays every blues lick they know, as fast and as loud as possible.

Try to get to know the person you are auditioning, both musically and from the standpoint of what it is going to be like working with him on a daily basis. Does he play other musical styles, like reggae or bluegrass that your band has never attempted? Get as much information as you can. Does he play any other instruments that could add spice to your sound? Many musicians have been through a high school band program where they've learned how to play a horn or a string instrument. Maybe that's just the sound you need to add to a song that has never sounded exactly right.

Be sure to check out the type of equipment your future band member owns. Does he have effects pedals? Is her amp loud enough for the types of rooms you will be playing? Does he have a van that could be used to haul equipment? Does she own any extra microphones or sound equipment? What kind of attitude do you surmise he will project on stage? Can you imagine rehearsing with her, day after day, for months at a time? Does he have a serious interest in music or is this something to pass away a little time before he goes away to college?

If you are the one who is auditioning for a band, try to see things from the band's point of view. Be frank about your strengths and weaknesses. Don't try to pretend that you are a hot jazz player if you don't know what a C6 chord is. Don't dwell on the negative, but try to figure out what you could add to a band that would convince them to hire you. Have you written any songs? Can you write arrangements? Do you own recording equipment? Do you have up-to-date equipment? Could the band rehearse in your garage? Finally, is this a band you want to be in?

Just because you're offered a job, it doesn't mean you have to take it. Don't waste time doing something that you don't want to do. On the other hand, if this is your first band, it may be worth your time to get some experience, even though you know the group isn't really going anywhere, or you don't like the bass player's attitude.

Joining a band is a matter of chemistry and goals. Sometimes, you'll run into a wonderful musician who is just not the right fit for your group. Perhaps when he learns something new his attention wanders or he plays too loud over the vocals. Possibly, he's too egotistical. You won't want to work with someone on a regular basis who only seems to think about how great he is, without relating to the other people in the group. Music needs to be a give-and-take thing—cooperation will help to produce musical and ultimately, financial results.

It's a different matter if you have a musical group wherein one person is featured and well known, such as Garth Brooks or Bruce Springsteen. In these cases, the leader has most of the responsibility, and the jobs that come in are largely a result of how managers and/or record companies have built up the name of that performer. The people in the band, out of necessity, are going to play a subsidiary role. In these situations, the featured artist usually writes all or most of the material and the only hope a band member has of getting something recorded is by co-writing a song with the artist. It is also not unusual for the "road band" to be replaced by studio musicians for the recordings.

There is nothing wrong with joining this type of band, so long as you have a realistic view of what is going to happen. You can then use this situation to help your own career move to another level.

Equipment

Whether you are an acoustic soloist, a jazz combo or a heavy metal band, you're going to need some sort of sound system in order to work. If you are a solo acoustic act, or even a duo, you may be able to survive temporarily without any sound reinforcement. Even then, you will be dependent on the not-so-tender mercies of second class microphones that constitute the sound system of most nightclubs or school gymnasiums. Most dances and quite a few concerts are held in high school and college gyms.

The first thing to do is to figure out what you need and what the equipment is going to cost. How many microphones do you need to properly reproduce your vocals and instruments? What kind of mixing board with how many microphone inputs will be necessary to send sound out to the audience? Do you require any special effects? Do you need to update your keyboard sounds by buying a new synthesizer? What about a computer and a sequencer? Does the drummer have a quality drum machine, octapads and electronic drums? Does your guitar player have an effects rack that's set up so all of her effects are ready to go? Is the rack activated by foot pedals that are easy to reach?

If you want your band to develop a contemporary sound, you will need to invest in equipment. How are you going to come up with the necessary cash or obtain credit to buy what you need?

If the group is going to be run as a cooperative, with each band member assuming areas of responsibility and with income equally distributed, then each player should try to save some money that can be set aside for equipment (such as sound equipment, microphones, a mixing board, speakers, and possibly a van). Sometimes, this money is set aside by the band's placing a portion of the receipts from each gig in a special bank account.

Each player should own his own equipment and amps, so if the band breaks up or if one or two people leave, they can either be bought out of their share of the sound equipment, or they can buy it from the remaining group members. It is a good idea to work out a rough agreement between the group members and formalize that agreement on paper in order to avoid future disputes. Remember, equipment loses its value as it ages and is constantly used, so a $3,000 sound system will certainly not be worth $3,000 in four years.

Back to the issue of raising money to buy the equipment—you may be able to buy some equipment on a credit basis, if your parents, an older brother or sister or a manager is willing to co-sign a loan at a music store. Another option is to buy the equipment on time, if a store owner is willing to trust you or if you have a good credit rating. Make sure that the interest rate, if there is one, is not excessive.

Where can you buy a good sound system or musical instruments at a fair price? Much depends on how many music stores there are in the area in which you live. Major cities have giant discount stores that offer large discounts off retail prices. However discount stores may not always be reliable about servicing the equipment they sell and are often too busy to offer much advice or consultation. This is even true of mail order discounters. If the store or mail order company that sells you equipment doesn't service it, you may find yourself in the annoying position of having to ship it back to the manufacturer, instead of the store dealing quickly with the problem. A good local store hopes to start a long-term relationship with you, while a big city discounter or mail order company is much more impersonal as they understand this may well be your only purchase from them.

Now that you are getting outfitted with better, larger and more expensive equipment, you may need a larger vehicle to carry it all, as well as group. You may even need a roadie to help you carry, load and/or unload the equipment, as well as operate the mixing board while the band plays. Your roadie or road manager can also take care of any questions a club owner or manager may have, in the absence of an agent or manager being there at the club to represent you.

Some people pay the road manager a percentage if their own gross income or a weekly salary, while others make him an equal member of the band. Initially, you may find a friend or brother or sister who is willing to help you out, but if the band starts to work regularly, you will need help on a regular basis.

How do you find a road manager? You can advertise in the newspaper or weekly entertainment guide or you can put up a sign at local music stores or in schools. Your road manager is as important a member of your team as anyone in the band, so you want to choose her with great care. You want someone who is dependable and even-tempered, but who won't put up with any outrageous nonsense from a patron or a club owner. Frankly, it helps if your road manager is big and strong, and looks it.

One last word about equipment, now that you are starting to play paid jobs, you need to keep good records of any equipment that is purchased: musical instruments; sound equipment; a van; musical accessories. Keep a record on any music lessons or classes that you are taking to advance your skills. Keep a record of all miles driven to and from jobs, auditions and rehearsals. You can deduct mileage driven to and from professional engagements, as well as promotional or business expenses from your taxes. You can also work out a depreciation schedule for your instruments and sound system and possibly your van, that can save you quite a bit of money on taxes. The Internal Revenue Service demands precise records. If you are audited and are unable to produce such records, you may not be able to deduct your expenses, even though they are legitimate business expenses. You will also have to pay interest penalties if the IRS disallows your deductions. Keep a log of all car, instrument and PA repair expenses.

Another deductible item you may be able to take advantage of is the cost of buying and maintaining costumes, provided that they are not worn off-stage. You will need to keep a record of what your costumes cost and a steady log of dry cleaning costs. Most bands designate the one person in the group who is most organized and careful to keep a record of expenses. Buy a car mileage log from your local stationery store, and record the miles driven on a daily basis.

Below is a sample card detailing an equipment purchase. Careful record keeping will give you a good idea of what you are spending on equipment and what it will take to service each piece of your gear. It will also refresh your memory when a problem arises as to whether servicing will be convenient or awkward.

Sample Instrument Record Card

Equipment & Brand	Guitar Amp., Global
Source	Joe's Music
Price	$800
Length of Warranty	90 days, ending June 1, 2000
Service, Availability of Parts	No repair, factory warehouse in Los Angeles

The chart on the next page is a sample of an expense log that includes a month's worth of income and expenses.

June, 1999
Income and Expense Sheets for Bitter Roots Band

Income & Source / Mileage / Musical Expenses / Other Expenses				
Date	Income	Expenses	Description	Miles
6/1/99	$400.00		OK Club	82
6/7/99	$650.00		Jackson PTA	39
6/9/99		$12.50	Dry Cleaning, Al's	
6/10/99	$500.00	$100.00	City Golf Club	61
			Commission to Fast Ed's Agency	
6/12/99		$28.50	Ralph's Printing (Business Cards, fliers)	6
6/14/99		$15.40	Guitar strings, Maine Music	12
6/15/99		$60.00	Local 14 quarterly union dues	
6/19/99			Audition, Mix & Max Bar	112
6/20/99		$80.00	Irene's voice lessons	20
6/22/99		$68.00	P.A. Repair, Maine Music	12
6/26/99		$100.00	Photo Session, Al Brunson Pictures	
6/28/99		$200.00	Rent, rehearsal studio	
6/30/99	$1,000.00		Bill's Bar	150
Total	**$2,555.00**	**$664.40**		**494**

Total Income:	$2,555.00	
Music Expenses:		$323.40
Business Expenses:		$341.00
Net Income		*$1,890.60*

      Mileage   494

Sound Systems

On these two pages are some diagrams of sound systems:

Sound System—Solo Performer

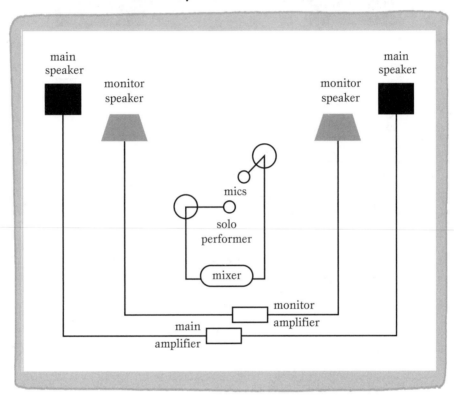

Sound System—Rock Quintet

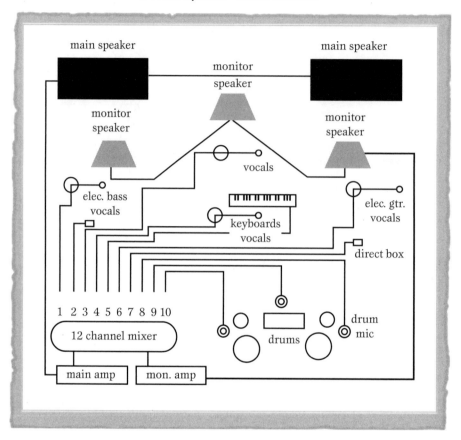

CHAPTER 2 RESOURCES

There are ever-increasing numbers of books that discuss how musicians can get a band together. They tend to be at their best when examining the protocol for rehearsals, and the way musicians can develop into better players through study and the acquisition of new skills and better instruments. Most of these books are less successful in their attempts to provide insights into the music business. Three of the better books that I have run into are:

Jourard, Marty. *Start Your Own Band: Everything You Need to Know to Take Your Band to the Top!* New York: Hyperion, 1997. Contains useful guides to equipment and some basic information about music.

Lineberger, Kathryn. *The Rock Band Handbook: Everything You Need to Know to Get a Band Together and Take It on the Road.* New York: Berkeley Music Co., 1996. If you've never been in a band before, and don't really understand what each instrument is supposed to do, this book is a good beginning guide.

York, Norton, Editor. *The Rock File: Making It in The Music Business.* Oxford: Oxford University Press, 1991. This is a collection of articles by various British writers. The first half of the book, which discusses the role of rhythm instruments, vocals and horns is equally applicable to American musicians.

Sound Reinforcement

Sokol, Mike. *Acoustic Musician's Guide to Sound Reinforcement & Live Recording.* Upper Saddle River, N.J.: Prentice Hall, 1998. A practical guide.

Taking It to the Street:

Packaging Your Talent for Potential Buyers

You now have the opportunity to test your performing repertoire, see which members of your group like to talk on stage and which ones need to concentrate simply on playing their instruments. You'll find out which of your songs seem to get the most reaction from audiences. Try experimenting by performing the same song in different keys at different tempos. You may be surprised to find out that a song you thought was a fine musical arrangement, works far better in a different tempo or key.

Once you have honed your performance chops to a fine point, perhaps after six months or more of free performances for various audiences, you'd like to get paid for what you do! How do you get this to happen?

There are booking agents in all local markets whose professional expertise is in matching performing artists with buyers of talent. These buyers exist in all sorts of venues, as you will see in the next chapter. How can you package your product to get the attention of buyers, whether you are booking yourself or working through one or more booking agents?

You will need to put together some sort of promotional or press kit that you can show to prospective clients. The kit should include:

- Pictures of the group
- A group biography, with some information about each member of the band.
- A list of music styles your band performs
- A set list (if the song titles are recognizable to a club or bar owner)
- An audio demo of your group on cassette tape or CD
- Videos (discussed later in this chapter)

Making Demos-Audio Tapes

First, analyze your intended audience. Where do you wish to work? If you want a gig in a Top 40 bar where bands perform current hits, you need to do Top 40 material on your demo. You may want to put together medleys of these tunes, performing excerpts from a number of songs, rather than trying to record the complete tunes. For example, you might have a '50s medley or a group of songs by a current artist. Medleys demonstrate the depth of your repertoire to a club owner.

How should you go about recording a demo? A good place to start is by having your own four track cassette studio, or an eight track A-DAT, if you can afford one. (There is about a $2,000-$2,500 difference in the equipment.) You can keep your mini-studio in your rehearsal space. It helps if someone in the group has some knowledge about the recording process and the sound mixing. There are several current books that deal with home studios listed in the Appendix D. As your talents develop and you become more critical, you may want to upgrade your equipment, mix your tape at a local recording studio, or do the whole project at a high tech professional studio.

If this is your first recording venture, prepare yourself for a shock. You may be about to discover that you don't always sing in tune, your vocal enunciation is unclear, and that wonderful $200 guitar you love sounds awful on tape. Don't despair. Part of the problem may lie with the microphones you are using. A cheap microphone can make you sound terrible. The spot where you place the microphone also radically influences the sound quality of your recording. For example, if you are recording a guitar with one microphone and place the mike very close to the bass strings of the guitar, the guitar will lack brightness. The microphone should be placed wherever it reproduces the sound in a way that reflects the vision of the player. If the player is striving for special effects, this may call for unusual procedures of microphone placement, or the effects may be obtained through equalizing the sound on the recording console.

After you have logged some time in your home studio "woodshed," it's time to evaluate what you have done. Are you getting a good enough sound to make a demo for your press kit? Have you captured the essence of your group's sound on the tape? If you are working with a four- or eight-track machine, unless you are dealing exclusively with a drum machine, it's going to prove very difficult to capture a real contemporary drum sound.

Now you have more decisions to face. Should you try to buy a better tape recorder, a second A-DAT machine or better-quality microphones? Should you try to enlist a friend who is a technical wizard to help produce your demo? Will she charge you for her help? Or, should you go with a professional studio recording with an experienced engineer at the controls?

Part of your decision, as usual, will be an economic one. Check the rates for studios in your city. Chances are that the cost for a sixteen-twenty four track studio with decent equipment will be anywhere from $35 to $50 an hour, plus tape costs. Remember, we're talking about a demo studio, not the place where they cut the regional McDonald's commercials or where the best producer in town works.

If you decide to go to a studio, be sure to talk with the engineer who is going to work on your project and get a feel for whether he will be comfortable recording your style of music. Above all, listen to other projects he's recorded in the same studio.

If you aren't sure whether you need a studio-quality demo to achieve your objective of getting work, take your home tape and play it for prospective employers and booking agents. How do they react to the tape? It's best not to rely on family or friends for this sort of information. They may not have the basis for making an informed judgment, or they may be afraid to be critical. They may also bring some unwelcome personal biases to the situations with comments like "I told you that bass player was no good—look at the way he dresses." This is not the sort of information you need.

Today there is a wide range of recording equipment available. Before you buy anything, it's a good idea to listen to what it can do. Listen to some tapes that other people have made using that equipment. If possible, try to arrange a rough demo session for your band, however brief, where you can check out what your band will actually sound like using that tape recorder and microphones. Find a music store owner who has the patience to work with you, then give him your loyalty by buying from him.

Another possibility for making a cheap demo is to do it at a local college's recording studio. You may be able to find a student majoring in audio engineering willing to do your demo as a college project. She'll get some experience as well as fulfill a course requirement, and you'll get a demo for the cost of the tape. Some of these college studios are well-equipped sixteen and twenty-four track facilities.

If the college ploy fails, look for a non-professional audio fanatic who spends much of his free time recording bands as a hobby. Many non-professionals love experimenting in a studio and buying high-quality professional gear financed through some other career. It may be work for you, but it's fun for them. For example, a few years ago an airplane pilot in Denver had a well-equipped eight-track studio which he rented out for next to nothing. There may be someone like that in your hometown or nearby. Some successful recording artists have home studios they allow their friends to use, just for the practice of recording music in that particular room, or as a favor.

At times, a new recording studio needs somebody to try out their equipment, and they will allow you to use studio time free or at minimal expense. A professional audio shop may also let you use their studio, and will use your demo as an example of what can be done with their equipment.

If you are paying for the recording studio, be sure that your band is well-rehearsed before you set foot in the door. A studio is not a cost-effective place to re-work musical arrangements or argue about repertoire. Know what you are going to do before you get there. It will probably take longer to record your project than you anticipate. You should work out the kinks of your repertoire in your home studio before renting elsewhere.

How many songs should be on a demo? No more than three, four at most. If you are recording cover tunes, you may want to do portions of a dozen songs or three or four medleys. If you want to work in a bar that features cover bands, limit or omit original music on your demo. If you won't perform it at the club, don't put it on your demo. Make sure your strongest song or medley is the first thing on your demo, because if the owner of a venue doesn't like the first song, he may never bother listening to any subsequent material.

Making Video Demos

Making a video is an expensive proposition, but there are some ways of saving money. The American Federation of Musicians (the Musicians' Union) has a number of locals that allow members to make videos cost-free, using equipment owned by the union local. Of course, you must be a member in good standing of the local to obtain such services. The union probably will not allow you to take possession of the video. They will show it to prospective buyers at union headquarters. This enables them to be sure that your group will file a union contract on any jobs you receive, but it also means you can't shop the tape yourself. There are many film, television and mass communications students at local colleges who may be able to use your video as a class project.

The community access division of your local cable television supplier may provide similar services. Many of the cable companies have agreements with the communities they serve that require them to teach people in the community to run video equipment and produce local shows.

A possible drawback that many of these free services share is a lack of editing facilities. Sometimes, a college or union local may have some editing equipment, but it is not usually state-of-the-art quality. Any sort of student project starts with the assumption that most students lack experience. This is definitely going to limit the scope of your video. Another problem with free or low-cost video services is the number of cameras involved in the shoot. A one-camera video shoot may portray your group accurately; it offers little chance of capturing unusual artistic or humorous effects that top artists use in their MTV videos. High-quality, professional videos require the use of three or more cameras, access to a sophisticated editing facility, a quality director and unfortunately, the expenditure of considerable sums of money.

If none of these strategies have enabled you to get a free or low-cost video, I recommend that you wait until the group has achieved a solid financial base before you make a video. It is too expensive to attempt such a high-risk proposition early in your career. It is safer and far less expensive to combine an audio recording with some quality photos to demonstrate your abilities and charisma.

Why bother with a video at all? Remember your goals: to communicate whatever visual strengths your group possesses, together with a good audio track. For one thing, you can sometimes use a video as a substitute for live auditions at clubs. If the video is reasonably good at capturing what your group does, you won't have to lug equipment across town for an audition. The alternative to getting video services free is to be prepared to spend $25,000 and up in order to capture your group in a thoroughly professional vein.

If your video comes out well, you may be able to promote it to be shown on cable television as part of the cable company's neighborhood access program commitment. Some public or private channels have programs that devote time to local videos.

Now you have a video and/or audio insert that you can place in your promo kit, what else do you need? You'll certainly want some good photos of the group, together with some biographies and some favorable critical reviews. If you want the photos to be useable in newspapers and magazines, be sure to use glossy photos. How do you assemble these materials?

Once again, you need to resort to whatever talent and ingenuity your group possesses. If you have done a video or any sort of local television performance or interviews, you may be able to use some stills for your promo kit. Be sure to get permission from the broadcaster or you may get a nasty letter from a lawyer threatening a lawsuit if you don't pay up. Do you know anyone with a good camera who is looking for experience? Remember, all you really need are one or two decent photos. The more copies of a photo you can get duplicated, the cheaper the cost per photo.

You can always hire a photographer. Try to find someone who has some experience working with musicians. Look at some of the work she has done before making any commitments. Check with the Musicians' Union or with local agents or other bands. The Denver local of the Musicians' Union provides free photos for members. They can be done either by a photographer the union recommends or one the group chooses. Student photographers at colleges and even high schools are another source of free or low-cost photos. It's most important that a photo captures the spirit of the group. It's a good idea to have the photographer listen to some of your music before she does the shoot. This will help the photographer match the image of your music with the "look" of the band.

Stylists

Costuming and appearance can be an important part of developing a group's image. Getting the attention of the public is an important step in building a performing career. Some of today's pop stars (not to mention athletes and politicians) expend considerable effort on creating a visual image that coordinates with their musical or personal style. To accomplish this, some groups hire stylists or costume designers who create a particular "look" that the public will identify with a musical act.

Although this may strike you as an extravagance, remember that getting the attention of the public (or for that matter, record companies) is one of the first major hurdles of your music career. Working with a stylist or costume designer can be one of the ways to overcome public indifference to accepting a new musical group. The visual aspect of the package that you present to the public can be as important to your career as its musical contents.

To save a bit of money, try writing your own biographies and/or group history. Tell what the members in the group have done which may be of interest to the general public; not only in the areas of music, but in terms of hobbies or unusual skills or interests. Maybe one of you collects snakes, plays professional table tennis or set a state record in women's javelin. As your career develops, you should include a list of satisfied clients.

If no one in your group has the ability to write well, you can always hire a professional writer or journalism student to compile your biographies.

Be sure to include a list of any musical credits. Has anyone in the group studied with a famous musician? Does anyone have music degrees, did someone play in an honor band or win a local or state music contest? Have any members of your band played with other well-known bands?

Publicists

Once a group has started an active touring career, it is often desirable to hire a publicist. The role of a publicist is to make sure that anything positive about an artist gets attention in the media. Even hobbies or skills that are totally unrelated to music may enable you to get publicity in magazines or on television shows that may not feature music. For example, athletic skills, cooking specialties or unusual hobbies can earn a story in an appropriate newspaper or magazine. The publicist attempts to control any media coverage of the artist to fit the image of the group which either the group itself or their manager are attempting to formulate.

Media attention leads to record sales and to public interest in a group. This, in turn, stimulates concert appearances and further record sales. Hiring a publicist isn't cheap, but in the long run can be quite cost-effective. (See the Resources page at the end of this chapter for books about publicity.)

Sample Press/Promo Kits

Now that you have taken a look at the various forms of publicity you will need, the following are some sample press/promo kits and photos. Note that different musical groups try to relate the style of their publicity to the style of their music.

The Van Manens

Includes photo and a background sheet.

The Van Manens

Skyline Talent & Events, Inc., is proud and pleased to announce the availability of a very special act for young audiences — a delightful singing duo, **The Van Manens.**

Children and adults alike can relate to Dave and Helene Van Manen's music. Their concerts showcase up-beat and tuneful songs from their albums, *"Healthy Planet, Healthy People," "Barley Bread & Reindeer Milk,"* and *"We Recycle and Other Songs for Earth-keepers."* Their songs help children build self-esteem and understand the need for caring for ourselves and our planet — all in a fun and musical way. The Van Manens affirm that music with a message is a great way to learn and reinforce important information while filling the heart with laughter and delight.

In 1991, the **Parents' Choice** Foundation awarded The Van Manens their prestigious **Gold Award**. This Newton, Massachusetts, foundation is a non-profit organization that reviews and selects the very best in children's music, books, videos and toys. The Gold Award is considered one of the most valuable and coveted honors in the children's music industry. Other well-known recipients have been performers **Raffi**, and **Sharon, Lois & Bram.**

As well as being performers, composers, recording artists and parents, The Van Manens are also music therapists. They love, understand and respect kids, and they communicate with them in a very special way. Children especially enjoy learning sign language along with the songs because Dave and Helene make it so much fun. Your kids will love them too!

printed on recycled paper

The Earthkeeping Show

This upbeat program celebrates nature and environmental awareness. Great songs, sign language, sing-alongs, story-telling and just plain fun are all a part of this well-crafted program. Kids actively participate as they learn about themselves and the Earth through songs and stories such as *"We Recycle," "Trees," "I Am an Earthkeeper,"* and *"Earth on Turtle's Back"* (a native American tale). A perfect show to support lessons on the environment and recycling!

The Warm Fuzzies/ Cold Pricklies Show

This program explores the many facets of taking care of ourselves. The Van Manen's diverse backgrounds as seasoned performers and clinical music therapists are expertly combined as they cover such important issues as knowing when to say "no," drug and alcohol prevention, prejudice, and building self-esteem. As students "sign and sing along," they are entertained, educated, and empowered to take a closer look at themselves and the beauty and richness of our diverse world. This program qualifies for "Drug-Free Schools money" in many states.

The Van Manens perform other programs on diversity and cooperation as well as in-service programs for teachers and health workers.

WHAT PEOPLE ARE SAYING...

"I watched their performance on Sunday morning and cannot wait to rebook them for future festivals."

Sharon Sheldon, Special Events Coordinator CitiFest, Toledo, Ohio

"When The Van Manens sing they connect so well with their young audience that you feel the children leave with a little more respect for nature…"

Karen Benson, Association of Vermont Recyclers

"Kids love the infectious, folksy tunes and lyrics from such songs as 'Earthkeeper,' 'Goin' to My Garden' and 'What is Peace?' Parents appreciate the duo's message of compassion and caring and respect for nature."

Country Living Magazine

"Your program is of great value to students and teachers who are concerned about the Earth and improving conditions for all living things."

Wayne Stone, Principal Hygiene Elementary School, Colorado

An informational video of a Van Manens live concert is available for you to audition.

Representation is provided by:
SKYLINE TALENT & EVENTS, INC.
1424 Larimer Street, Suite 300
Denver, Colorado   80202
303/595-8747 Fax: 303/595-8744

Alex Komodore

Includes photo and bio.

Alex Komodore

Biography

Alex Komodore began studying the classical guitar at age 8 and began performing at 10. His career included performances in New York's Town Hall and the United Nations. He took first prize at the 1985 competition of the National Music Teacher's Association and was featured on a solo documentary for PBS television. Alex's talent for chamber music has enabled him to work with many fine ensembles, including the Central City Opera, Colorado Ballet, Denver Chamber Orchestra, Colorado Festival Orchestra at Chautauqua and St. John's Episcopal Cathedral Choir. He is featured on several recordings, two of which are with St. John's Choir on the prestigious Delos label. He is also featured on jazz pianist Kenny Passarelli's CD "Visones de Mis Antepasados," which was aired on the 1992 Summer Olympics broadcasts worldwide, and on "Redstone" with flutist Rod Garnett. Alex has received significant press attention, having been awarded *Westword's* Best Classical Recording for "Redstone" and *CD Review's* "Highest Recommendation" for Recording Quality and Artistic Expression.

Alex has taught on the collegiate level for many years at institutions such as New York University, the University of Colorado at Denver and Metropolitan State College of Denver, and is in demand as a Master Class Instructor nationwide. He is currently a contributing editor for "Fingerstyle Guitar" magazine.

Gush

Includes performance photos, press clippings, band logo, background sheet.

Fyah Wyah

Includes press kit cover with color photo, information sheet, press clippings, music award, flyers, photo on this and the next page.

Expense

Includes business card, information sheet, song list, press clippings.

CHAPTER 3 RESOURCES

See the Chadbourne and Levine books in Chapter 1 Resources.

Two reasonable books about music publicity are:

Gibson, James. *Getting Noticed: A Musician's Guide to Publicity & Self-Promotion.* Cincinnati: Writer's Digest Books, 1987. Readable and intelligent.

Pettigrew, Jim Jr. *The Billboard Guide to Music Publicity.* 2nd ed. New York: Billboard Books, 1997. An up-to-date guide, including sample press releases, and information about technology and media guides.

chapter 4

Selling Your Act in Places You Never Dreamed Of

At this point, you have developed a promo kit that includes group photos, bios and a demo tape and you have a sound system and a vehicle in which to transport it. What you need now are more jobs.

There are two ways to go about finding work. One way is to do it yourself, or have one person in the group represent the band. The other way is to be represented by a booking agent.

Booking Yourself

Getting a musical organization together is a full-time job in itself. You need to work out musical arrangements, choose the tunes you want to perform, buy equipment, select clothing to be used in your performances, and set aside many hours (and a place) for rehearsals. If you are doing original material, then you will need to set aside time for writing and re-writing songs.

If you plan to book yourself, you will need to:

- Do a good deal of leg work, such as making numerous phone calls to check out all sorts of leads from friends or other bands.

- Figure out ways to advertise your talent. This may include ads in the Yellow Pages of the phone book, printing posters and flyers, designing T-shirts with your logo, and contacting schools, clubs, religious groups, social and business organizations, caterers, etc.
- Be prepared to negotiate prices. You want to make as much money as possible; the client wants to get great entertainment at a low price.

Of the hundreds of musicians I've known, I can only think of three or four individuals who actually enjoyed booking themselves or their groups and were good at it. The most successful sales person of the bunch books himself and does a brilliant job of it. This is mostly because he has an office and six full-time assistants who have maps on the wall, huge card files, and who return phone calls immediately. They run their operation like a business. The owner-band leader only involves himself during the final stages of the negotiation.

Another person who was good at booking his group quit doing it after a couple of years. He found that it took up too much of his time. It was easier to hire someone else who didn't need to spend his time practicing, rehearsing, performing and recording. Booking a job is a full-time job, if it's to be done well.

Setting a Price

The most obvious factor in setting a price is to know as much as possible about where you're going to perform. Is there a cover charge or a minimum number of drinks the customer must buy? What kind of money do they charge for drinks? Does the cover charge apply for the whole evening, or just one show? Do you know other bands or soloists who have played this particular room?

If you're working for an organization at a party or a charity event held in a room they've rented out, what sort of people are hiring you? Are they well-heeled doctors and lawyers, truckdrivers at a Christmas party, or a group of environmental activists? Obviously you don't charge a regional convention of IBM the same price as you would a benefit for a safehouse.

This brings up the subject of benefit concerts. Many of the local chapters of the Musicians' Union follow the rule that a group can only do a benefit if *all* of the people at the facility—the ticket-takers, stagehands, ushers, etc.—are contributing their services free of charge. This is a great out for you, if you feel that you are being taken advantage of. One final ploy I have used when the client is being particularly aggressive about getting me to donate my services is to tell the client I will be happy to do a benefit for them if they can get my dentist and auto mechanic to donate free services for me. Many clients have a terribly inflated idea of how much money an average musician earns. They may figure that if you are charging them $100 for an hour, since the ordinary work week has forty hours that you are earning $4,000 a week. If only this were true!

The Alan Remington Pricing Formula

Alan Remington is a friend of mine who teaches music and music business at Orange Coast Community College in Costa Mesa, California. Alan has had a long and successful career as a conductor, composer arranger, and head of his own band. His own band was so successful in playing one night casual gigs that he sent out as many as a dozen bands to different events in the Los Angeles area in the same night. This is the formula he devised after playing at many clubs and talking with other bands and club owners.

1. Figure out the number of patrons during the peak hour. By Alan's reckoning they will usually consume two drinks per hour. Typically, two drinks will average out to a cost of four to five dollars.
2. Double this figure, because the average customer will stay for two hours. Let's say the room holds two hundred people. During the two hours they will spend $8 a head, bring in $1,600 to the club.
3. Since there are two shows, the total receipts will be $3,200. Alan's formula is that the band should get about a third of the bar receipts. In this case, just under $1,100.

This assumes that there is no cover charge. If there is a cover charge, the band should either get the amount of the cover charge, or 75% of it, plus an additional percentage of the receipts from the bar. If the room doesn't serve alcohol, the numbers must be adjusted to reflect the prices of coffee and dessert, or whatever constitutes the bill of fare.

One way to convince the owner your band is earning its keep, is to try to establish how many people are coming to the club because the band is there. Of course the club owner will say they would come to drink and party anyway, but he is usually quite aware that this is not necessarily true. Another argument that can be used is that the club has to have entertainment because it is available at competing venues.

Booking Agents

What do booking agents do and how do they do it? A booking agent is someone who sells acts to a variety of clients on a short-term or long-term basis. Agents service wedding receptions, parties, conventions and special events such as political rallies. They also work with caterers and halls, schools, county or state fairs, and anyone or anyplace that might require the use of live entertainment.

Some booking agents specialize in clubs, others in conventions. An agent may book one type of entertainment, or provide anyone under the sun on request. That could range from an Hawaiian hula group to a pair of trained bears and a juggler. Agents generally have offices, although a few may work out of their homes (depending on state laws). They charge the musician a commission of 15-20% of the musician's gross wages. The higher fee is what is paid for a one-night engagement, and the lower one is what the agent takes for a long-term booking in a club.

Agents build up a certain clientele who give them repeat business. For example, an agent might book the local IBM Christmas Party every year, unless his contact at the company leaves or they're dissatisfied. Agents may book a particular club on an exclusive basis or compete for the account with other agents.

How do you find an agent to represent your group? Some agents may be willing to give your group a live audition in their office, at a rehearsal studio or club. Others may prefer to see you working in front of a live audience. This means you may have to go out and get some work yourself before you can get an agent. You will find agents listed in the *Yellow Pages* and you can get a list of those who have union franchises from the nearest local of your union.

One way to find out who the viable agents in your town are is to ask some of the local groups who work regularly for recommendations. You'll probably hear the names of two or three agents repeatedly, unless you live in a very large metropolitan area where there are dozens of them.

If you have friends in working groups, ask them to recommend you to an agent, or if you can use their name when calling the agent. There's a much greater chance of an agent coming out to see you if someone they know and trust suggested doing so.

Provided an agent has some interest in your band, she will need some selling tools in order to represent you to the best of her ability. If you have a good promo kit with attractive photos, a few reviews, a set list, some letters from satisfied clients, and a good audio or video demo, an agent is more likely to take you seriously than she would with an act who simply wanders in the off the street and says "book me."

It is crucial for you and your agent to reach a clear agreement on a number of issues. What kind of music do you like to play? What sort of music can you play in a pinch and what styles of music are you unwilling or unable to perform? Do you want to work in bars or is this impossible because of some of the band's day jobs? Are you willing to do some travelling, at least on weekends? In many areas, travel is a necessity. There may be more work available in neighboring ski resorts or beach clubs than exists in the town where you live. Some agents simply don't deal with out of town accounts. Others may send you on a six-month Holiday Inn tour, if that is what you want.

You also need to reach some agreement on the price of the band. Initially, the agent may have a better notion of what your band can make than you do. After all, she's been booking bands in the area for a while. She also knows the clients and the size of their budgets. It is her business to know.

This brings up another subject. It doesn't much matter who books you for your first few gigs, but don't let a buddy or a relative book your band on a long-term basis. It's very unprofessional. Although they may be enthusiastic, they probably have little business knowledge or skill. Agents know when to lower the price and when to hold out for top dollar. They recognize when a client is bluffing and could easily afford to pay the band double the initial offer.

In many sections of the country, conventions are a daily event. They may be gatherings of local business people, regional meetings of medical or sales groups, or even national meetings. Convention gigs often pay more for one hour of work than you could earn working in a club for three days of four one-hour sets.

If some of the people in your band work day jobs and some don't, you may be able to form a smaller group within your regular band. You might also be able to do a solo lunch hour show, or a duo during "happy hour," usually from around 4 P.M. to 6 P.M. Happy hour gigs are common in many downtown areas or near the airports of cities where business people may be quartered. After a hard day of meetings and selling, they like to go to the motel bar and unwind. You can provide the (usually happy) background music. Many "singles bars" also offer happy hours. However not all happy hours include entertainment, some just feature special deals on food or drinks. If that is the case, try to convince the manager of the venue to feature music at least one day a week or ask your agent to check it out. Friday is usually a good bet, because it marks the end of the work week and the start of the weekend.

Never try to steal jobs from an agent. If your agent has booked you on a gig and someone comes up and asks what the band charges, it is best to hand them your agent's card. She was the source of the job and is probably more adept than you are in negotiating deals. If the people for whom you are performing say that they would like to book you again and ask if they can contact you directly, do the honorable thing and say "no." If the agent finds out you are booking jobs directly, she will probably never call you again. She may even bad-mouth you to other agents in your locale, who will then be reluctant to book you.

What can an agent offer you? Sometimes, agents book certain clubs exclusively, so they may be able to get you booked in a club on a long-term basis. If you are seeking consistent gigs, either for financial reasons or to make the group musically tight, this can be a great opportunity. If you sign an exclusive agreement with an agent, she may be willing to share the costs of your promo kits or photos, or even to invest in helping you to make a better demo.

Some agents have ready access to work outside your hometown or in the region you live. Most agents will insist on an exclusive agreement if you expect them to perform this kind of service. They will also want to place their name and phone number on your photos and promo materials.

If an agent has been booking you on a non-exclusive basis and everything is going well, it may be worthwhile for you to sign an exclusive deal. An exclusive deal means that the agent is the only one with the right to book you or your band, and he will collect commissions on any job you work, even if you book it yourself.

It would be foolish to sign an exclusive agreement with an agent who has seldom, if ever booked you unless the contract contains some guarantees of work or income. For instance, if your band has been together six months and you have been able to make $500 a week for the four of you, an agent will have to get you work that pays over $620 in wages to compensate for her 20% commission. You can and should work out an agreement that gives the agent a certain amount of time to get your income over, say, $750 a week, or the contract can be dissolved. If you are a Union member operating under a Union agreement, the agent has to get you a certain amount of work or the agreement can be dissolved. Check with your Local to find out about this requirement.

In the "dirty tricks" department, watch out for this maneuver. Rather than talk about commissions, an agent may ask you what your group charges to play at a particular event. You will quote a price and they will accept it. What you don't know is thjat you are getting the $600 fee that you requested, but the agent has sold the group for $1,200, pocketing 50% of the fee. This sort of trick is difficult to prove. The client is rarely interested in getting in the middle of a dispute between an agent and a band. All they know is that they were billed for $1,200, and the band showed up and did a good job. I've had friends who played convention gigs where an out-of-town client gave the band a check and asked them to give it to the agent. Much to the band's surprise, they found out that the agent was making as much money as the band received for playing the gig. Do your best to find out what the job pays, rather than quoting a price up front to the agent.

Another issue you should discuss with your agent is the question of doing repeat jobs at a higher fee. If you've played the Cheyenne Elks Club twice and each time the band drew bodies like flies, then it's time to ask for a higher fee on the next go around. The trouble is that sometimes the agent's loyalty to the client is stronger than his attachment to the band. If he books a club 100 nights a year and you only play six or seven of those nights, chances are he will be more concerned with the club manager than with your band. Under these circumstances, you may have to get tough with the agent and turn down the gig. If the agent is representing your interests, she should fight to get you more money. If she doesn't, perhaps you should look for new representation.

A contract for a gig, with or without an agent, should specify the hours of employment, specify breaks during the course of the evening, offer discounted or free food or drink, provide lodging or a lodging allowance if the gig is not near your home base, and should specify how and when the band will be paid. It is a good idea to get a 50% deposit on any contracted job. If something goes wrong, at least you will get to keep that money. What sort of things can go wrong? Occasionally a club owner spaces out and forgets that he booked a band, or books two bands for the same gig at the same time. Sometimes, the person who hired you quit his job or was fired. The new manager or owner may not even be aware that you have a signed contract. The American Federation of Musicians (AFM) will provide legal help and even pay you the union minimum if you get caught in such a situation. However, this requires that your band all be members of the union, and use a signed union contract filed in the jurisdiction of the local where the gig is taking place. The AFM also franchises certain booking agents, limiting the percentages of their commissions. If you decide to use a Union agent, it is best to join the Union. Though some Union agents will book non-union talent, they are not supposed to do so.

The truth is that many local rock bands don't bother to join the Union, thinking of it merely as a bunch of old swing and symphonic musicians. In some locals that's probably true. It's also true that if younger musicians would join the Union and take a more active role in it, they might transform the shape of their locals. A number of locals are making more of an effort to deal with young rock and country musicians. Almost all of the big-time rock and country musicians belong to the Union, because their recording contracts and TV appearances require that affiliation.

In cooperation with the record companies, the Union co-sponsors local concerts through a fund called the Music Performance Trust Fund (MPTF). These concerts are free and open to the public. They take place all over North America in shopping malls, hospitals, schools, parks, nursing homes, prisons and other locations. They pay whatever the Union minimum for that local provides, Each local sets its own wage scales, and as you would expect, wages in New York or Los Angeles are higher than they are in Dubuque or Tupelo. Working a couple of MPTF jobs a year will often pay enough to cover your Union dues. Of course, you may get other jobs as a result of playing these gigs.

MPTF can be a great "cop-out" for all the requests you get to do benefits. These clients can be referred to the Union with a recommendation to apply for MPTF funds. You will still be paid minimum scale, and the client only pays part of the tab. If an organizationm is truly poverty-stricken, it may even be able to get MPTF to pay most or all of the costs of the gig. Note that MPTF jobs must be requested 45 days in advance, recommended by the local Unions, and approved by the trustees of the fund in New York.

There is an organization called NACA (see Resources) that books colleges. They hold regional and national conventions which showcase acts for college buyers. A similar group exists in Canada. The attendees at these conferences are buyers for college entertainment, so a successful audition can result in weeks of work at colleges.

It is possible to do NACA auditions without an agent. Once again, you need to face the question of whether you are the best person to do the necessary bargaining. If they like an act, a group of several colleges will try to "block book" it. This means that several colleges will get together and offer you a series of concerts at a reduced fee. You get more work, and they'll get a bit of a bargain. Whether this will prove to be worthwhile depends upon the distances you traveled to get the job, the distance between the various jobs, and the amount of work that they are offering.

Personal Managers

Agents get jobs for acts. They function as an employment agency for the act, as well as bargaining agents who need to satisfy both the buyer and sellers of talent.

Generally speaking, agents don't offer acts long-term career plans. Their work is to get jobs and keep the buyer happy by providing good entertainment.

A personal manager, on the other hand, does attempt to build long-term careers for his acts. She is usually the one who gets a record company contract for the artist and negotiates that contract with the help of a music business attorney. A manager is also a sort of buffer between an act and the booking agent, monitoring the agent's work to make sure that everything benefits the act. Managers do not usually function as booking agents, except in the classical field, where it is customary to do so. State laws vary on the exact limitations of a booking agent and personal manager, but some are very stringent. It's to your advantage to check them.

Since the premise of this book is that you want to stay in your local music market, either by choice or necessity, you probably won't require the services of a personal manager, unless you expect to record and tour on a national level. Also, to put it bluntly, you usually cannot afford the additional commissions that a manager will require. A good personal manager charges anything from 10 to 50% of your gross wages, with 15-20% being the most common amounts required. If you put this on top of the 15-20% fees you are paying to your booking agent, there isn't much left for the band to split.

Why do people hire managers? When an act is on the road, they rarely have time to take care of their business. Someone has to make decisions as to which jobs to take and which to turn down. Negotiations with a major record company can take months of hard work, negotiating offers and counter-offers. In short, for a full-time touring act that is after national exposure and big-time record deals, a manager is a virtual necessity. Record companies may judge the viability of an act by the reputation of the group's manager and/or attorney. The best and most influential managers have immediate access to major record company personnel.

For an act whose aim is to work only in a secondary market, a personal manager may be an unaffordable luxury. Most local managers have other full-time employment commitments and may not have the time to commit to developing an act. Examine your goals. What can a manager do for you that you aren't already doing? (Long-term goals are covered in depth in Chapters 11 and 12.)

Business Managers

Superstar acts usually hire a business manager to deal with their investments and tax problems. This usually represents another 5% off the gross income of the act. Since the lion's share of the people reading this book are not competing in the superstar arena, it is not really something that you should worry about at this time. If a high degree of success comes your way, believe me you will get many people soliciting you to provide these services.

Other Creative Opportunities

In the category of special projects a number of cities have commissioned songs to celebrate their history, attract tourists or to build local pride. Local chambers of commerce and tourist bureaus are possible sources of such work. If you get any nibbles, send a demo of any songs that could be considered appropriate or write a fragment of a potential song. Do some research to check out historical events in your town, and what musical style is popular in your community and appropriate for the subject. It is always good to throw in a few references to local tourist attractions or prominent landmarks.

Other similar projects can include state songs, celebrations of historical events or songs built around tourist attractions. These songs can be lucrative and are fun to write. If you excel in writing melodies or in crafting lyrics (but not in both), you may find it helpful to find a collaborator to complete the project.

Two other sources of local recording work are industrial films and slide shows. Industrial films usually require only instrumental music. They are usually short films, running from five to fifteen minutes. Occasionally, a song may be appropriate at the beginning or end of the film, much as in a feature film.

Slide shows usually also focus on a product or event, but they are done with smaller budgets and less elaborate productions. With either slide shows or industrial films, you should include creative fees as part of your budget, as well as the Union scales for yourself and any other musicians. These wage minimums vary in each medium, so you should get the necessary information from your Union local. Many of the clients for these projects will not be signatory to Union agreements, so you may have to do the necessary paperwork. If the client uses the film in another medium, for example, in a commercial, there will be additional payments that need to be made to the musicians. Be sure that your agreement with the client specifies that he will be responsible for any payments if the work is used in a new medium.

Local news programs and cable television will sometimes buy snippets of music for use during five to fiftten second segues that run between shows or behind credits. Check your local cable supplier or news station to see if they need such music, and what kind of musical style they prefer. In Chapter 7 there is an extended discussion of work available doing local or regional commercials.

One final source of jobs is film editors. They put the final touches on film and video products, and often they have input on who will provide the music. in some instances, they may even do the hiring and payment for such a service. You can find who the film editors are in your community by consulting the better photo and film processing labs, or by checking with college film departments or any recording studios that are capable of recording sound with picture. Occasionally recording studios hire composers to work on projects the studio is recording.

Other Sources of Employment

There are some organizations that do not work through booking agencies—one of them is called Young Audiences. This group hires groups or soloists to do school concerts. (See Appendix A for their various offices.) It is often necessary to audition in order to work for them. They want a combination of a lecture and a performance, oriented to children of various ages. You may be asked to spend a portion of your program demonstrating vocal or instrumental techniques or answering questions. It is a good idea to do a brief history of the musical styles that you perform or to talk about the history of the music you are playing.

The great advantage of Young Audience performances is that almost all of them take place in the very early hours of the morning (try 8:00 A.M. on a snowy day in a distant suburb)! The performances are usually the length of a school period, 40–50 minutes, and you usually do two consecutive performances at the same school.

Income from Young Audiences won't make you rich, but it's a nice way to supplement your income. Many of the Young Audience jobs are limited to Union members, because they are partially funded through MPTF.

There are organizations in some cities that deal with disadvantaged people or special populations. Some of these shows are for people in correctional facilities, or physically or mentally disadvantaged people. Typically, these performances also take place during the day. They provide a wonderful opportunity to get paid for what is really community service. They are a reminder of the tangible evidence that music is something that almost anyone can relate to, no matter what their age, intellectual or social level, physical or mental handicap. One organization that has offices in various cities that provides these services is Hospital Audiences, sometimes called Very Special Audiences. Denver also has an organization called Artreach, that brings the arts to special populations varying from halfway houses for juveniles to senior centers. Check with the Department of Social Services in your local city government to see if there are similar organizations in your community.

Artist in Residence Programs

Another significant area of possible employment is available through government or foundation-supported grant programs. Every state in the United States has an arts council and a humanities council. Similar programs are available in Canada. Arts councils exist to promote an appreciation of the arts and to help local artists and arts organizations to achieve recognition. Each state arts council has a program called Artists in Residence (AIR), Or Artists in the Schools. These programs hire artists to work in schools for periods ranging from half a day to an entire school year.

A "residence" means that you work in a school or community setting. In order to do this, you must live in or near that locale. If you live in a large state, the residency may require you to temporarily relocate. The arts council may provide you with free or low-cost housing, but you may lose the ability to work at your normal evening musical gigs in your home town.

Each state administers this program in its own way, using broad federal guidelines. There are many employment opportunities available through these programs. The state gives a local school district some "matching funds" to pay for an artist to work in a school. The extent of the match varies from state to state.

Usually these jobs are for soloists; not for groups. The reason more work is available for solo acts is that the Arts Council and the local school district must come up with more money for each member of the group. In these days of budget-cutting for school programs, this is unlikely to happen.

The AIR aims to offer new experiences to children in a particular school. Music is only one of a number of disciplines represented. Dance, drama, creative writing, video and visual arts specialists may also apply for the programs.

The usual procedure for an AIR position is to submit a form, together with a resume and a tape of your work. (See the sample of the Colorado Council on the Arts form at the end of this chapter). The Arts Council staff then screens the application. If you get past the preliminary screening, the Council calls you to do a short audition. The judges are selected from people with previous working experience in the program, some of whom will undoubtedly be musicians. Others on the panel will include Council staff members, and some educators who have had artists in their schools and are familiar with the program.

The judging of your work is based on an evaluation of your talent together with some consideration of whether your work will fit into a public school program. You need to be able to communicate with children, as well as demonstrating that you have artistic ability.

The forms will ask whether you can work in different areas of the state, and what lengths of time you are willing to commit to the work. The less restrictions you place on where and when you are willing to work, the better your chances of being employed in the program. However take into account the size of the state in which you live, and whether travel will be a hardship.

One of the things you can do to try to improve your chances of getting AIR work is to contact a school and work with them on proposing a program. The school goes through roughly the same process that you do with the Council. Their grant proposal is scored by a panel on the basis of the validity of the program and how much it can contribute to the artistic learning of the children, together with some judgments as to whether the program has been well-planned and is workable as described in the grant form.

There are some pitfalls to getting a school to do a grant proposal. They may be funded and you may not have passed the artist audition. Or you might be chosen, but the school's grant is rejected as being poorly planned or insufficiently interesting. It is still wise to get schools to write grants, however, because it increases the odds in your favor.

Is all of this worth the trouble of doing the paperwork and an audition? Most of the AIR programs pay the artist approximately $500 a week, plus mileage. They may or may not provide a housing allowance if you need to travel many miles away from your home. The local hosts will usually, at the very least, attempt to assist you in finding low-cost housing.

The beauty of the AIR program is that almost all events take place during the day, leaving your nighttime hours free for practicing, writing, or even performing. There are also generally no weekend obligations, so if you are not far from home, you can at least continue to work weekends.

Some states allow applicants from other states. You are less likely to actually get work unless you have a fairly unique skill or have developed a reputation that has spread to that state. You will have to do more hustling and try to contact schools in the other state to be sure that there are some requests for your services. Unfortunately, it is possible to be listed on the AIR roster, but not to actually get any work from it.

Each state has its own specific procedures. Some states encourage community arts residencies, where your residency is in a city, rather than in a school. The same general rules apply, except that you will be working with adults as well as children.

Once you are accepted into an AIR program, you have entered another network that can supply you with additional opportunities for employment. The state arts councils often get requests from local arts councils or from various areas of the state to recommend musicians to play at festivals or special events. Once the people working at the arts council get to know you, they may well recommend you for other work. Many of them are artists themselves, and they have a pretty good idea of how artists work. Best of all, since they are state agencies and not for-profit companies, you do not pay any commission on this work. Other arts council grant programs are discussed in Chapter Six.

Other sources of grant money include city arts programs and private foundations. Consult your local librarian, particularly at a college library, for a list of private foundations in your state. Often, the money offered by private foundations is related to education or disadvantaged populations. For example, they might be willing to fund a songwriting program for juvenile delinquents, but they are not apt to fund a demo of your band. Many uses of music are appropriate in the area of mental health programs, such as improvising music with disturbed children. Use your imagination, and consult with the foundation office for help.

There is also a fair amount of work available performing music for "special populations," such as people in penal institutions, seniors, disturbed children and numerous other groups. Performing for special populations involves more than setting up a sound system and getting everyone to "boogie." Seniors are apt to be interested in hearing songs that were popular when they were teenagers or young adults. Research your audience, much as you would do in a normal performance. You wouldn't play bossa nova in a country bar, would you? Check with local seniors' organizations and with your city or state Department of Social Services.

Through working with special populations, you may develop skills and an interest in learning about music therapy. Some friends of mine have been able to get steady work performing for and with patients in mental hospitals. They find the work is very satisfying. There are a number of full and part-time jobs available in the field of music therapy. Should you become more interested in this area, you may want to take some college courses, or even get a degree in this field.

Arts Council Form

Colorado Council Form, used by permission.

1998-1999 ARTS IN EDUCATION GRANT APPLICATION

APPLICATION TITLE PAGE

<u>DEADLINE: POSTMARKED OCTOBER 1, 1998</u>

PLEASE TYPE OR PRINT CLEARLY/NO STAPLES

NAME OF SCHOOL _____ SCHOOL PHONE _____

SCHOOL ADDRESS _____ SCHOOL FAX _____

CITY _____ ZIP _____ COUNTY _____ SCHOOL DISTRICT NAME/NUMBER _____

IS THE SCHOOL: PUBLIC? _____ PRIVATE? _____   GRADES IN THE SCHOOL: _____

TOTAL # OF CLASSES: _____   STUDENT POPULATION: _____

FACULTY POPULATION # _____ # OF _____ VISUAL ARTS SPECIALISTS _____ MUSIC SPECIALISTS

_____ THEATRE/DRAMA   _____ OTHER ARTS: _____

STUDENT DEMOGRAPHICS:
_____% AFRICAN AMERICAN _____% LATINO/CHICANO _____% ASIAN/PACIFIC ISLANDER
_____% AMERICAN INDIAN/ALASKAN NATIVE _____% CAUCASIAN/WHITE _____% OTHER

IS THE SCHOOL DESIGNATED A TITLE 1 SCHOOL? _____ YES _____ NO
(NOTE: VERIFICATION OF TITLE 1 DESIGNATION MUST BE INCLUDED WITH APPLICATION)

☐ REPEAT SCHOOL (HAS HAD A YA RESIDENCY PROJECT WITHIN THE PAST THREE YEARS)

☐ NEW SCHOOL

PRINCIPAL/AUTHORIZING OFFICIAL: _____ HOME PHONE: _____

CONTACT FOR GRANT APPLICATION: _____ HOME PHONE: _____

CONTACT PERSON FOR THE RESIDENCY: _____

HOME ADDRESS OF CONTACT PERSON: _____ CITY: _____ ZIP: _____ HOME PHONE: _____

INDICATE THE REGION SERVED BY YOUR PROPOSED ACTIVITY:
☐ EASTERN/SMALL COMMUNITIES   ☐ SOUTHERN/SAN LUIS VALLEY
☐ FRONT RANGE/URBAN AREAS OF WELD, LARIMER, PUEBLO AND   ☐ WESTERN/AGRICULTURAL
   EL PASO COUNTIES   ☐ WESTERN/MOUNTAIN & RESORT AREAS
☐ METRO DENVER/URBAN AND SUBURBAN AREAS IN SCFD   ☐ STATEWIDE OR MULTI REGION

LEGISLATIVE DISTRICT(HOUSE)*: _____ NAME OF REPRESENTATIVE: _____

LEGISLATIVE DISTRICT(SENATE)*: _____ NAME OF SENATOR: _____

U.S. CONGRESSIONAL DISTRICT*: _____ NAME OF CONGRESS PERSON: _____
*CONTACT THE LOCAL BOARD OF VOTER REGISTRATION OR LEAGUE OF WOMEN VOTERS FOR THESE. APPLICATIONS WILL NOT BE PROCESSED WITHOUT THEM.

PROJECT OVERVIEW

RESIDENCY:
TENTATIVE DATES OF RESIDENCY:_____

DESIRED LENGTH OF RESIDENCY:_____

DISCIPLINE DESIRED:_____

NAME OF ARTIST/S (IF DETERMINED):_____

IF THE ARTIST IS CURRENTLY DETERMINED, ATTACH 3 COPIES OF A
LETTER IN WHICH HE OR SHE DESCRIBES EXPECTATIONS FOR THE
RESIDENCY AND INVOLVEMENT IN THE RESIDENCY PLANNING

RESIDENCY PLUS:

☐ SCHOOL IS REQUESTING STAFF DEVELOPMENT
IF SCHOOL IS APPLYING FOR THE STAFF DEVELOPMENT OPTION - NAME
OF BRIDGE BUILDER (IF DETERMINED)

☐ SCHOOL IS REQUESTING EDUCATIONAL
PERFORMANCES
IF SCHOOL IS APPLYING FOR THE EDUCATIONAL PERFORMANCES OPTION
NAME OF EDUCATIONAL PERFORMANCE (IF DETERMINED)

☐ SCHOOL IS REQUESTING COMMUNITY EXPERIENCES
NAME OF COLLABORATING COMMUNITY ORGANIZATION:

IF A COMMUNITY ORGANIZATION IS INVOLVED, ATTACH 3 COPIES OF A
LETTER IN WHICH IT DESCRIBES EXPECTATIONS FOR THE RESIDENCY
AND INVOLVEMENT IN THE RESIDENCY PLANNING

LIST OF PLANNING COMMITTEE:
NAME/TITLE/AFFILIATION

LIST OF TEACHERS WHO HAVE ATTENDED
ANY OF YA'S TEACHER TRAINING
INSTITUTES:
NAME/TITLE/AFFILIATION   INSTITUTE & YEAR

	BUDGET	
	PLEASE REFER TO BUDGET TABLE IN GUIDELINES	
A.	TOTAL *RESIDENCY* COST:	$
B.	TOTAL *STAFF DEVELOPMENT* COST:	$
C.	TOTAL *EDUCATIONAL PERFORMANCE* COST:	$
D.	TOTAL *COMMUNITY EXPERIENCES* COST:	$
E.	TOTAL COSTS (A+B+C+D)	$
F (1)	REQUIRED SCHOOL MATCH (50% OF LINE E)	$
OR F(2)	TITLE I SCHOOL MATCH (30% OF LINE E)	$
G	VISUAL ART MATERIALS (IF APPLICABLE)	$
H	TOTAL SCHOOL MATCH: [F(1) OR F(2)] + G	$

ASSURANCES

The Applicant assures that it is eligible under the Colorado Council on the Arts guidelines. All information contained herein is accurate or represents a reasonable estimate of future operations based on information available at this time; and there are no deliberate misstatements or misrepresentations in the information submitted herein or as supplement to this application. The application is a part of the public record.

The Applicant assures that the Colorado Council on the Arts and the State of Colorado, their employees and agents, shall not be held liable or responsible for damages to or loss caused by the negligence of the Colorado Council on the Arts, the State of Colorado, their employees and/or agents. The Council will make every effort to return slides, video/audio tapes, photographs and other materials as stipulated by the applicant. Questions regarding the return of support material should be directed to the Associate Director by the applicant organization. The applicant will provide an adequate self-addressed stamped envelope for mailing.

The Applicant assures that it will comply with Title VI of the Civil Rights Act of 1964 which provides that "…no person in the United States shall, on the grounds of race, color, or national origin, be excluded from participation in, be denied the benefits or, be subject to discrimination under any program or activity receiving Federal financial assistance."

Age Discrimination Act of 1975 provides that no person in the United States shall, on the basis of age, be excluded from participation in, be denied the benefits of, or be subject to discrimination under any program or activity receiving Federal financial assistance. . . .

Title IX of the Education Amendments of 1972 provides that no person in the United States shall, on the basis of sex, be excluded from participation in, be denied the benefits of, or be subject to discrimination under any program or activity receiving Federal financial assistance.

The Applicant assures that it will meet the requirements of Sec. 504 of the Rehabilitation Act (P.L. 93-112) which provides that "…no otherwise qualified handicapped individual in the United States…shall, solely by reason of his handicap, be excluded from participation in, be denied the benefits of, or be subjected to discrimination under any program or activity receiving Federal financial assistance. . . ."

The Americans with Disabilities Act became law on July 26, 1990. The Act extends civil rights protection to people with disabilities, assuring that they cannot be excluded from participation in any program or facility that is open to the public. Because the achievement of access for people with disabilities, as directed by Federal law, frequently requires long-range planning and budgeting, the Colorado Council on the Arts encourages applicants to consider access issues in early planning stages of programs and services.

The Applicant assures that it will comply with the Fair Labor Standards Act in regards to the employment of professional performers and related supporting professional personnel, mechanics and laborers employed for any construction on a project, and the health, safety and sanitary laws of the State.

The Applicant assures that it will continue to provide a "drug-free workplace" as a condition of receiving a grant from the Colorado Council on the Arts as required by the Drug-Free Workplace Act of 1988 (P.L. 100-690, Title V, Subtitle D).

Signature of Principal   Date

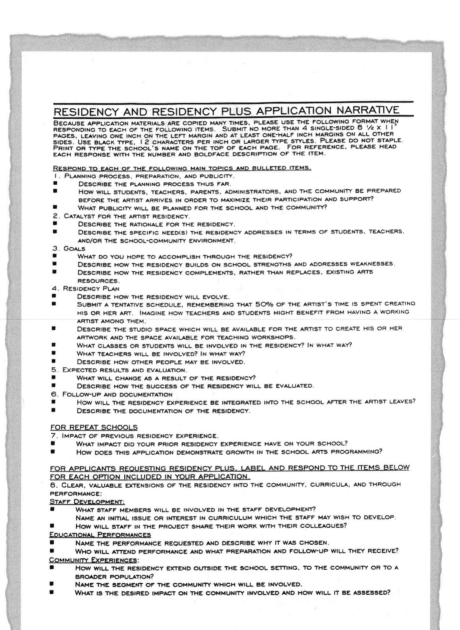

RESIDENCY AND RESIDENCY PLUS APPLICATION NARRATIVE

Because application materials are copied many times, please use the following format when responding to each of the following items. Submit no more than 4 single-sided 8 1/2 x 11" pages, leaving one inch on the left margin and at least one-half inch margins on all other sides. Use black type, 12 characters per inch or larger type styles. Please do not staple. Print or type the school's name on the top of each page. For reference, please head each response with the number and boldface description of the item.

Respond to each of the following main topics and bulleted items.

1. Planning process, preparation, and publicity.
   - Describe the planning process thus far.
   - How will students, teachers, parents, administrators, and the community be prepared before the artist arrives in order to maximize their participation and support?
   - What publicity will be planned for the school and the community?

2. Catalyst for the artist residency.
   - Describe the rationale for the residency.
   - Describe the specific need(s) the residency addresses in terms of students, teachers, and/or the school-community environment.

3. Goals
   - What do you hope to accomplish through the residency?
   - Describe how the residency builds on school strengths and addresses weaknesses.
   - Describe how the residency complements, rather than replaces, existing arts resources.

4. Residency Plan
   - Describe how the residency will evolve.
   - Submit a tentative schedule, remembering that 50% of the artist's time is spent creating his or her art. Imagine how teachers and students might benefit from having a working artist among them.
   - Describe the studio space which will be available for the artist to create his or her artwork and the space available for teaching workshops.
   - What classes or students will be involved in the residency? In what way?
   - What teachers will be involved? In what way?
   - Describe how other people may be involved.

5. Expected results and evaluation.
   - What will change as a result of the residency?
   - Describe how the success of the residency will be evaluated.

6. Follow-up and documentation
   - How will the residency experience be integrated into the school after the artist leaves?
   - Describe the documentation of the residency.

FOR REPEAT SCHOOLS

7. Impact of previous residency experience.
   - What impact did your prior residency experience have on your school?
   - How does this application demonstrate growth in the school arts programming?

FOR APPLICANTS REQUESTING RESIDENCY PLUS, LABEL AND RESPOND TO THE ITEMS BELOW FOR EACH OPTION INCLUDED IN YOUR APPLICATION.

8. Clear, valuable extensions of the residency into the community, curricula, and through performance:

Staff Development:
   - What staff members will be involved in the staff development? Name an initial issue or interest in curriculum which the staff may wish to develop.
   - How will staff in the project share their work with their colleagues?

Educational Performances
   - Name the performance requested and describe why it was chosen.
   - Who will attend performance and what preparation and follow-up will they receive?

Community Experiences:
   - How will the residency extend outside the school setting, to the community or to a broader population?
   - Name the segment of the community which will be involved.
   - What is the desired impact on the community involved and how will it be assessed?

APPLICATION CHECKLIST

☐ Applicant is a public or private pre K-12 elementary, middle, or high school

☐ The applicant understands that it must provide time during a school day for orientation and groundwork, with the principal and the planning team present

☐ The proposed project takes place within the project period defined in the guidelines

☐ The school's typed and signed application is postmarked on or before October 1, 1998 (one original and two copies)

☐ School Arts Profile is completed (Three copies)

☐ Each of the project questions 1-6 from the application narrative is answered in the specified typed format (Three copies)

☐ Verification of Title I designation is included in the application (if applicable)

Required letters are attached or sent under separate cover

☐ Letter from the artist - if a particular artist is being requested
Artist describes his/her expectations for the residency and involvement in the residency planning.

   ☐ Letter is attached with this application

   ☐ Letter is coming under separate cover

☐ Letter from Community Organization - If the school is applying for the Community Experiences option in conjunction with a non-profit organization, indicating the involvement of the organization in planning and implementation

   ☐ Letter is attached with this application

   ☐ Letter is coming under separate cover

☐ The assurances have been read and signed

One of the following is true:

   ☐ The school HAS received a residency through YA in the previous 3 years and answered the application question related to repeat school (Answer question #7)

   ☐ The school HAS NOT received a residency through YA in the previous 3 years

One of the following is true:

   ☐ The school is applying for one or all of the residency plus options (Answer appropriate items in question #8)

   ☐ The school is NOT applying for any of the Residency Plus options

For assistance in completing your application, call Young Audiences at (303) 922-5880. Mail to: Box 205 Loretto Station, 3001 S. Federal Blvd, Denver, CO 80236-2711

CHAPTER 4 RESOURCES

The Buttwinick, Chadbourne and Levine books recommended in Chapter 2 are also relevant to this chapter.

The annual book, *Songwriter's Market*, published by Writer's Digest in Cincinnati, lists producers of audio-visual materials and short films who are looking for music. It is an invaluable resource.

Most state arts councils are located in the capital city of your state. Check for their addresses in the telephone book under "State Government."

The address for NACA is: National Association for Campus Activities, P.O. Box 6828, Columbia, SC 29260.

chapter	5

Developing Versatility

Developing versatility is the key to expanding your opportunities to work in the music business. Whatever you know how to do or are doing, there are ways to expand your employment opportunities by using the skills you already possess.

Start with the most basic and obvious skills. What instrument do you currently play? How many other related instruments could you add to your arsenal? If you are a guitarist, do you also play banjo, mandolin or ukulele? If you play electric guitar, do you have both jazz and rock-type guitars, a rack of effects pedals, a MIDI adaptor, or a guitar synthesizer? Do you own both acoustic and electric guitars? What about a twelve-string? If you play acoustic guitar, do you own both nylon and steel string models? Can you play both pick and finger style? Can you use finger picks or play slide guitar?

Even if you only play a single instrument, there are options open to you that can increase your musical scope and ability to tackle new musical projects. The fact that Jimmy Page could play excellent acoustic guitar, as well as his wild electric rock leads, enabled Led Zeppelin to use a wider sound palette that was not in the repertoire of most of their rock competitors. Expanding your musical sphere will help vary the musical arrangements of your band and make you a greater asset for any future musical endeavors.

Other rhythm instrument players have similar opportunities. If you are an electric bass player, do you own both fretted and fretless bass instruments? Can you play an upright acoustic bass? Do you know how to use a bow? Do you have effects pedals that will expand the range of the music that you play? Do you play the newer five and six string electric basses? If you play drums, do you own a drum machine or synthesized drums? Can you follow a chart? Do you play Latin percussion, or own any exotic percussion instruments, such as an Irish bodhran or African or Greek percussion instruments?

Family of Instruments

Instrument Family	Instrument	Related Instrument or Skills
Rhythm	Guitar	Acoustic; various electric; 12-string; 5-string banjo; tenor banjo; dobro; mandolin; ukulele; effects pedals; MIDI; synthesizer; pedal steel guitar
	Bass	Fretted; fretless; acoustic; use of the bow; 5-string; 6-string; tuba
	Keyboards	Acoustic; synthesizers; piano; organ; harpsichord; celeste; clavinet; sequencers; samplers; accordion
	Drums	Congas; bongos; woodblocks; tympani; tambourine; drum synthesizers; drum machines; Latin & African percussion
Woodwinds	Saxophones	Clarinet; flute; oboe; english horn; bass clarinet; alto flute; recorder family; piccolo; tenor, alto, baritone, soprano and bass saxophones; EWI
Brass	Trumpet	Flugelhorn; piccolo; trumpet; mutes; EWI
	Trombone	Bass and tenor trombones; sackbut, mutes
Strings	Violin	Viola; mandolin; electric violin; cello
	Bass	See rhythm bass above
All		MIDI adaptors are now available for virtually all instruments, enabling players to achieve effects that were previously impossible. Sampling devices allow players to achieve the sounds of any instrument.

Keyboard players, do you own one or more synthesizers? Do you have your various keyboards hooked together via MIDI? Do you play organ, harpsichord and acoustic piano? Can you read and improvise with equal skill?

On the previous page is a chart of various instrument families, designed to indicate ways of improving your employment prospects and musical skills. Adding variety will help keep you excited about playing music, and will also lead to more and better-paying jobs.

Some of the work in smaller music markets may actually demand more versatility than is required in a major music market. For example, in New York it is possible to make a living (though admittedly, usually a modest one) simply by playing jazz. If you live in, say Idaho Falls, you will need to explore additional options. Teaching is one of the more obvious ones.

Teaching

If you have a college degree with a major in music education or you are getting one, you may want to consider teaching in the public school system. In order to get certification, you must have completed courses in music education and completed practice teaching in a school. The course work includes the basics of study in different families of instruments, so that you can work with school ensembles. No one can play many instruments with equal facility, but taking method courses in the various families of instruments will enable you to develop a basic understanding of the orchestra. Other parts of the music education curriculum include the study of conducting and music transposition. These subjects are essential in dealing with a school band. The same general sort of study leads to jobs conducting school choral groups. In small schools a teacher may have to conduct both a chorus and an orchestra.

Public school music generally includes music programs to celebrate the holidays; a spring and/or graduation program; and music during sporting events.

Work is also available as a substitute music teacher. The advantage of subbing is that you can work when you choose, providing work is available. The disadvantage is that although the pay is reasonably good, you probably will not qualify for dental or medical benefits, nor will you be paid during summer vacations. Part-time or substitute teachers are unlikely to accumulate pension benefits.

Teaching in private schools is another possibility. Private or religious schools may not demand state certification and their programs may have a bit more flexibility than the standard public school offerings.

Many teachers continue with active playing careers, working weekend gigs and even touring in the summer. Summer music camps offer teachers additional opportunities to earn extra income. Many musicians thrive on teaching music; it actually fuels their enthusiasm to play. Others find that teaching music all day is not conducive to inspiring one to practice or perform music on a regular basis. You need to decide for yourself which sort of reaction you are apt to have to a full-time teaching position. It is also important to keep in mind that opportunities in public school teaching seem to be diminishing. Despite research that validates the importance of music in a school program, state legislatures and school boards seem to always cut music and art budgets as their first steps towards balancing the budget. On the other hand, if you are able to find full-time employment as a music teacher, you will receive pension, medical and dental benefits, and a fair amount of vacation time. For the average musician, these benefits are unheard of, outside of teaching or employment in a major symphony orchestra.

If you do decide to pursue a career in teaching music in the schools, it is a good idea to study ways of integrating music into the overall school curriculum. This includes the use of music in teaching American history, as well as the mathematical and acoustical foundations of music.

Private Teaching

Many musicians set up a private teaching practice in their own homes. Some teachers even go to the student's home, which may represent a considerable investment of your time, not to mention the price of gas and car maintenance. However, you may be able to charge more and get a more upscale group of students. Many music stores employ teachers to give private lessons, but usually charge the teacher from 10-20% for recruiting students and setting up lessons.

Working for a music store can provide you with a regular income, but it also can be a deadening experience. Many store studios are small cubicles and spending hour after hour in such an environment is not particularly conducive to your physical or mental health. This condition is aggravated in warm weather, if the studio is not air-conditioned.

One way to avoid teaching burnout is to schedule 45 minute lessons, leaving 15 minutes at the end of the hour for relaxing, getting outside for a breath of air, making notes on the last lesson, making phone calls, or talking to the student. Although this will cut into your income, it will make you a better teacher and a saner person.

For children under the age of fourteen, a half hour is a good amount of lesson time. Many children don't practice enough to justify a longer lesson or don't have a sufficient attention spans to get through a longer lesson. Naturally, there are exceptions, such as children who are unusually mature or motivated. In such circumstances, you can always experiment with a longer lesson time.

If you play keyboard or guitar or write songs, you may also be able to teach group classes. Teaching groups of people is sometimes less musically satisfying than teaching individuals, because people who take group lessons are usually less serious about the work involved. Groups can be fun, though, because of the interaction between the various personalities in the class. They also pay better than private lessons, even though the fee per person will be smaller.

My favorite group lesson experience took place with one adult male student. He seemed to grasp everything quite well during the lessons, but each week he would come back and seem to be at exactly the same level of skill. After three weeks of this I tried to diagnose the problem. As it turned out, he never practiced at home because he thought since he was learning the material in class, there was no need to spend time at home repeating the same things he had learned in the class.

In order to teach classes, you will need a location suitable for approximately five to ten students. Community centers, religious institutions, community colleges or music stores are possibilities. You can advertise the class through sponsoring organizations, or you can rent the place yourself and advertise the classes by printing up fliers or making posters. The advantage of having a sponsoring organization is that they will publicize the class on bulletin boards or in their own catalog or newsletter. They usually have large mailing lists, which give you a good chance of filling your classes.

You should set a limit on the size of your classes, so people are comfortable in the space and can get to know one another. Several friends of mine have run successful guitar classes lasting two hours. The second hour is a sort of sing-along social hour, combining beginners with students who have a bit of playing experience. Since many people who take group lessons are adults and have no illusions about becoming guitar heroes, the second hour is sometimes more fun than the actual lesson. The Old Town School of Folk Music in Chicago offers large group classes, combining various stringed instruments and several teachers. They have had success with this format for over forty years.

What should you charge for lessons? You will need to check the going price in your area, which may be anywhere from $10 to $25 for a half-hour lesson. It is possible to teach two students in one lesson, especially if they are friends or siblings. A fair arrangement is to charge less than you would for two private lessons, but more than you would for a regular group lesson. Group lessons usually cost $5-$10 per person, and the fee is usually paid ahead of time. Most group lessons run in series of six to eight weeks. The biggest problem with group lessons is being sure you have enough enrollment to offer the classes. One way to accomplish this is to offer a pre-payment discount for classes, in the same way that many shows charge more at the door than if tickets are bought in advance.

Many teachers collect by the month, on the first lesson of the month. Some teachers give a slight discount for prepayment, such as offering all "lesson months" as though they had four lesson days per month. This gives the student a free lesson every third month when there are actually five lesson days during the month.

Make-up lessons are a ticklish issue. A teacher should not allow make-ups unless the cancellation takes place 24 hours in advance. If you do not adopt this policy, you will get last minute cancellations from parents who forgot about beauty parlor appointments or golf dates. Some teachers simply don't offer make-ups, but that's probably pushing things a bit too far. Make-ups can be scheduled on a day when you normally don't teach. If you have a large teaching practice, trying to schedule make-up lessons on a hit-and-miss basis can be disastrous. Don't allow students to cancel because they haven't practiced. Use that situation for a lesson in improvisation, sight-reading or analyzing records.

Another consideration in teaching is your own attendance. If you are going to teach on a regular basis, then you can't leave to take a last-minute luncheon gig. Deal with your students in the same way you expect them to deal with you. If you need to make a last minute cancellation, you can offer a free lesson to the student who you have inconvenienced. If these changes in your work schedule keep happening, you should consider cutting down on your teaching load.

Summer is a time when many students drop out of lessons. They may leave because of vacations, work, social commitments or athletic interests. You need to anticipate this drop-off in your income. Very few students will want to take lessons during holiday breaks. If you charge by the month, you should charge for these "vacation times."

If you are consistent about following most of the policies outlined, you can count on teaching as a good supplementary source of income. It can even provide your major bread and butter, if you want it to, if you can develop a regular clientele. Music stores that don't offer lessons are a good source of referrals. Another source of potential students is advertisement in the local entertainment weekly, or even in the daily newspaper.

You will need to find a source of rental instruments, especially if you are teaching group lessons. If you rent any instrument yourself, be sure to get a deposit to cover damage and to make sure that the instruments won't disappear. Renting provides a reasonable alternative to the jaded parent who has watched her child go through many fads and temporary hobbies or interests.

If you are teaching for a music store or studio, you will be encouraged to have the student buy instruments and supplies there. There is nothing wrong with this, provided the store does not tack-on unreasonable mark-ups. Be sure to advise the store as to what supplies and sheet music you'll be recommending to your students. You should resist the tendency of some store owners to get you to pressure the parent to spend money for a higher quality instrument, even if the store owner offers you a commission on the sale. A good teaching relationship that can continue for several years is worth a lot more to you than ten or twenty dollars in commission from the sale of an instrument that is not needed. It is the teacher who should be the judge of when the student is ready to up-grade their instrument.

Record at least a portion of your music lessons on a cassette tape. The student can then refresh her memory by playing the tape at home. This will also prevent unnecessary phone calls between lessons. Be sure to have some blank tapes available, because students invariably forget to bring their tapes. It is also a wise idea to have the student write down all lesson assignments in a notebook. You should also have a notebook in which you keep track of each student's progress. Sometimes, when a teacher gets busy, he too can forget what pieces he has assigned, or what sections of a piece the student needs to work on.

Sample Pieces at Medium Skill Levels

Below and following are examples of what you are apt to meet with on a normal club date or on a record date. Here's an original be-bop line in Db for a lead player.

Here's a sample of a regular piano part for a standard tune.

Take Me Out to the Ball Game

Here's a typical example of a rhythm lead sheet for guitar, bass or keyboard. (Note that the key signature only appears on the first line.)

CHAPTER 5 RESOURCES

There are dozens of books about teaching music in schools. The best resource I have found about private teaching is the book *Making Money Teaching Music*. It was written by David R. Newsam and Barbara Sprague Newsam, and published by Writer's Digest in Cincinnati in 1995.

chapter 6

Making Use of the Union and Other Organizations

Many musicians see themselves as purveyors of some sort of glamorous lifestyle, rather than blue collar workers. When the question comes up of uniting with their colleagues in a labor organization, they invariably ask, "What can the Union do for me?"

Union leaders often resort to blue collar answers to what is really a white-collar question. The Union sets wage scales, offers pensions and benefits for those participating in national contracts, and provides a measure of job protection. A number of AFM locals also offer pensions based on contributions for work done locally.

Many younger musicians see the Union regulations as restrictions on their work life. A member is not supposed to work with non-union musicians, contracts are supposed to be filed on all jobs played, members must pay work taxes on these jobs, and many of the younger musicians feel the cold shoulder from older union officials, whose idea of a contemporary rock tune is "Kansas City."

However the union is what its members make of it. The truth is, many musicians are out in the cold if they're working without the protection of a signed contract. Unfortunately, there are a fair number of sleazy agents out there booking jobs at low wages, and a considerable group of club owners who tend to treat musicians like mildly-educated cattle. The real question is not whether a serious professional should join the Union, but how she can make it work to her best advantage.

Some professional engagements absolutely require Union membership. Professional symphony orchestras work under collective bargaining agreements. These contractual agreements not only cover wages, but every aspect of working conditions. They are hammered out in complex negotiations between lawyers representing both sides. Players in such orchestras require Union membership within 30 days of employment. When you consider that symphony orchestras employ from 60 to 105 musicians, it would be a disaster if each musician had to negotiate such matters as length of rehearsals, instrument insurance, dental and medical plans, disability, and a procedure for arbitrating disputes. Fortunately for the symphony musician, the Union negotiates such agreements on a daily basis around North America.

What about musicians in pop or country music? Anyone recording for major record companies must be a Union member because the major record companies have all signed Union agreements that require it. Musicians who want to appear on national or syndicated television performing on-camera are required to join AFTRA, the American Federation of Radio and Television Artists, as well as the AFM.

Should those who wish to make their own records bother with the Union? Meet the Special Payments Fund—one of the least understood benefits of Union membership, one that can actually assist you in financing your own recordings.

The Special Payments Fund pays a yearly bonus to all Union musicians who participate in recording sessions with filed Union contracts. The bonus is based on the amount of each musician's gross wages earned in recording sessions. It has nothing to do with the sales of the recordings you played on, but is a small percentage of the sales of **all** recordings. The payments continue on a reduced scale for an additional four-year period after the first year.

How can this help a four-piece country band in Boise? If this group files union contracts, pays work dues and makes the ten percent pension contribution to the AFM Pension Fund, they will then receive bonuses based on their gross wages during the recording sessions. The pension money is put into the AFM Pension Fund and comes back to the musicians involved, between ages 55 and 65. To qualify for a pension, a musician needs to have earned $1,500 in pension-covered wages for a period of five years. One-quarter, one-half and three-quarters of a year's credits are given for those who earned $375, $750 and $1,125 in covered wages. Thirty five locals have pension plans for work done in their jurisdiction, so the amount of your pension will escalate if you are a member of one of these locals.

Self-contained groups (those who do all of their own playing) generally file six sessions for each album recorded. One album a year will cover you for a full pension credit. Any commercials, film scores, television shows, slide shows or industrial film scores in which you perform that utilize union contracts will also add to your pension credits.

How important is the Special Payments Fund? A few musicians make over $30,000 from their bonuses, and many others clear anything from $50–$1,000 and up. The size of your check depends upon how many Union sessions you played. A similar bonus plan exists for musicians who play on feature film scores that utilize union contracts. In the bonus fund for film, you are paid bonuses based on the gross of the particular film you performed on, rather than the gross of all films.

The chart on the next page summarizes some of the other advantages and disadvantages of Union affiliation.

Radio and Television Commercials

Under Union agreements, commercials pay residuals, i.e., repeat payments for extended uses. These payments are made every 13 weeks, and are governed by agreements between the Union and advertising agencies. Local commercials recorded under AFM agreements used in a single market are allowed to run for as long as 18 months with the payment of residuals. Local commercials have a markedly lower payback than national commercials because:

1. There is a great deal of recording going on in the secondary music markets, and the Union had to modify the rules to compete with non-Union producers.
2. The Union has recognized that the budgets for recording local commercials and the money involved in buying time on local TV or radio is relatively small. A small bank in rural Nebraska cannot afford to make the sort of repayments that a national beer company regards as part of the cost of doing business.

How significant is the income from residuals? In New York, the center for recording commercials, studio players estimate that two-thirds of their income comes

Advantages of Union Affiliation	Disadvantages of Union Affiliation
The Union provides you with a standard form contract	You pay work dues of 1-3 % on all jobs played. These work dues are based on the local Union minimums.
Commissions are limited by the Union	You are not supposed to work for agents not franchised by the Union
The Union sets the minimum wages	Too many groups are willing to work for the bare minimum and some agents are all too accustomed to negotiating minimum wage
The Union may recommend you for jobs. Many locals have a job availability book and will also help you to hook up with other players	Some Uunion locals make rock or country players feel unwelcome
In the event of a breach of contract, you have some legal recourse. Some Union locals will even pay you the minimum wage and help you to institute legal proceedings to collect the rest, if the wage is "over scale."	
You can get unscrupulous employers put on the Union blacklist. An emergency phone number, (800) ROAD GIG, provides 24-hour assistance for traveling musicians.	
The owner cannot fire you without notice.	
The Union local in your town may participate in the AFM pension plan. It may also offer access to a credit union, discounts on such items as musical supplies, tires, etc.	

from residuals and only a third from new commercials. (I have had the pleasant experience of earning as much as $2,000 in repayments from a single one-hour recording session, and have had commercials that have run for as long as ten years.) Other repayment schemes govern the use of film scores on television.

Singers belong to either the American Federation of Television and Radio Artists (AFTRA), or SAG (the Screen Actors Guild.) Singers receive much higher residuals for their work than musicians and their Union contracts are much more complicated. They have many categories of use (including local, regional, national, prime time and so-called "wild spots"), that allow for unlimited use during a specific period of time. A single national campaign for a major product which includes both radio and television and runs for an extended period of time, may earn a singer tens of thousands of dollars.

Returning to the subject of the AFM, most musicians do relatively little recording. What about the players whose bread and butter comes from freelancing or performing in clubs?

The Musicians' Union As a Source of Work

When you live in a larger city with 250,000 people or more, there are usually various types of traveling shows that come through your town. Among them are ice shows, touring artists who require small or large groups to augment their performances, the circus and traveling companies of Broadway shows. In every town there are musicians called "contractors" whose function is to put together bands for such touring entertainment. In return for performing this service, the contractor earns from 1½ to 2 times the union wage paid to the other musicians. Contractors usually play the job with the rest of the band; although in larger towns, they may not play, but simply supervise the proceedings. Contractors call rest breaks, see that everyone arrives on time with the proper instruments and supervise both the Union paperwork and collection of tax forms. The employer relies on the contractor to handle any emergencies, such as dealing with absent or late musicians and any other personnel problems.

Almost all of this highly professional work is funneled through the local Musicians' Union. If you are serious about trying to find this sort of freelance employment, you will need to join the Musicians' Union, unless you live in a Right-To-Work state. A Right-To-Work state is one that has passed legislation stipulating that membership in a union may not be a condition governing employment.

Even in such states, there is nothing to prevent a local contractor from "accidentally" hiring a band that consists entirely of Union members. This procedure may sound unfair to you, but it is the Musicians' Union that has established the wage scales and working conditions covering these jobs. This often requires long and extensive negotiations, even strikes or arbitration. If each musician had to negotiate with the employer as individuals, they might be at a disadvantage. Few musicians are aware of the expenses of mounting a show, its possible gross, or any special conditions that pertain to a particular production or venue. This is where the Union comes in, negotiating the agreements on a national or local basis, protecting musicians against capricious actions.

For instance, because the conductor of a traveling show is unlikely to see you again, he may make unreasonable or peculiar demands. The Union contract is designed to protect musicians against such eventualities, or at least to set up an arbitration process whereby your employment cannot be arbitrarily terminated.

In the case of the circus, the wage scale depends upon the population of the city. Cities are categorized as A, B, or C, according to population. The A or larger cities have higher wage scales than the other categories.

When you join the Union, you should inquire about local contractors. If you spend a little time with the secretary-treasurer of your local, you can learn how the freelance business functions in your town. A contractor may be retiring or may be replaced because the client was unhappy with the last band she hired. Once you have found out who the contractor is, try to get a recommendation to her from someone who knows her. You should at that time be ready to present a demo tape and resume to her. You may be hired initially as a sub, someone who is hired when the regular player-of-choice is sick, on vacation, or unavailable to work. If you play well and act professionally, the contractor will probably call you again. It is also quite possible that other musicians on the job will call you when they in turn are in a position to hire musicians.

Your teacher may be just the right person to refer you to a contractor, though teachers are sometimes reluctant to refer a student for fear their lack of experience or professionalism will create problems on the job.

Dealing with employers can be a tricky process. You need to be friendly and willing to take direction, yet it can be a mistake to be either too pushy or a pushover. Don't make too many suggestions or behave flamboyantly.

Be sure that you have an answering machine or voice messaging to take calls when you are out, and a calendar book in which to keep all of your bookings and commitments. Not showing up for a job on time or at all, can ruin your career even before it starts. Be sure to have written down when and where the job is, what you are supposed to wear, and what instruments you were asked to bring or rent. If a contractor needs you to play an unusual instrument which you do not own, he should be willing to pay for or split the rental cost.

One of the advantages of Union jobs is that they usually pay extra money for doubling on other instruments. A wind player may end up playing three or four instruments in a show. The additional money can really mount up.

Don't expect immediate results when dealing with contractors. The contractor may want to see you play before hiring you, but often don't bother to seek you out to observe your playing. Your best recommendation is through word-of-mouth by other professionals.

Making Contacts through the Union

It's already been mentioned that most of the freelance gigs that are major bookings, such as traveling Broadway shows, require Union membership as a condition of employment. However, if you're a local country, casual or rock group, would Union membership be meaningful, for you, too?

First, in all honesty, there are locals of the Union indeed run by ex-accordion players or by musicians who will seriously argue that the Glenn Miller Orchestra was the last great music organization. How do you combat that kind of attitude?

Two suggestions: first, play the best shows you can, and impress these dinosaurs with your professionalism. Some union leaders really do think that rock musicians are animals that have been temporarily been let out of their cages, and country musicians are people with boots and sideburns who learned how to play guitar in between milking the cows.

The other step is a bit more extreme. Not only should you come up with the cash to pay the union's initiation fee, you should think about becoming active in your home local. **Don't** join the Union with the attitude that they have your money, now it's time for them to change their attitudes. Help to turn your Local around to the place where you want it to be. The worst kind of Union members are the ones who join and complain about the organization, but can't be bothered to lift a finger to change it.

Why bother to join the Union if you're a rock or country musician? There are a number of locals in the Union that are run by (gasp) rock or country pickers. Locals in various areas of North America have officers who are tuned in to the music business in the 21st century.

On a more mundane but very practical level, as a rock or country musician, you are in a wonderful position to get employment referrals from the Union. The Union invariably gets calls for musicians to play weddings, dances, conventions, luncheons, birthday parties, store openings, political campaigns, nightclubs, etc. If you are the only Union rock band in town, so much the better for you. Go down to the office of the local and get to know the Secretary-Treasurer. Explain to her what your band does, ask for any appropriate job referrals, and give her a promotion kit and a demo. Ask to play MPTF jobs, and even find charities or malls that want to hire your band. Encourage them to apply for MPTF funds and make sure that the Secretary-Treasurer gets their application.

Many young bands often set up a sort of antagonism between "our" music and "their" music that often exists only in their own minds. Not all older musicians hate rock and roll, although it may not be the main ingredient in their major musical meal.

Is it really possible to change anything in an established group like the AFM? **Yes!** I was an inactive member of Local 802 in New York for about ten years, a Union couch potato. I paid my work dues, collected my recording checks, and played a few live gigs. I even went to one or two meetings of the Local. I didn't care for its autocratic and old-fashioned leadership; I figured I had better ways of spending my time than getting involved with the opposition.

When I moved to Denver, I became quite active in that local of the Union. I received many job referrals (though none in New York), and went to most of the meetings. I ran for office and was elected to three terms on the Executive Board. I lobbied in the local to fight for the creation of local jingle scales, because the national scales were unrealistic for the employers in our market.

About 17 years ago, I originated a concept that provided for lowering wage scales on limited pressings of records. Although this proposal was not accepted at that time, the Union accepted this idea a few years later, and had by then, achieved the support of the RMA, the Recording Musicians' Association. (The RMA is an organization of top studio musicians who work in the major recording centers.)

The original limited pressing agreement provided for reducing wages for pressings of 5,000 or fewer records. In 1995, the Union expanded the agreement in providing for another scale for budgets of $90,000 or less. These two agreements have enabled music in specialty areas to be recorded under Union agreements, with the musicians enjoying benefits as well as reasonable wages.

This example indicates that rules are subject to change if the people who desire change have the commitment to fight for what they believe in, with the factual material to back-up their feelings. You have the ability to turn your whole Union local around. You can propose ideas, get on committees, run for the Executive Board, or even be president of your Local in a few years. You can change the way your Union acts and is perceived in your marketplace.

How else can you make use of the Union? Try to persuade your Local to pass a "contract guarantee" clause. This rule stipulates that your Local guarantees to pay you the Union minimum if you work a job and the club owner cannot or will not pay you. This is one of the most significant ideas to come out of the Union in years. It was originated by Richard Totasek, then President of the Spokane local, now an officer of the Los Angeles Local. Naturally, you can't take advantage of this benefit unless you have filed a Union contract for the job in the first place.

Filing a Union contract is as important to your welfare, as well as the Union's. It provides you with a convenient form without needing the services of an entertainment business lawyer. A violation of the contract gives you ammunition to sue the non-paying employer in Small Claims Court or in a regular court of law.

Implementing innovative ideas in your Local is as simple as formulating a creative idea and having the staying power to fight for it. For instance, get your Local to build a small recording studio available to members at bare-bones cost, or convince them to produce a sampler of local groups on a cassette. Parlay that cassette into a recording deal for your own group.

Use the Union to network with other musicians, songwriters, contractors, and recording studio producers or engineers. Be sure to tell the Secretary-Treasurer of your Local that your band wants to receive referrals for gigs. Some locals have even started to *book bands*.

Musicians who live in an area equi-distant between two locals are often unsure as to which local to join. You should be aware that there are some restrictions on your ability to work in a local, other than the one of which you're a member. Work covered under national contracts, such as recording jingles or television scores, can be done with a Union card from any local. However, you may not play a steady job, one lasting more than two weeks, or a number of consecutive weekends unless you are a member of the local in the town in which you are playing. Some locals have residency requirements of up to six months before they will allow membership in the local.

Smaller union locals often charge less quarterly dues than larger locals. However, if you or some of your band are members of a local other than the one you are now working for on a regular basis, the union is unlikely to toss MPTF jobs your way or to refer work to you. They will generally adopt the attitude that work coming through the local's office should go to their own members. Many musicians who refuse to join bigger locals because of the additional expense find this decision has cost them lost referrals and MPTF jobs.

Here is a sample of a Union Local contract and a page out of the Denver Local's availability list (open to any current members).

AMERICAN FEDERATION OF MUSICIANS OF THE UNITED STATES AND CANADA

(HEREIN CALLED "FEDERATION")

CONTRACT
(Form L-2)

FOR LOCAL ENGAGEMENTS ONLY
(NOT FOR USE IN CANADA)

Whenever The Term "The Local Union" Is Used In This Contract, It Shall Mean Local Union No. _____ Of The Federation.

THIS CONTRACT for the personal services of musicians on the engagement described below is made this _____ day of _____, 19 _____, between the undersigned purchaser of music (herein called "Purchaser") and the undersigned musician or musicians.

1. Name and Address of Place of Engagement: _____

   Name of Band or Group: _____
   Number of Musicians: _____   Number of Vocalists: _____

2. Date(s) of Engagement: daily or weekly schedule and daily clock hours:

3. Type of Engagement (specify whether dance, stage show, banquet, etc.): _____

4. Compensation Agreed Upon: $_____
   (Amount and Terms)

5. Purchaser Will Make Payments As Follows: _____
   (Specify when payments are to be made)

_____ (Continued on reverse side) _____

IN WITNESS WHEREOF, the parties hereto have hereunto set their names and seals on the day and year first above written.

X_____ | X_____
Print Purchaser's Full and Correct Name (If Purchaser is Corporation, Full and Correct Corporate Name) | Print Name of Signatory Musician   Home Local Union No.

Signature of Purchaser (or Agent thereof) | Signature of Signatory Musician

Street Address | Musician's Home Address

City   State   Zip Code | City   State   Zip Code

Telephone | Telephone

Booking Agent   Agreement No. | Address

Names of All Musicians	Local Union No.	U.S. Social Security Nos.	Direct Pay
			$

Form L-2, Rev. 9/15/95   59-C   Rekord Printing Company, Shamokin, PA (717) 648-3231

6. No performance or rehearsal shall be recorded, reproduced or transmitted from the place of performance, in any manner or by any means whatsoever, in the absence of a specific written agreement with or approved in writing by the American Federation of Musicians ("Federation") relating to and permitting such recording, reproduction or transmission. This prohibition shall not be subject to any procedure of arbitration and the American Federation of Musicians ("Federation") may enforce this prohibition in any court of competent jurisdiction.

7. This contract, and the terms and conditions contained herein, may be enforced by the Purchaser, and its agents, and by each musician who is a party to this contract or whose name appears on the contract or who has, in fact, performed the engagement contracted for (herein called "participating musician(s)"), and by the agent or agent(s) of each participating musician, including the Local Union. It is expressly understood by the Purchaser and the musician(s) who are parties to this contract that neither the Federation nor the Local Union are parties to this contract in any capacity except as expressly provided in 6 above and, therefore, that neither the Federation nor the Local Union shall be liable for the performance or breach of any provision hereof.

8. A representative of the Local Union shall have access to the place of engagement covered by this contract for purposes of communicating with the musician(s) performing the engagement and the Purchaser.

9. ADDITIONAL PROVISIONS: _____

_____

_____

_____

_____

Names of All Musicians	Local Union No.	U.S. Social Security Nos.	Direct Pay
			$

(IF ADDITIONAL SPACE IS NEEDED, ADD SEPARATE SHEET(S).)   （Form L-2)

REFERRAL SERVICE INFORMATION SHEET

Date_____

1. Name of purchaser:_____

2. Address:_____ Zip_____

3. Phone: Day_____Evening_____

4. Type of engagement:_____

5. Date:_____Time:_____

6. Place:_____

7. Style of music:_____

8. Number of musicians:_____

9. Budget:_____

10. Number of people attending:_____Age:_____

11. Where did you hear about the Union_____

12. **PLEASE LET US KNOW WHEN YOU FILL THE REQUEST!!!!!!!**

13. Special instructions/requests:_____
    _____
    _____
    _____

14. Referrals:_____
    _____
    _____

AMERICAN FEDERATION OF MUSICIANS REPORT FORM
TELEVISION AND RADIO COMMERCIAL ANNOUNCEMENTS   RP № 026255

Date:_____

ORIGINAL SESSION:

Recording Date: _____ No. of Mus. _____

Recording Studio: _____

City: _____ State: _____

AFM Local: _____

Hours Employment: _____

RE-USE, DUBBING, NEW USE OR OTHER:

Original Report Form No.: _____

Original Recording Date: _____

Producer: _____

Producer's Address _____

Signatory of Record: _____

Employer of Record: _____

Employer's Address: _____

MEMO

Payment Type	Medium	Rates
____ Original Session	____ TV	____ National
____ Re-Use	____ Radio (13 weeks)	____ Regional (Nat'l Adv)
____ New Use	____ Radio (8 weeks)	____ Regional (Reg Adv)
____ Dubbing	____ Foreign	____ Local (Nat'l Adv)
____ Dubbing (Longer/	____ Non-Broadcast	____ Local (Loc Adv)
Shorter Version)	____ Other	Indicate region or
____ Short Term Use		local area in memo box.
____ Spec Factual Info	Check here if:	
____ Local Info	____ Commercial made for cable only	
____ Mech Edit	____ PSA status confirmed by AFM	
____ Sideline Session	____ Session performed solely on synthesizer	
____ Other		

ADVERTISER_____

PRODUCT _____

ADVERTISING AGENCY _____

ADDRESS _____

LOWEST NO. OF REPORTED HRS W'KD._____

NO. OF ANNOUNCEMENTS CLAIMED_____

IDENTIFICATION Titles and Code Nos. (Include track lengths for original sessions only). When identification changes give prior and new.

	Original (or Prior) Identification	TRK LGTH	New Identification
A.			
B.			
C.			
D.			
E.			
F.			
G.			

First Air Date _____

Cycle Dates Being Paid _____

The Producer understands and agrees that the terms and conditions of the engagement covered by this Report Form include the terms and conditions of the AFM Commercial Announcements Agreement in effect at the time of such engagement.

Producer's Signature _____   Leader's Signature _____

	EMPLOYEE'S NAME (AS ON SOCIAL SECURITY CARD) LAST FIRST INITIAL	CARTAGE	LOCAL UNION NO.	SOCIAL SECURITY NUMBER	HR'S W'KED	NO. OF D'BLE PER SESS-ION	SPOT. ID. BY LETTER ABOVE	ID. OF SPOT PER DOUBLE	SCALE WAGES (1)	PENSION CONTRI- BUTION	H & W WHERE APPLIC- ABLE
1	(LEADER)										
2											
3											
4											
5											
6											
7											
8											
9											
10											
11											
12											
13											
14											
15	ARRANGER										
16	ORCHESTRATOR										
17	COPYIST (SEE PAGE 2 FOR ADDITIONAL COPYISTS)										

(1) Insert X if wages being paid are overscale

FOR FUND USE ONLY:

Date pay't. rec'd. _____   Amt. paid _____

Date posted _____ By _____

Form R-6 Rev. 1-89

REKORD PRTG. ® ⬤ 59C

Total H & W Contributions _____

Total Pension Contributions _____

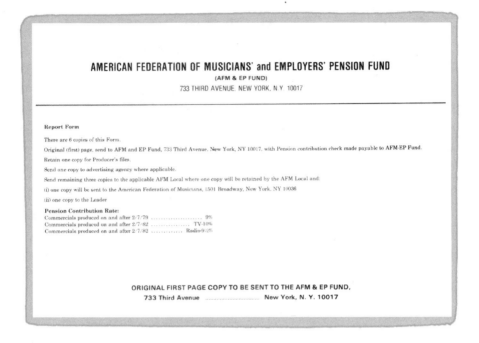

AMERICAN FEDERATION OF MUSICIANS' and EMPLOYERS' PENSION FUND
(AFM & EP FUND)
733 THIRD AVENUE, NEW YORK, N.Y. 10017

Report Form

There are 6 copies of this Form.

Original (first) page, send to AFM and EP Fund, 733 Third Avenue, New York, NY 10017, with Pension contribution check made payable to AFM-EP Fund.

Retain one copy for Producer's files.

Send one copy to advertising agency where applicable.

Send remaining three copies to the applicable AFM Local where one copy will be retained by the AFM Local and:

(i) one copy will be sent to the American Federation of Musicians, 1501 Broadway, New York, NY 10036

(ii) one copy to the Leader

Pension Contribution Rate:
Commercials produced on and after 2/7/79 .... 9%
Commercials produced on and after 2/7/82 .... TV-10%
Commercials produced on and after 2/7/82 .... Radio-9.4%

ORIGINAL FIRST PAGE COPY TO BE SENT TO THE AFM & EP FUND.
733 Third Avenue .... New York, N. Y. 10017

Arts Councils and Grants

Another source of help, and sometimes money, is your state's arts council. In addition to the AIR programs described in Chapter Four, there are other grants for which you may be eligible. Some states offer individual grants programs for artists. In music, these programs are typically open to composers. Most arts councils are supportive of musical exploration. Grants offer an opportunity not often readily available in the marketplace. The grants are judged by a group of panelists who have expertise in the field of composition. They tend to favor "artistic" rather than commercial projects. Many of the panelists are deliberately chosen from other geographic areas to eliminate favoritism in awarding grants. Call your state arts council to find out if they have a grant program for individual artists. An alternative is to get a commission from an organization that has received a grant. This is the option you need to adopt if the arts council only funds non-profit organizations. Sometimes, the sponsor will receive a portion of the grant in return for administering the program and assisting you with the paperwork. Possible sponsors could be local symphonies, a Mayor's Arts Commission, or a local arts council. Usually, the organization must be a 501 (C) (3) category non-profit organization under the federal tax code.

By using your imagination, you may be able to find a community organization, such as a facility for battered women, to sponsor you in a program of songwriting or music performance. There are also an increasing number of cities which offer grants to individual artists, so be sure to check with your city government or a local arts magazine to see if your town supports the arts with its wallet.

There are many workshops offered on the subject of grantspersonship, which is the art of writing successful grants. Your state arts council may offer free workshops several times a year. There are also professionals who charge fees to impart similar information. (See the Resources section at the end of this chapter and the Appendix D for books on grants.)

The key to writing successful grants is clarity and the ability to match your proposal with an organization that funds grants like yours. It is vitally important that your project description be understandable to an intelligent person who may not have a music background. Your budget and the means of implementing your project must also be clear. Be sure that your resume, which is usually required along with your grant application, clearly supports your capability to execute the project.

For example, if you are applying for a grant as a composer or songwriter, provide as much supporting evidence as possible showing successfully completed work. For this type of grant, teaching experience is not necessarily a plus and should not be stressed. On the other hand, if you are doing an educational project, it is wise to provide as much documentation as possible evidencing your teaching skill and experience. It is a good idea to have a friend who is not a musician read over your grant proposal. If she doesn't understand it, you need to re-work it.

The National Endowment for the Arts (NEA) and the National Endowment for the Humanities (NEH) are sources of a great variety of grants. NEA offers grants to jazz and classical composers, and specialists in the folk arts. They even have a grant program for small record companies. NEH gives grants to college teachers and independent researchers for critical studies in the arts.

NEA and NEH grants can offer a considerable amount of money. The College Teachers' Program, for example, pays up to $30,000. Consequently, the competition is liable to be tougher for a national grant than for a grant in a small state. Don't be afraid to apply. The state or national arts councils can often answer your questions about aspects of the application. Call and ask them, or visit the office of your state arts council for in-depth information. Although NEH and NEA budgets have been cut by Congress in the past few years, private foundations offer another possible source of funding.

NARAS, the National Academy of Recording Arts and Sciences, offers grants for projects that relate to the history of recording and American music. Membership in NARAS is a useful tool for information and networking. Active membership is restricted to those who have recorded six cuts of an album in national distribution. Categories of membership include singers, players, record producers, engineers, album note writers, songwriters, spoken word artists, video and music arrangers, comedy album artists and album cover artists. The category of Associate Membership is available for those who do not qualify as active members. Current chapters of NARAS are located in Austin, Atlanta, Chicago, Los Angeles, Memphis, Miami, Nashville, New York, Philadelphia, San Francisco and Seattle. Active members of the Recording Academy can vote in the Grammy Awards process, and are able to order records at an appreciable discount. (Chapter addresses are in the Appendix.)

Specialized Casual Work

Referrals for casual playing jobs can be obtained through local music stores, other musicians, caterers and happy clients spreading your name around. Another performer may find herself unable or unwilling to take a particular job, so don't be shy about letting other professionals in town know about what you do.

Sometimes casual jobs require research into some specific subject matter, like music of the American Revolution. It is customary to charge the client a fee covering the extra time you may need to research and rehearse this material. Be sure to explain to them why you are charging something above your normal fee.

Some of these may involve your normal performing group; others might require you to put together a group for this performance only. Use the Musicians' Union or the local college's music department as a resource to meet your needs.

Don't be afraid to set a reasonable price for your skills. The average person doesn't realize that a musician doesn't work a forty-hour a week job, and must practice regularly to sustain his talent. $100 for a solo artist may seem like a lot to a client for a one-hour evening performance, but it may be your only job during that particular weekend and will probably prevent you from taking another job on the same evening. Since Friday and Saturday nights are prime times for musicians, you need to factor that into your price.

Remember, too, that a single $100 job is actually better than two $50.00 jobs. You'll only have to drive to one location and will set up and take down your P.A. system only once. If you don't respect yourself by setting an appropriate price, your employer probably won't treat you with respect either. Find out what the local

Union scale is and charge above it. Scale is a minimum wage and should not be the upper limit of your income potential.

The same general principles apply to negotiations with agents. Set a minimum fee and never go below it. There must be some room for negotiation between the wage you'd prefer and the one you will reluctantly accept. If you go below your own minimum, you will probably resent playing the job and not perform up to your abilities. This can hurt you and prevent you from getting further job referrals.

Set a fee, negotiate to a point, then stick to your guns. You will lose some jobs, but probably ones not worth your time.

Through unions and other professional music groups, you can make useful contacts that will influence the direction of your career in a variety of productive ways. Networking with other sympathetic professionals can benefit your musical growth and be financially beneficial as well.

CHAPTER 6 RESOURCES

Unions

Most of the books about the music business have brief discussions about the Musicians' Union; but I can't think of any that offer enough details to be worth your time.

Grants

Your best bet in exploring the world of grants is to contact your state arts council and the reference librarian at your local college or central branch of the public library. There are numerous books about grants and lists of grant opportunities in the library. It is also a good idea to find someone in your town who has developed a reputation of being successful at writing music grants. Chances are, there is someone at your local college who has developed this skill.

chapter 7

Expanding Your Recording Opportunities and Developing Skills

No matter where you live and whatever work you are currently doing, there are probably opportunities to earn some money doing recording work. In this chapter, you'll see how you can utilize these opportunities to increase your income and develop your abilities as a composer.

The rate of technological change in the music industry has developed with amazing rapidity. Recording equipment is now affordable and the equipment is relatively portable.

At one time, if you wanted to make a demo tape of a song you had written, you would have had to hire a rhythm section and rent a local studio. Studio time may have cost you from $25 to $65 an hour for eight-track recording, or slightly less for four-track time.

Anyone who has ever been involved with any kind of recording project knows that it invariably takes more time to complete the project than you expect. An instrument may be out of tune, singers may be tired or not phrasing in the way you wish, or other musical or technical problems may occur.

In today's music world, you can buy a small four-track cassette studio, a synthesizer and a drum machine for $3,000 or less. Or you can buy an eight-track

A-DAT machine for about $3,000. These machines are designed to be easy to use, so that even a novice can quickly master them. If you have basic keyboard skills, you can literally be a one-person band—playing keyboards, electric bass parts on the synthesizer, and drums with a drum machine. You can perform similar feats with a guitar synthesizer. If you are also a good singer, you *are* the chorus and orchestra. Your major investment will be the limitations of your patience as you record track after track to refine the song to your own taste.

A MIDI setup, a computer and a sequencer will adjust for any rhythmic problems. If your own timing is less than perfect and you don't own that gear, you should record a click track on one of the tracks as your first step in the recording process. A click track is simply a constant beat and you can use a metronome to provide it. When you have filled up the other tracks, you can erase the click track and use that track for an additional vocal or instrumental part.

There are several books by qualified engineering experts that can help you to manipulate home gear to its maximum potential. Some of these books are listed in the Resources section at the end of this chapter, and more are in Appendix D. There is also a list of some regularly-published magazines that will assist you in developing your engineering skills and keeping abreast of the latest technology.

Below is an example of a small, home-studio set-up.

Rick Moss

Jingles

What other local recording opportunities exist in the marketplace? If you are able to write songs, there is really no reason why you shouldn't attempt to master the art of writing jingles. As a matter of fact, the current trend in commercials is towards capturing the contemporary sound of recordings. If your aim is to do "commercial" pop music, what better way of learning than to write a "hook?"

How can you crack the local jingle market? Virtually every city in the United States has advertising agencies. First, listen to local radio and television ads; then call your local advertising agencies; and if possible, make an appointment to see the creative director of the agency. What kinds of jingles are being recorded in your area and who is writing them? Often, the agency's creative people write the lyrics for a commercial, or at least come up with the concept for it, and usually hire other people to do the music. If you have a good demo tape, leave it with the creative director of the agency. Agencies are listed in the Yellow Pages. In larger cities, there may be a local advertising organization that brings local agency people together for meetings or lunches. Take a look at the map and check out agencies within a fifty mile radius of where you live.

With your home studio and synthesizer, you should be able to turn out good-sounding demos for commercials. Most commercials are done in demo form before the agency and/or the client actually approves the work. Do not invest too much in a demo, unless the agency is willing to pay the costs you may incur, such as hiring musicians or singers. Most agencies will not be willing to pay a creative fee for doing a demo. In fact, they may be shopping around and asking several other production companies to make demos, too. You can see the advantage of having a home studio, since renting a studio to produce five or six unsuccessful demos could quickly put you out of business.

It is also possible to deal directly with an advertiser, instead of an agency. Some small manufacturers or service outlets may not use agencies. If the advertiser is dealing with an agency, it is unwise to go directly to the client. If you try to bypass the agency they may bad-mouth you, and certainly won't hire you to service other accounts. Agencies get commissions on all the work they do for a client, and will mark up your bills to get their portion of the take. If you bypass the agency, you're cutting into their income.

When the advertising agency receives a demo, they take it to the advertiser, who will approve, disapprove or ask for a revised version of the jingle. On a number of occasions, I have witnessed a client spending considerable money by adding additional instruments or vocal parts to a demo, only to reject the "improved" product and return to the demo.

In order to maximize your profits and protect your own interests, it is best to record under Union contracts. Locals of the AFM are empowered to create their own wage scales for commercials used in a single market. If your jingle is played in more than one city, it is considered a regional or national jingle—you must pay higher wages to the musicians and singers. Consult your local AFM and AFTRA offices for the correct local or national wage rates. The leader of the band, who is often the producer-composer, must sign a contract for each recording session worked.

When the same commercial is used both on radio and television, the musicians need to be paid separate fees for each use. Under Union contracts, a musician receives a session fee, currently $94 an hour. When the commercial is broadcast, there is an additional payment of $24. Reuse payments on national and regional jingles are subsequently paid every thirteen weeks of broadcast use. On local jingles, these residuals are paid every eighteen months. Consult your local union for the current union minimums.

In addition to your union wages as a musician, you are entitled to a creative fee for writing the music and/or words for a jingle. Creative fees can range from a few hundred to thousands of dollars, depending upon the client and the nature of the campaign. In order to know what to charge, you need to have some idea of how much money will be spent in buying time on radio and television, and how long the campaign is expected to run. For example, if your client has budgeted $100,000 for time buys on local radio and television, a creative fee of $250 is much too low. It is a good idea to set a minimum creative fee for your services, and to adjust that figure upward if you work for a major client or if you are required to perform extra work. Extra work might include an excessive number of conferences with the advertising agency or rewrites based upon disagreements between personnel at the agency itself. Some of your clients will choose not to deal with issue of a separate creative fee, but will simply ask for a budget for the project. It is up to you to include your creative fee in the total package. (See the sample budgets on the next pages.)

If you sing on any commercials, file contracts with AFTRA, the American Federation of Radio and Television Artists. AFTRA has regional offices rather than local ones, and you will be surprised to find their wage scales, and especially their residuals, are much higher than those musicians get. These contracts are also more complicated in the ways that they deal with reuses. Most major jingle writers insist on singing on jingles, even if they are only lip synching, in order to collect these juicy reuse fees. Sometimes, an agency will not pay a creative fee, but will allow the composer to appear on the contract as a singer, even though he didn't sing.

In order to file Union contracts, someone must be signatory to Union agreements. It is to your advantage for the advertising agency to be the signatory; otherwise, it is your obligation to police and administer the payment of residuals and do all the paperwork. Major advertising agencies are all signatories to the Union agreements, although their local branches may prefer that you sign off on the contracts. Try not to do this, because it then may involve you in disputes between the singers and musicians and the agency.

Sample Budget

Brand X Super Toys (Home Studio)

Hours of Recording Time at $25.00 per Hour

Instrumental Tracks to Include Guitar,
Bass, Drums, Keyboard—Musicians Fees:

Union Scales:

Pension & Welfare:

Health Payments:

Cartage—Bass Amp and Drums:

Doubling Fees:

Singer's Fee for Jane Doe:

Singer's Pension & Welfare:

Singer's Health Insurance:

Tape Costs:

Creative Fees:

Total:

Brand X Super Toys (Professional Studio)

Studio Time: RPM Sound 24-Track: _____

Tape Costs: 24-track tape, 2-track Final: _____

8 Radio Station Tape Dubs for Agency: _____

Creative Fee: _____

Musicians:

Guitar, Bass, Drums, Keyboard, Flute, _____
Synthesizer, Bongos—Union Scale:

Cartage Fee for Drums, Bass Amp, _____
Guitar Amp

Doubling Fees: _____

Pension Fees: _____

Arranging and Copying Fees: _____

Health Payments: _____

AFTRA Fees for 3 Singers: _____

Pension & Welfare: _____

Health Payments: _____

Other: _____ _____

Total: _____

Other costs might include legal fees for contract with advertising agency

If a small-budget client who is not using an advertising agency insists that you be the signatory, the local Union can show you how to get a franchise that will enable you to sign Union agreements. When you sign these agreements, they require pension and health payments, payments for cartage of certain musical instruments, and doubling fees. Be sure to have included all of these fees in your budget to the client or agency.

Do you really need to do these sessions via the Union? It is my opinion that you are foolish not to use Union agreements. The wage scales are good, the repayments are beneficial, and you can build up pension credits by using the Union agreements. If the employer defaults on payment, you can often get the Union to assist you in collecting the money, and, as a last resort, put the employer on the unfair list to protect other musicians in the future. The reason for doing commercials is to make money. Songwriting projects or records may have many emotional aspects involved in their conception and execution, but jingles are done for the "big bucks."

Sometimes, a client will object to repayments, but not to the Union minimums. Initiate the help of your local Union officials in explaining the rationale behind residuals to the client. Many clients are somewhat paranoid about some mythical monstrous repayment scheme. The truth is, if the campaign is successful, the client will probably record new versions of the jingle. The chances are that the repayments to musicians and singers will amount to considerably less money than the client spends on buying radio and television time.

A few words of advice about the advertising business: Don't try to get into the jingle business unless you can write well under very short deadlines. Sometimes, a client will give you only a couple of days after they have approved a demo to complete the final product. They also think nothing of making lyric and even musical changes during the actual recording session. Don't expect a great amount of loyalty from an agency or a client. You may save an account for an agency, and four weeks later not be able to get in the door to bid on another job. Remember that many agencies are virtual revolving doors, and the person who worked on the account you saved may be working at another agency. Another possibility is that the client moves the account to another agency because the client's own personnel shifts; the new kid on the block may have other loyalties.

On the following two pages are sample budgets for demo and final versions of a jingle. Be sure that you bring your project in at or under the estimated budget. A good idea is to add a 10–20% over-ride or contingency fee to resolve any unpredictable problems. It also should be clearly stated in the contract that if the agency and/or client makes changes in the content of a commercial on or after a session, they will be responsible for any additional costs.

Even if the recording session takes place in your own home studio, you should still bill the client for studio time. He will expect this charge and after all, you did invest money to create your own recording facility. If you are renting a studio, you may be get reduced rates by using off-hours or by buying large blocks of studio time. Most studios have a written rate card, but will deal with clients based on how busy the facility is and how much work they feel the client can bring into the studio.

Hiring a Sales Representative

If you want to get into the jingle business, but don't wish to handle the selling of your own talents, there are three possible options:

1. You can hire an agent to represent you, in return for paying her a percentage of whatever work she brings in. You will be responsible for her expenses, which may include business cards, lunches, trips and many tape dubs. You must negotiate with your prospective agent to determine whether her percentage comes off the top of the budget, or simply comes out of your creative fee. You should expect to pay between 20% and 33.33% if you want a salesperson to spend much time representing you.
2. Your second choice might be to find a partner to be responsible for the selling. You then go into business together and share all costs and income.
3. A third option that might work in a smaller market is to utilize a booking agent and to pay him a fee, just as you would for a band booking. Be sure the agent understands the jingle business, because it is a different ballgame than selling an act to a bar. A good agent should be able to sell your services for more than you would charge.

The third option is a bit unusual. Choosing between the first and second options depends on the people involved and what motivates them. Would you rather have a partner or be in control and be the "boss?" An agent is not apt to do a good job of representing you unless he is making a sufficient amount of money to justify her time and energy. On the other hand, many partnerships, like many marriages, end in bitter separations, even legal actions.

Writing to Pictures

How can you develop your skills for writing music to picture for film, television or commercials? Classes in TV and film scoring are offered at some colleges, like the University of Southern California in Los Angeles or the Berklee College of Music in Boston, among others. You can also experiment on your own by writing a music to existing videotapes. You will need to develop an awareness of the relationship between music and the visual aspects of a production. Some composers foreshadow events about to happen on the screen; some mimic them; others choose to work counter to the visual events in order to create an element of surprise. Generally, a client will present you with a finished video—the music usually being recorded after the filming is done. There are exceptions, especially for dance sequences which may be too complex to synch the music with the dancing after the fact.

Get the agency to put a window on the screen with a running clock. This will save you many hours of demarcating when each step of the action is happening. If they can't or won't do this, you need to prepare a cue sheet for yourself that describes all of the visual events in the film commercial. A simple cue sheet for a 30 second commercial might look like this: estatically

Time (in seconds)	Event
0.00 to 1.50	Tennis match
1.50 to 4.00	Women player smashes ball at net
4.00 to 6.20	Players walk to veranda
6.20 to 10.00	Two players ecstatically sip tea
10.00 to 14.10	Voiceover touting wonders of Playglo Tea
14.10 to 19.00	More tennis scenes
19.00 to 28.50	Jingle with product tag

Most 30-second commercials actually run about 28½ seconds. The balance of time is taken up by the tape winding across the sprocket.

If you own a sampler, sequencer and synthesizer, you may be able to do some film/video projects and commercials without using other instrumentalists. Owning your own studio is a very practical alternative; if you have to rent a studio,much of your savings will be eaten up by additional studio time.

It takes a certain amount of experience before you can readily estimate the amount of studio time a project may require. If you are hiring other musicians, look for those who can master a part quickly, and have quality instruments that play in tune. Utilize musicians who can take direction, but who will also offer constructive, intelligent ideas when called upon to invent a part or suggest a solution to a musical problem. A creative, but even-tempered musician can save your session, or bring it to life by virtue of offering an idea. Sometimes, a subtle little musical fragment can make a track sparkle.

Occasionally, feature films are produced in a local market, and with luck and a bit of sleuthing, you may get to score one. If the creative fee is low, try to retain the publishing to your original music. While this is difficult in Hollywood, it is sometimes possible to pull off in a small town with a producer who realizes he is not paying you a Hollywood price.

Some of these locally-produced features may never be distributed locally, let alone nationally. It seems as though every local market has a "rich kid" whose parents have financed all or part of a film. It is usually poorly executed, badly produced, and will die a quick and merciful death. On the other hand, don't be surprised if some of these dogs show up on cable television at 3 A.M. on a Monday morning. If you are lucky enough to score a feature that gets on local or cable TV, you should realize some income from one of the performing rights societies. (Details about these performing rights societies can be found in Chapter 17.)

You can also utilize your composing reel to solicit work as a player or singer from local record producers. Studio work isn't stressed in this book, since fewer and fewer musicians will be employed in this capacity, because of increasingly sophisticated and reasonably-priced samplers, sequencers and synthesizers. This is the age of the composer-musician, the person who can fulfill both roles successfully. Nevertheless, you can never tell what sort of work might be available at a particular place in time.

If you are deeply involved in local productions, the chances are that few of your competitors will want to hire you as a player or singer, They will generally be reluctant to expose their clients to the competition.

Don't overlook the possibility of renting your home studio to other musicians to do demos of their songs. You may also want to look into opportunities to produce records for other artists, This is discussed further in Chapter 9.

Final Thoughts on Advertising & Film

Don't be surprised when bizarre events occur in film and jingle sessions. I once played in on a session in New York for Gleem Toothpaste. The jingle was one of the best-written pieces I have ever played on, with a beautifully-written contrapuntal rhythmic duet between an oboe and a soprano saxophone. The client didn't like it—Mitch Leigh, the composer went back to the drawing board and gave them some mediocre Stephen Foster parodies which ran for nine months or so.

On another occasion, I did a score for a horrible film in Colorado. Another musician and I played about fifteen instruments. The client became very angry because even though he was paying badly, he expected to see a large orchestra at work in the studio.

CHAPTER 7 RESOURCES

It is a good idea to subscribe to *EQ, Mix,* and recording magazines to keep up with new developments in recording. Though some references on jingles appear in Appendix D, the most current book is Jeffrey P. Fisher's *Scoring Soundtracks and Jingles*. The book was written in 1997, the publisher is Mix Books, and it is distributed by Hal Leonard Corporation.

chapter 8

Working in Multiple Contexts

Working in multiple contexts means you can find employment in more than one musical organization, even if you are a member of a group that performs on a regular basis. If you are capable of playing a number of instruments and have mastered several musical styles, you can probably find opportunities to work in a number of ways.

By this time, it should be apparent to you that your ability to work as a soloist can be a tremendous boon to your income. You should recall that on Union jobs, the leader of a group gets double or 1½ times Union scale. Even if you are not a Union member, it is still possible for you to charge quite a bit more than you would make as one-third of a trio. The way groups can split income has been outlined in Chapter 2, which covered the role of leaders, co-op groups, and side musicians. If you play in more than one group, you may assume more than one of these roles.

Suppose, for example, you play electric bass in a trio called The Red Elephants that plays '50s rock and roll. The three of you have played together since high school. You work as a musical co-op, splitting the money and owning the sound system in common. You may also be able to play guitar and sing. In that role you work alone as "Henry Lewis, singer-songwriter." Since you are a solo act, you will certainly function as the leader. You also play decent bluegrass banjo, and utilize that skill as a side-musician playing with the Blue Devil Bluegrass Band on the first Monday of the month at a club.

Another example of the same sort of musical lifestyle might exist for a versatile trumpet player. On Friday nights, you are a side musician with the Ultimate Kicks Dixieland Band. Most days of the week, you lead your own lounge combo, and play modern jazz concerts on flugelhorn with a co-op group. Occasionally, you do freelance work for the ballet in a neighboring town or play for touring Broadway shows.

The leader of a group takes the responsibility of dealing with a client or booking agent. Often, the check for the job will be made out to the leader; she, in turn, must pay the rest of the group. She must keep careful tax records, because the earnings will be reported by the client as having been paid to the leader, not to the members of the band. At the end of the year, if group members have earned over $600, the leader must send Tax Form 1099 to all the members of the group, stating the earnings and whether any withholding taxes have been deducted.

Since the leader usually selects or rejects any jobs offered (with or without the input of other group members), there should be general agreement in the band as to what jobs the group wants to play and what minimum wage they will accept. In some groups, the leader handles the negotiations without discussing the matter with the other members. In others, the majority opinion of the group prevails. The democratic option can be complicated if some members are difficult to reach or frequently out of town.

In Chapter 7 about the Union is a standard union contract for a one-night casual gig. If you are a member of the AFM, you are expected to file a contract for each engagement you or your group plays. If you are not a Union member, you still need some sort of contractual agreement with your employer. The contract should cover days and times of employment, the length of shows, wages and any special considerations, such as having a piano tuned on a regular basis. You should also have a letter of agreement with the club manager that sets forth whether the band is entitled to free or discounted food and drink.

On convention gigs lasting for three or four hours, that require you to set up your equipment several hours in advance, establish an agreement with the client or the agent that sets forth whether you will get a meal. Sometimes, the client is agreeable to feeding you, but doesn't want you in the dining room with a group that may be having a formal dinner or a business meeting.

Be particularly careful when dealing with out-of-town convention gigs. You may be asked to come early, and literally have no place within driving distance to grab a sandwich, let alone eat dinner. It is a good policy to demand (and receive) extra payment if you must arrive early and sit around for several hours before you play.

Some agents have a peculiar attitude about the dinner issue. They seem to feel musicians are socially inferior to the client and should never mingle with guests in a social situation. In fact, the guests often enjoy talking to the performers, because most business people are curious about musicians' lifestyles. It is also true that if you are the leader, you should make an effort to see the musicians don't eat so much food as to make pigs of themselves. It is best if the band limits (or better yet avoids) drinking alcohol during the gig.

It is important the band and the client both honor the starting time, within reasonable limits. "Reasonable limits" could be defined as within ten minutes of the contracted starting time. Breaks should also be worked out by the agent or leader with the client. When a client wants continuous music, it is often possible to split the breaks so no one in the band has to play for two or three straight hours without a break. Upon the band's arrival, the leader should arrange where the band members will dress, if they need to change clothes. He should also ascertain where the band can go to relax during breaks.

If you are playing out of town, especially if you haven't worked for a particular employer before, you should get a 50% deposit paid up-front before you pile into the van. The same applies to a club you know to be in shaky financial condition.

It may seem like an obvious point, but if you are going to work in multiple contexts, you will need a variety of suitable clothes. A bluegrass band doesn't dress like the combo at a debutante's ball.

Working for "The Door"

Some club managers will try to induce you to work without a guaranteed set fee, instead recommending you take a percentage of the money collected at the door. They may tack on a cover charge and give you 50%, 75% or even 100% of the door charge. This is usually a poor idea. First, you may not get an honest count of how many people were actually there. You can place a friend or your road manager at the door to count the patrons, but your friend's count may not agree with the manager's numbers. This may be because your friend counted some guests who got complimentary tickets or because you are getting a "short count." It is difficult to resolve this kind of dispute because it's a "are you calling me a liar?" type of situation.

Be aware that the Union strictly prohibits a band playing for the door charge alone. You can, however, effect a sort of compromise: play for the minimum Union scale, plus a percentage of the door. If you follow this plan, then when the owner makes money, you will share in the profits, so at least you'll go home with some money in your pocket. You can also create a situation where the band builds a following. Your income and the club's profits can then both escalate each time you appear there.

For some years now, an outrageous custom has arisen in Los Angeles and New York. In some of the clubs in these cities, acts actually have to pay money in order to play at a club. This is a sort of perversion of the notion of playing for the door. The club manager polls the audience as they come in and the band is awarded some of their money back, based on the number of people the manager says they have drawn to the club. Not only do the bands often end up with no money, they may actually have to pay to work. Another way some clubs handle this is to make the band sell tickets to the club.

The Musicians' Union has tried to prevent such practices. They have even picketed "pay to play" clubs, but often bands are their own worst enemies. Not only should you never accept such a deal, you ought to use any influence you have over other bands to keep them from working under these outrageous conditions.

How can you keep a client from bouncing a check on you? You can specify in your contract that payment must be in cash or certified check. This is particularly desirable with out-of-town jobs, where collecting bad checks can be an extremely difficult chore. A certified check is one a bank has issued or guaranteed. Your agent should share your feelings on this issue. You can't pay commission on a job that hasn't paid you any money.

The Musicians' Union has established an 800 number, 1 (800) ROADGIG for bands that are stranded on the road when a club owner stiffs them. This number is staffed 24 hours a day, and the union will provide emergency relief, pay the band minimum scale and pursue legal action against the club. The band must be operating with a Union contract, and if the wage specified is above scale when the Union wins the lawsuit, they will pay the band the balance of the money.

Contracts

Under no circumstances should you play a club or a concert without a signed contract. "Casual" jobs, such as weddings or parties, should all be treated the same way. A contract for a casual gig should always specify that you be paid upon completion of the job. The happy couple at a wedding may disappear on their honeymoon, and a month later will barely remember the name of your band.

If you are the leader of a band, it is a good idea for you to introduce yourself to the client immediately upon your arrival at a casual. Arrange for a place where you can meet the client after the job is over. There is nothing more annoying than playing a four hour gig, then having to wait another hour to find the person who is supposed to write the check.

Leaders and Side Musicians

If you are using a Union contract, remember the leader of the engagement is required to file a copy of the contract at the Union local **before** the engagement. If you have played the job without a Union contract, it is difficult or impossible to get the Union to assist you in any dispute over unpaid wages.

Since you may be working both sides of the leader/side-musician fence, here's another angle of the leader issue. Many groups actually split the extra money a leader receives in a Union contract. If you play with the same group of people on a regular basis, that may be a reasonable idea. It avoids any jealousy or arguments about "who does more for the band, whose car the band is using," etc.

If one person truly does the biggest share of the work, is clearly the featured star and invests more in the group's future, then it is reasonable for him or her to take the leader's fee. The whole concept of leaders goes back to the big band era, when a band consisted of a leader, like Benny Goodman, and the musicians he hired. The leader was usually the featured musician, provided the P.A. system, the music arrangements which were often specifically commissioned for the band, the music stands, and even the band bus and the costumes. The side musicians brought themselves and their instruments.

Anyone who has invested in all of these items was obviously entitled to a healthier share of the receipts than the guy who simply blew his trombone on the gig. Today's music is usually played by combos rather than big bands, so the situation described may not be apropos. Ultimately, you will need to make your own decisions on how to distribute money and authority.

Old-style band leaders often followed another quaint custom: they would hire a ten-piece band for minimum scale, perhaps $50 per person for a night, and sell the group for $1,000 to the club. This meant that the leader pocketed $500, or exactly ten times what the side musicians received. If an agent was involved the leader might net only $300.

As long as a leader pays Union minimums, there is not much the Union can do about the situation, but the band member should explore what their services are worth to the leader. There is no law that says you can't charge a wage above the Union minimum!

If you happen to be the leader on a particularly juicy gig, it is a wise practice to let the band share in your good fortune. For example, in the ten-piece $1,000 situation described above, if each musician had been paid $75, the leader still would have gone home with $325, more than four times the wages of the band members. All of this may come as a surprise to some rock and country musicians, but many of the old-time dance band musicians never received a dime above scale wages.

Each local of the Union sets work dues, which must be paid after any engagement. The leader of the band is responsible for employing only Union musicians, and it should be understood up front who is going to pay the work dues-the leader or the musicians. Some musicians prefer that the leader deduct work dues from their paychecks, because they are apt to forget about them. Others prefer to take care of their own business.

One problem that can occur in a band where all of the players work in many contexts, is one person getting an outside gig may interfere with work opportunities for the rest of the band. It is impossible to totally solve this problem. The band should have a clear agreement that certain dates should be set aside for the group, and some sort of minimum notice should be given if one member decides to take a two-week gig with a touring Broadway show. If too many conflicts arise, it may be necessary for the offending member to leave the group. There is a fine line between taking what musical opportunities you want, and being responsible to three, four, or more other musicians. Finding competent subs for your position in a band can give you more flexibility in accepting other opportunities, while fulfilling your responsibilities to you regular group.

CHAPTER 8 RESOURCES

The Buttwinick, Gibson and Levine books referenced in Chapters 2 and 3 cover some of this material.

chapter	9

Producing and Marketing Your Own Record

The assumption governing this chapter (and this book) is that you do not wish to leave your local music market. If this accurately describes your current situation, then you will most likely not be in the running for a recording contract with a major label. In order for you to understand why this is, here's a brief discussion of the contemporary record business.

Record Distribution

As of this writing, there are five major record labels that function in North America, do their own record distribution and have branches, affiliates or subsidiaries in most of the world. They are: Bertelsmann (BMG), Capitol (EMI), Sony (Columbia), Universal, a recently formed amalgam of MCA and Polygram and WEA-Warner/Elektra/Atlantic groups. Bertelsmann is a German company that took over RCA; Sony is the giant Japanese electronics firm that bought Columbia; Capitol is owned by the English label EMI; MCA-Universal is 80% owned by the Canadian liquor company Seagrams with a 20% share belonging to Matsushita, another Japanese electronics firm; WEA is the only American owned label, even though American popular music has dominated the world music market for some time.

All of these labels have branches that distribute their product to stores throughout North America. They also distribute recordings owned by other labels. At the close of the 1980s, many the largest independent labels were bought in whole or part by the majors, and this trend has continued in the '90s. For example, BMG bought Windham Hill and Warner Brothers bought Tommy Boy Records.

When rock and roll replaced the more middle-of-the-road musical styles that preceded it, there were quite a number of important small independent record labels, like King and Sun Records in the 1950s. They distributed their records through independent record distributors. By the 1970s, the larger independent labels turned to the distribution divisions of their own competitors.

One of the primary reasons for this seemingly strange choice is that even the larger independents have always had trouble collecting money from independent distributors. Records have always been sold with return privileges and, until recently, there was no time limitation on the return of records. This meant stores could return a large percentage of unsold product to the distributor, who in turn returned the records to the label. Record stores were often late in paying distributors, who, if anything, delayed even further in paying the record companies. Supposedly, this situation drove even the notorious Phil Spector, producer of a "million and one hits," out of business. How was this possible?

All of the people involved in recording and producing a record-studios, engineers, producers, studio musicians, arrangers, pressing plants, album fabricators and designers, etc., expect immediate or rapid payment upon delivery of the product. The AFM contracts with record companies even specify that musicians who play on sessions must be paid within three weeks of the recording date. Many studios will not allow a master tape to leave the studio until full payment has been made.

Distributors are generally billed on a 30–90 day payment schedule, with small discounts given for early payment as an enticement to pay bills as soon as possible. At times, record distributors have taken the position that they would only pay quickly to companies that had consistent hit records. As soon as a company went into a "dry spell," the distributors would become increasingly reluctant to pay their bills. This happened because the distributor no longer cared if a company stopped shipping records. What good were a bunch of records that sooner or later would be returned? This left record companies in double jeopardy: they could neither collect on monies owed nor could they even get new product into the stores.

A company that owned its own distribution network did not need to concern itself with this problem. It simply paid the parent company on demand. Another aggravating factor was that up until very recently, a record company needed to have a dozen distributors in different cities. Their willingness to pay bills and their aggressiveness in getting the records into stores varied accordingly. Although independent record distribution has a much smaller piece of the pie today (usually in the 10-15% range), a few of the current independents, like Koch, actually distribute nationally. From time to time, various companies threaten to establish a national independent distribution network, though this rarely occurs.

The chart below outlines the way record distribution works. Note there are different categories of distributors. A rack jobber buys in huge quantities and stocks discount or department stores. Sometimes, rack jobbers rent space in the store and utilize the store's sales personnel to stocking the shelves.. A one-stop is an operation that carries labels of all manufacturers. It generally sells them to "mom and pop" record stores at a slightly higher price. The advantage to a small store is they can do one-stop shopping for everything they need.

Record Distribution

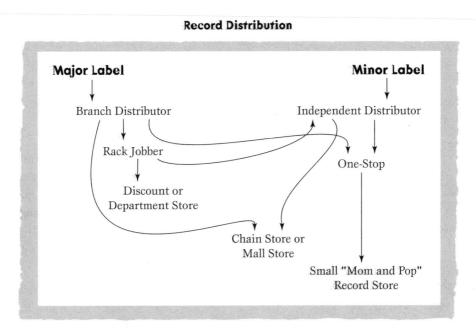

It is important to understand the economics of the record business. A major record company expects to spend $150,000–$200,000 on the creation and production of an album. In order to promote the record, it anticipates spending an equal amount on advertising and promotion. Along the way, it will give away more than 5,000 copies of an album to radio stations, and music critics, as well as copies given to stores for in-store play or listening stations.

Generally records are sold through radio play, by videos on MTV and other TV outlets, and by play in the stores. Discos provide an outlet for dance music, and jukeboxes are still another way to introduce records to the public. However, a recording rarely appears in a jukebox unless it has already achieved hit status.

Singles

Up to and until the late '80s, record companies made substantial amounts of money from hit singles (seven-inch double-sided 45 RPM records). These singles were the opening wedge for an artist's albums, which were plastered with stickers that said "contains the hit single _____ ." It was not unusual for hit singles to sell a million copies. Therefore singles were regarded as a way of breaking an artist and promoting an album. They were also profitable in their own right.

Today there are few singles that sell over 250,000 copies. The function of singles has come down to breaking an artist and calling attention to her through saturation radio play of the single. Twelve inch dance records provide a more profitable outlet for record companies. These records are singles that are re-mixed to be more danceable. Sometimes the length of the song is extended and the rhythm tracks are highlighted. There are even producers who specialize in these re-mixes for the dance market.

Getting a Record Deal

What do record companies look for in a new artist? They want the artist to tour, they prefer she write her own songs, and that she have professional management. Most of all, they feel the artist must have a "breaker," the song that can break the artist's career wide open. They are also looking for artists who are seemingly stable enough to write more than one hit, and who can survive the rigors of the business to record more and more hits.

Let's now to return to the situation in which most of the readers of this book find themselves: you have chosen not to tour all over the country, you probably (almost certainly) don't have the sort of high-level personal manager that will bring a smile to the face of major record company executives, you are not living in a major music market and you don't have ready access to record companies.

There are still some strategies you can employ to get the attention of a major record company, which are covered in Chapter 12, "The Urge for Going." However the odds are heavily against you or your group finding a major record deal in your location and outside of the major music markets. Let's explore some alternatives.

Producing Your Own Recording: Finding a Producer and an Engineer

The easiest way to get your recording to the marketplace is to do it yourself. You can use a home studio or rent one in your town. It is crucial you spend a good deal of time selecting songs and working out the musical arrangements you plan to use in the studio. This will save you a good deal of money and will enable you to intelligently utilize your time in the studio.

Try to find an experienced record producer to help you, since you are going to need all the help you can get! What should you look for in a record producer, what will it cost and where can you find one?

Talk to other local musicians and bands and recording studio personnel about who they have worked with and what it was like working with them. Listen to some recorded examples of their work. If possible, visit some sessions they are producing. When you talk to a producer, pay careful attention to the interactions between your group and the producer. You don't have to agree with one another on all issues, but you need to develop a spirit of mutual trust. If this trust doesn't exist, you may waste expensive studio time and end up with a product that satisfies neither you nor your producer. A good producer should be able to enhance the sound of your group without violating the spirit of the group's music. Above all, she needs to be someone who listens to the band and understands what their vision of the project is.

Choose your recording studio and engineer as carefully as you chose the producer. Make sure your producer and engineer work well together—it is best if they have have already worked on some projects together. Be careful that both your producer and your band are happy with the engineer who will record your album. It takes a team effort to come out with a recording that is representative of your group.

Home studios may be adequate to record your album, but usually don't have the capability or equipment to do quality mixing. If you are using a home studio, be sure that you have quality microphones, especially microphones that will be used for the vocals.

Beware of producers and engineers who seem to be trying to fit your group into a predetermined format. Are they really listening to the songs? Do they seem to have a sense of the direction in which you want to go or do they jump to inaccurate conclusions? Do you feel you are being hyped whenever you raise any serious questions? It is natural for the producer and engineer to want you to appreciate their knowledge of studio gear, but don't be snowed by the use of too many effects, or by playbacks of your music at deafening levels of volume. Do the producer and the engineer communicate well in the studio? If they do not, you will burn up lots of precious studio time. When you rehearse with the producer, what sort of suggestions does she make? Are they sensible and logical creative ideas or she is trying to move your sound in another direction? In short, is she trying to manipulate you?

On a relatively modest local or regional project, you should expect to pay a producer from $1,000 to $3,000, plus a royalty of anywhere from 2% to 3% of the retail selling price of your recording. The royalty should not go into effect until you have recouped the amount of the original advance. For instance, if your producer has a 3% royalty, and you have paid him a $2,000 advance and your CD sells for $15, he will be earning 45 cents per album, but he would not receive royalties until you have sold 4,444 copies of the CD.

You may think this is a lot of money to pay a producer, but your album probably represents at least a month's work, between pre-production, recording and mixing. You should not begrudge your producer her percentage. If your work becomes a hit, why shouldn't she reap the profits of her work?

I recommend that you do not hire a producer by the hour. It is much better to create an atmosphere where the only hourly charge you need to be concerned with is the rental of the studio. The producer needs to work as hard as is necessary, without any concern for the hours involved.

Engineers are usually included in the price of the studio and do not get any royalties for their work. (Engineers are among the most poorly rewarded people in the industry.) Only a few highly-skilled practitioners in the major cities operate independently and enjoy royalty deals. That is why so many engineers turn to production, where they can get a piece of the action. Whenever possible, you should record and mix your product at the same facility, using the same engineer. If you don't, the sound can be disconcertingly jumbled, and you will waste more money while the new engineer is figuring out exactly what is on the tape. The sound of your record is partly determined by the way the room is set up, what microphones are used and how they are placed, the recording format (analog or digital), and the type of tape recorder and console you use. Don't take foolish risks.

Recording Formats: Cassettes, Compact Discs and Vinyl

The previous edition of this book had a chart demarcating the advantages of each recording format. These days there isn't much choice. Vinyl is consigned to dance music and to the relatively few audiophiles who are in love with the format. The only advantage of cassettes is that they are the most portable format and can be played in cars. CD is the format of choice for anyone in today's record business. The manufacturing costs for CDs have come way down, as well. The only real difference in costs is that it is not cost effective to duplicate CDs in quantities under a thousand, while cassettes can be duplicated in short runs of several hundred copies or even less. CDs look far more professional than cassettes; most radio stations won't consider playing cassettes; and the cassette format is so small that cover art is virtually meaningless. If you are looking forward to a serious career and you want people to buy your product, CDs are the inevitable choice.

Mastering Records

Mastering in the process where tapes are converted to disc. Until recently this process always took place in a separate recording studio, one that had a whole array of different equipment. Only a handful of major cities had this sort of facility. Today, there is an alternative to the use of a separate mastering studio. More and more CDs are being mastered at studios that have a facility for cutting a master CD, called a CDR. The CD can then be manufactured directly from this CD reference disc. It is also possible to make a handful of CDs at these facilities for early play on radio stations or for sending out an album to a particularly important music critic.

It *is* possible to influence the sound of a record during the mastering process, whether it is done at the still-existent high-priced facilities like Bernie Grundman's LA studio or Gateway in Portland, Maine, or a CDR-equipped local studio. This can be done through computer programs like Sonic Solutions, or by the use of re-equalization or outboard gear. The problem is that by the time you have mixed down a multi-track tape to a stereo tape, the changes tend to be gross. Re-equalizing the bass on the left channel will re-equalize the bass frequencies on any other instruments on that channel.

If you decide to use one of the mastering studios, I advise you to attend the mastering session. This will ensure that the engineer understands what you want and gives you a voice in the decision-making process. If you plan to produce cassettes, you'll need to choose between high speed or real time duplication. Real time sounds better, but costs more. "Real time" means it takes 37 minutes to duplicate a 37 minute cassette. In high speed duplication, your tape is copied in vary-ing time ratios, usually at least as high as one minute for every eight minutes of running time of your original tape. The faster the speed, the more the possibility of compromise in the sound of your finished product. Be sure the facility serv-ices their machines regularly, so they run at the correct speed.

Budgets

Do a budget before you ever go into the recording studio. From your experience working in your home studio, you should have some notion of how long each song will take to record. Include time for instrumentals, vocals, mixing, and some provi-sions for possible re-mixing. The smaller the group of people involved in the mix, the faster your production will move.

It's difficult to estimate how long it will take to record a song. Some people are very nervous in the studio and seem to take forever to do their best work. Others enjoy the freedom from audience response that is part of the studio experience. Just as with rehearsals, don't allow a bunch of visitors in the studio, particularly those who feel compelled to give you the "benefit" of their often useless opinions and suggestions. If you have friends to whom you feel obligated to involve in the sessions, invite them at the very beginning or end of a session, making it clear you don't expect them to hang out there. Visitors can also be a nuisance to producers and engineers by asking incessant and often foolish questions. You hired these people to do the work—not to entertain your friends.

In working out your budget, consider hiring additional musicians who are not regular members of your performing group. A group doesn't need to be able to duplicate every sound on their record. Generally what the listener will latch on to is a particular sound that represents a sort of trademark that identifies an artist. It can be a vocal sound like Sting's or Bob Dylan's, or an instrumental sound like Phil Collins' drum sound. The average listener won't care if Sting adds a flute to one track of his album, but if his vocal in performance differs radically from the sound of the recording, it will annoy many people.

Don't radically change the way your group sounds in a performing situation on your tape. If you don't have a mandolin player in your band, don't use mandolin on eight cuts of the album. Remember, also, the listener is probably more aware of your group's vocals than any other component of your sound. Don't hire three or four great background singers and substitute them for your regular vocalists. In short, use studio musicians or singers to enhance the sound of your group, but don't use them in such liberal doses that the public becomes confused about what your sound truly is.

You should go into the studio with some notion what your CD ought to sound like. Use the following track sheet before you get into the studio as a guide to what you are going to do. Typically, in a 24-track rock set-up, drums occupy seven or more tracks of the tape. By filling out a track sheet, you will develop a notion of what each song will need, and whether for example, too many of the songs have an identical instrumental set-up.

Track Sheet for 24-Track Recording

Track Number	Instrument	Name of Player or Singer
1	Click Track	
2	Snare Drum	
3	Snare Drum	
4	Bass Drum	
5	Cymbals	
6	Tom-toms	
7	Overall Drum Set	
8	Electric Bass (with Amp.)	
9	Electric Bass (Direct to Console)	
10	Keyboard (Low Strings)	
11	Keyboard (High Strings)	
12	Rhythm Guitar	
13	Lead Guitar	
14	Synthesizer	
15	Lead Vocal	
16	Background Vocals	
17	Background Vocals	
18-23	Other Lead Instruments, Special Effects	

Note: Tracks 1 and 24 are often the last used. It is generally thought that the outer tracks are more apt to produce technical difficulties. Be sure to allow 2 to 4 hours to mix each tune down, more if you are a perfectionist.

A group that has a single lead vocalist, guitar, bass and drums is going to have trouble varying their sound enough to come up with an interesting album. This is where versatility becomes important. If the guitarist has several nylon, steel string acoustic twelve string guitars, as well as jazz and rock electrics, and if the drummer is also a decent percussionist, you will be able to achieve a variety of textures even from a group this small. You should also avoid the temptation of overwhelming your audience with your versatility. Neither consumers or record companies are able to cope with popular music artists who have a dozen vocal sounds, and sing or play in three different musical genres. This may be a sad reflection on popular taste, but it is true. Even in jazz and classical music the public usually identifies artists with particular musical styles or periods.

Financing Your Project

How do you raise the money for your project in the first place? If you can't afford to do it yourself, you'll need to find other funding sources. The group itself may be one source of funds. Projects can be financed by friends and family of the artists, by loans or outright gifts, and even by selling stock in an album. To avoid any hard feelings, you should make it very clear to anyone investing in the project that they are very unlikely to make a profit on this investment. In fact, they may never get their money back. Whether you will pay interest on loans or give investors a percentage of your profits is up to you, but remember, anytime you give someone a piece of the action, you may regret it later. If Sony picks up your album, and you have to pay someone 10% of your royalties because they lent you $100 three years ago, you will regret making such an agreement.

Sometimes a manager or agent will invest in a project. Because they are professionals with experience in the business, they may want a larger piece of the action than you wish to relinquish. Any deal is possible as long as all the parties understand their obligations.

How can you budget for your sessions? The next page shows a sample budget for your CD, including expenses for artwork and promotion.

Choosing a Studio

The first budget decision will be to determine what type of studio you should use. Many cities have 24-track A-DAT studios that are not expensive to rent. Some of these small studios with up-to-date gear cost as little as $35–$50 an hour. A-DAT tape costs are minimal, about $40–$50 for forty minutes of tape for three interlocked A-DAT machines. Analog tape is much more expensive, costing $125–$150 a reel for 15–30 minutes of tape. It depends on what speed you choose to run the analog recorder at, 15 or 30 IPS. With care and planning, even if you use analog tape you should be able to make an album using three reels of tape. It is possible to rent used tape reels for less, but this used tape can lower the quality and brilliance of your sound, part of what you are selling.

Recording Budget (CD)

Each Song: _____
Name of Song: _____
Basic Tracks (instrumentation): _____
Vocals: _____
Vocal and Instrumental Overdubs: _____
Fees Paid to Musicians or Vocalists, including
any Pension and Health Payments _____
Mixing Time: _____
Tape Costs: _____
Studio Hours: (total hours at _____ an hour): _____
Total Cost of Ten Songs: _____
Mastering Costs: _____
Pressing Plant: _____
Album Art—Photo or Art: _____
Design Costs: _____
Printing of Labels: _____
Delivery Costs _____

Total: _____

Recording Budget (Cassette)

Song Budget (Same as CD items): _____
High Speed or Real Time Tape Duplication: _____
Cost of Tape Boxes: _____
Cover Art—Photo or Art: _____
Design Costs: _____
Printing of Labels: _____
Delivery Costs: _____

Total: _____

Another analog option is to rent a 16-track studio that uses one-inch tape. If you are recording rock, this is the absolute minimum of tracks you will need. It is also possible to "ping pong" your recording on a 4 or 8 track machine. This will require constant re-mixing to create open tracks. This is time-consuming work. It can ultimately degrade the quality of your product, and may actually end up costing you more money because of the re-mixing than you will save in the per hour studio charges. One-half inch tape of these machines should run you about $35 a reel.

Many artists know audiophiles, high-fidelity hobbyists and amateur musicians who will happily donate their time and equipment for the cost of the tape. Whether this is a good idea depends on the quality of the studio, and of the engineer. Sometimes what appears to save money simply ends up wasting time.

Trying to limit the amount of tape you use forces you to make quick decisions. Some artists never erase anything in the studio, figuring that they may use some amusing snippet at a future time. You won't be able to bask in that luxury, especially if you are using the analog format. If you are in doubt as to whether a take is good, your best bet is to trust in your producer and engineer. That is why you hired them, isn't it?

Hard Disc Recording & MIDI

If your product is keyboard-generated and doesn't require additional instruments, it may be convenient and cost-effective for you to record on a hard disk. Through multiple keyboard parts, the use of computers, MIDI files and sequencers you may be able to come up with a respectable product with the greatest expenditure being the time and energy you put into the project. This works particularly well with dance and techno music projects, where there may not be a need for live instrumentation in either recording or performance.

Time Lines

It will probably take you about a month of full-time work to record an album. This is a general guideline. It depends on what sort of music you are recording, how many instruments and vocals are on the tracks, and how much of a perfectionist you are. Don't try to record music that is at the very edge of your technical abilities, unless you have virtually unlimited time in the studio. It takes too long to get a good performance, and you may not be able to perform the material live.

Cover art and fabrication are likely to take another two months. Try to find a graphic artist who has already designed CD and/or cassette covers. There are many technical and special specifications for these types of art layouts. Increasingly this design is done with the help of computers. Be sure that the artist you work with talks to the people who will actually print the covers.

Promoting and Selling Your Album

Now that you have completed an album, it's time to market it. Start by writing a press release describing the concept of the album, where and how it was recorded, and your plans for distributing it. If it is feasible, induce a local television station to come to the studio to report on the progress of your project. In local markets, this can be an excellent human interest story.

Your press release should be simple and direct. Send it out to radio and television stations, daily papers, entertainment weeklies, and to neighborhood or suburban newspapers in different sections of your town or its suburbs. You should send a copy of your CD with the press release and an extra copy of the album cover. This can be expensive, but you are trying to build interest in your music. Be sure to send out the release (and the CD) to similar media in any neighboring cities where your band has worked.

This first and most obvious way to bring in some cash to pay for all of this is to sell the recording every time you perform. Depending on the type of venue, this can be done by the band itself, by your road manager, friends or even the club manager or her staff. You should offer a commission to the club if it handles the sales, which may not be accepted. Anything that spreads the word about your band and makes it seem more professional will help any club where you play regularly. Announce the availability of your recording during each set that you perform. Don't gloss over your product—you want people to remember it. By the same token, don't be a nuisance and over-hype it. The club may even want to host a record party when your product is first released. Invite any local media people, fans, friends or people on your mailing list. This is the perfect time to sell your product.

I have known some musicians who play in the streets primarily in order to sell their albums or cassettes while they are performing. Make sure your city doesn't require a license to do this, and be prepared to pay sales tax in your city or state.

Your largest single profit center consists of selling your CD at shows. If you want to put a recording in local stores, they may accept it on consignment or buy it from you. On consignment deals the store usually wants 20–25% of the retail selling price of the album. If they are paying up front for the albums, you can expect them to want about a 40% discount off the retail selling price.

Although it's a good idea to consign records in stores, you will need to keep an inventory of how many records are in each store and collect the money when the albums are sold. This will entail the use of your time and gas in your car, together with an endless round of phone calls. There is often only one person in the store who is authorized to pay you—sometimes it will seem as though he is never there. If your records are consigned in stores out of town, you will find it even more difficult to collect the money in a timely way. It will also be more expensive to check on sales when your calls are long distance.

It is also possible to work through independent record distributors. You will have to sell them CDs at about half the retail selling price; they in turn will contact individual stores and make about a dollar and half per CD. You will not get paid by the distributors until after they have collected from the stores.

Why bother putting records in stores at all? Improved distribution will broaden the sales potential of your product. If you know a store employee, he may be willing to give your CD some in-store play or even display your cover on the wall. If you are getting airplay, the radio stations will virtually compel you to have your records available in stores. When people like a record they often call the station to get the name of the artist and the album and if they can't find the record in stores, they tend to get irritated at the station. When Windham Hill Records began, their first recording was never intended to be a nationally-distributed item, so was pressed in very small quantity. When the album began to be played regularly on a station in Seattle, they received many calls from annoyed listeners who couldn't find the record in stores. The station notified Will Ackerman, the company's founder and first artist that he either had to get the records in stores or they would stop playing it. That is how this large and quite successful record company actually started!

Realistically, you have a smaller chance of getting your CD into chain stores. These large-scale operations have taken over a big piece of the business from old time "Mom and Pop" stores. The chains often do their buying from one national warehouse location. They get high discounts and operate with computerized buying programs. It is a nuisance for them to stock local or regional product. However depending upon the policy of the particular chain and who is managing the local store, you still may be able to get your album on the shelf.

You should send your recording to every radio station within a hundred miles of where you work, along with a full press kit of the group. (See the excellent press kit example at the end of this chapter.)

Some stations like to do interviews with artists, so try to induce them to interview your group. Public record stations will even sometimes play cassettes, but most commercial stations are unwilling to do so. By the way, when you are sending review copies of your product, whether they are going to radio station people or newspapers, always find out the name of the proper music critic, music director of the station, etc. Otherwise your product addressed to "New Jersey Gazette," may end up in the trash. Public radio stations and more adventurous free-form commercial stations may allow disc jockeys to do their own programming. If this is the case in your town, find out which people might be apt to play your record. It's worth giving away a few more CDs to get some airplay. Also ask reviewers if they want extra album covers. Sometimes they'll reprint the cover in their newspaper or magazine.

What about radio stations in areas where you haven't played? Unless your product is in record stores, most stations will be reluctant to play it. There are books that list alternative radio stations and suppliers who will sell you appropriate labels. They are listed in the Resource Section at the end of this chapter and in Appendix D of this book.

Find out which stations are actually playing your record. It's not a bad idea to send out prepaid envelopes or postcards to stations outside your area. If you discover they are playing your album regularly, you may be able to parlay that airplay into a booking at a club or college in that area.

Another way to attack the record market is to put out a vinyl dance single, a cassette or CD single. Although the manufacturing costs won't be drastically different than the cost of producing an entire album, the cover art is usually pretty basic and the recording costs should be much lower. You can get into trouble if your song starts to hit and you don't have an album available to capitalize on this success.

You can hire local or regional promotion people to help get airplay for your product. In Shad O'Shea's book, *Just For The Record,* he points out that you can force airplay in your town by deliberately concentrating on towns 50–100 miles way. He suggests all sorts of gimmicks, such as mobiles, T-shirts, teasers sent to music directors, etc. You can create your own list of radio stations by going to the library and consulting *Broadcasting Yearbook.* O'Shea also suggests that when possible, you personally deliver the recording to the station, and that you take the time to write personal thank you notes to stations that play your recording. You can hire local promotion people to assist you in getting airplay, but this is an expensive ploy.

Loretta Lynn achieved great success by personally visiting small stations all across the country, as she points out in her book, *Coal Miner's Daughter.* Not only did the stations play her records, they continued to do so after she became a big star.

How far you want to go in promoting your product is a function of how much you believe in it and how much time and money you have to spend. If your recording sells heavily in a city or region, you may be able to get a distribution deal with a major label, that may even sign you to an exclusive contract and re-release your record.

Another way to promote your recording is to build up a strong mailing list through your performances. Many touring acts keep such a list on a computerized data base, broken down into categories of whether the fan has ever bought any recordings of the group. They keep the people on these lists abreast of new recordings and performances in their area.

Don't consider making a record until you have a well-formulated plan for how you will promote it and some method of distributing it. Merchandising involves its own sort of creativity. Shirts, matchbooks, pens, jackets and mugs are all readily available if you can afford them. Advertising can also be effective, especially if you can identify a group that has a particular affinity for your music. For example, New Age music would obviously appeal to the people who subscribe to a journal on holistic healing. Chris Le Doux is an ex-champion rodeo cowboy who built his core following with people who follow the rodeo. If you have songs that appeal to particular groups, whether they are jet pilots or baseball players, find the magazines or newsletters that go out to those people. You may be able to play their conventions, in turn, selling more albums.

It is doubtful that a self-distributed album will make you rich, but stranger things have happened. George Winston became a major player in New Age music on the then barely-known Windham Hill Records label. Hootie & The Blowfish had an independent regional album that did well on the beaches of the Carolinas and Virginia before they achieved major success and a major label deal. The same thing happened to the Colorado-based band Big Head Todd and the Monsters.

All of these artists were ready and willing to do national tours. National exposure can fuel the success of a record or it can follow from a successful album. If you don't plan to tour extensively, then don't expect national impact from your CD.

Producing and merchandising your own recording validates your professional standing to club owners, concert promoters, agents and even the general public. It also provides you with a permanent landmark of where you are musically at the time that you recorded the album.

Insert and Promotional Material for a Self-produced CD

Used by Permission

Publishing and Performance Rights

If you put out a tape or CD, you will need to copyright the songs and the perform-ance. You will also need to join ASCAP, BMI or SESAC—the performing rights organizations that monitor the payment of royalties for airplay and public perform-ances to writers and publishers. In Chapter 11, "Making Inroads on the National and Regional Scene," the ins-and-outs of publishing, songwriting and perform-ing rights organizations are discussed.

If you don't write your own songs, or have used some songs composed by others, you will have to pay the statutory royalty rates of 6.95 cents to the writer and publisher of each song.[1] This is usually arranged through the Harry Fox Agency at 711 3rd Ave., New York, NY 10017. If you are recording songs written by friends, you may be able to publish the songs yourself, which cuts the royalty payments in half.[2]

Finally don't overlook the possibility for marketing your CD on the Internet or creating your own web page. For more details, see the article by Ron Sobel in the last chapter of this book.

CHAPTER 9 RESOURCES

There are a number of books on making your own record listed in the appendix. My favorite one is still Diane Sward Rapaport's *How to Make and Sell Your Own Record,* published by Prentice Hall. Get the most recent edition available.

There are several books out that discuss record producers. The most recent is one that I co-authored with Jim Mason called: *The Record Producer: The Magic in the Music.* It was published by Music Maker Publications in Boulder, Colorado and comes with a CD of recorded examples.

---

1. As of the printing of this book. It varies from year to year.
2. For further information on this process, see my book, *The Music Business: Career Opportunities & Self Defense,* 2nd Revised Edition, 1997.

chapter 10

Polishing Your Skills

Many musicians and singers who work in local markets find that after doing much of the same thing over a period of years, they lose interest in music. Some become bitter about the music industry, constantly comparing their skills to that of some popular music superstar who they regard as an untalented fake. This is a fruitless pursuit. Although it is not possible to predict whether or not an artist will be successful, it is clear that in the field of popular music, image, physical attractiveness, and other non-musical qualities play a major role in the public's rather fickle tastes. (On the positive side, networking and good business relations have also helped these people.) Some musicians become so obsessed with the idea that people who have little musical talent become successful that they leave the music business and look for a more "stable" profession.

There are two ways to counteract the drudgery of playing music in the same or similar venues. One concept already discussed was that of developing enough musical versatility to pursue other musical opportunities in areas such as recording work, writing music, or freelance playing or singing.

Studying Music

Another way to retain a fresh approach to music is to seek out a new area of music, perhaps one that has always interested you, but one you have never taken time to pursue. This might entail the study of arranging or composing, taking vocal or instrumental lessons, or finding classes in audio engineering or video production.

To find the best teachers in your area, talk to other musicians, music store owners and teachers at local colleges. Consult musicians who you respect and whose opinions you value. Most cities have stores or repair shops where the best players hang out. The proprietor of this type of place has usually spent many years in town, and has a good idea of who the best teachers are.

Sometimes there's an underground network or grapevine from town to town about who the master teachers are. These people may be unknown to the general public, even in their hometown. Some rarely perform, but enjoy the stability of passing their skills on to motivated students.

It is possible to take music lessons at most colleges without enrolling as a degree student—this is usually handled through a department of "continuing education" or "extended studies." In some instances, continuing education lessons are taught by graduate students. Check out the teacher, his skill level and experience before you sign up. Be sure to keep in mind that great players don't always make great teachers, and some great teachers don't themselves play all that well. What a great teacher does have is a profound knowledge of his instrument, a strong dose of patience and a real love for music.

Colleges also offer classes in arranging, composing, electronic music, songwriting, music on the personal computer, jazz history and classes about the music industry. Try sitting in on a class before you sign up. This will give you an idea as to whether the teacher will be teaching things that are useful for you.

Many community colleges or four year schools have jazz bands. If you wish to improve your sight-reading or doubling skills, or simply want a chance to play in large ensembles, they can provide you with new challenges. Similar opportunities exist in vocal ensembles and orchestras.

A music arranging course provides you with a good opportunity to explore the sounds of other instruments and to learn to write for them. Similar courses can teach you the basic skills for writing music for film or TV. Provided that some of the musicians with whom you are working read music, you may be able to utilize some of these arranging and composing tools writing for your band.

World music, or music of non-Western cultures, is another fascinating study. Although learning about the music of Africa is not apt to give you specific ideas that you can immediately put to use at the local Holiday Inn, it can result in your learning some things about percussion that you can use in your band. (I have a friend in Denver who picked up a steel drum and took a few lessons while he was visiting a relative in the West Indies. He now gets additional work playing calypso music.) The study of exotic music from other parts of the world will broaden your perspective about the role of music and musicians in various cultures and contexts.

Jamey Abersold, Music Minus One and Hal Leonard Corporation are companies that provide recordings which have fine rhythm sections. Sheet music is supplied with the CDs, and you jam or read written music along with the band. Materials are available in most styles of music and for vocalists as well.

Sight-reading

If you want to play freelance gigs, it is a good idea for you to develop superior skills at reading music at sight. When you are a rhythm section player, like a bass or guitar player or a drummer, you may be able to get away with being able to follow a chord chart. If this is the case, you will be expected to make up (improvise) your own part. No matter what instrument you play, you are going to need a basic knowledge of chords and chord progressions, and you need to be able to respond instantly to chord symbols. Even in a recording situation, you may get a chart that consists of a group of chord symbols with a particular rhythm pattern indicated. You shouldn't have to stop and think before playing the correct chord.

The late Tommy Tedesco was one of the outstanding studio guitarists in Los Angeles for many years. His method books for guitar describe how a guitarist develops studio skills. He suggests that when someone hands you a difficult part that you not try to play every note the first time through. Rather, he feels you should try to grasp the essence of the part, and then play a bit more of what is written during each run-through. It is essential that you keep your place rhythmically, because being ahead or behind the rest of the band is an obvious tip-off that you are having trouble with a part.

The rationale behind Tommy's approach is that by playing a sort of "Reader's Digest" condensed version of the part, you will give the arranger and producer the basic sound they want while you become accustomed to the nuances of the music. During the first few rundowns, the engineer is usually working on instrumental balances, so no one is apt to be listening to your complete part.

Many good sight-readers point out that it is important to read slightly ahead of where you are actually playing. By doing this, you psychologically prepare yourself for any truly difficult passages, rather than coming upon them by surprise.

The best way to become adept at sight-reading is to spend time each day reading new music. Read the most difficult parts you can find. This will help prepare you for anything that you might see in a show or at a recording studio. It is also a good idea to buy yourself legitimate (legal) "fake books." A fake book is a collection of melody lines, lyrics and chords of hundreds of popular songs in every conceivable style: rhumbas, rock tunes, country ballads, etc. It is a very useful tool on jobs like weddings where the audience is liable to request virtually any musical style. Fake books also provide a common source of music between players who don't know one another well and may not have a common repertoire. Anyone with even a basic knowledge of music notation and chord symbols can play out of a fake book.

Songwriters' Organizations

A list of songwriters' organizations is in the Appendix. What can you get out of such groups?

You may be able to locate a collaborator in the ranks of your local songwriting group. Today's collaborations are not usually separated between lyricists or composers, but involve input in both areas. Two writers may sit around trading ideas in a small room. They may have a couple of guitars, a keyboard instrument and a drum machine. The process consists of two people coming up with ideas and hammering them out, until they hone their song to a point where both parties are happy.

Some people deliberately write with more than one collaborator in order to explore fresh influences in their writing. Some writers excel at creating rhythmic grooves; others have a talent for chord alterations and substitutions. Some lyricists focus on story songs; others may work best on love ballads. By writing with different collaborators, you develop the opportunity to attempt different musical and lyric styles.

Songwriting organizations offer writers the chance to honestly critique each other's work. Most people are not sufficiently objective or analytical to see the limitations or defects in their own work. This is particularly true of people who write songs that are based on current or recent emotional experiences. These songs may be extremely meaningful to the writer, but may not hit home to a casual listener. You may resent receiving criticisms of songs that are close to your heart, but it may be very helpful to your development as a songwriter.

Many songwriting associations sponsor seminars. They bring professional songwriters, producers and publishers in from a major market who can provide you with some insight on what is happening in these larger markets. Some of this information may be about the business-copyright matters, how songs are recorded, or what song contracts should offer the writer. A speaker may take an interest in a local writer and actually publish her music or take it to an artist or a producer.

Try to attend as many of these seminars as you can. Listen carefully to what the speakers say, then evaluate the information in terms of your own goals and development. It is sometimes a mistake to accept advice without being critical of it.

Many of the speakers at songwriting seminars live in the major music markets. Their advantage over you is that they have access to who and what is currently viable in the marketplace. The disadvantage is that in a city like Los Angeles, there is a plethora of would-be writers and artists. They all go to the same seminars and hear the same lectures. It is quite common for lecturers to deal in generalities that may or may not apply to your particular situation. Sometimes a writer develops a viable style because of his isolation and individual experimentation. Many of the best songs or musical styles would have never been accepted if they had been born in a major music market. The "suits" would have deemed such work uncommercial.

Local colleges or community colleges sometimes offer seminars or classes in various aspects of the music business. Such classes can be quite useful, but be sure to find out who the teacher is and what she has done. Is the teacher currently active in the business or did she produce hits fifteen years ago? The fact that someone is teaching a class doesn't prove what he has to offer will be relevant to today's music.

There are several songwriting organizations that can be helpful. The Nashville Songwriters Association International (NSAI) plays an important role in the Nashville songwriting community. It sponsors numerous seminars and provides a source of contacts with publishers and record companies in Nashville. The National Association of Songwriters (NAS) plays a similar role in Los Angeles. It sponsors a weekly Songwriters Showcase that provides access for songwriters to publishers, producers and peers.

The Songwriters Guild of America (SGA) is a source of help by providing suggested contracts that tend to favor the writer, as opposed to what most publishers will tend to offer you.

BMI and ASCAP sponsor seminars in different parts of the country that cover various aspects of songwriting, recording and the music industry. These events provide local writers with an opportunity to meet top pros who come in and donate their time to teach about the business. To find out about such seminars, contact

BMI or ASCAP directly, or talk to the music professors at the college nearest you that offers any programs in the music industry, audio engineering or music merchandising.

If you pursue some of these suggestions, they may also open up some new employment opportunities. This may include teaching at a local community college, scoring local television commercials or industrial films, or even doing workshops on songwriting.

If you are trying to sustain a long-term musical career, don't get locked into one musical style or set of musical mannerisms. Music is an ever-changing world, and you should strive to be involved in its evolution.

Improving Your Skills As a Songwriter

If you are trying to polish your songwriting skills, there are some things you can do without taking classes. There are a number of books about songwriting that explain how songs are written and merchandised. Many of these books are concerned with the actual structure of popular song. Some of these books are marred by an over-emphasis on the song forms of the 1930s and 1940s, forms of limited use today, except in the writing of Broadway shows. Many of these authors have trouble acknowledging that in today's music it is often difficult to separate a song from the production of it on a recording. For some recommended books see Resources at the end of this chapter.

I particularly recommend Bill Flanagan's *Written in My Soul.* Flanagan has an encyclopedic knowledge of contemporary songs, and his interviews with songwriters transcend the generalities usually found in books where major songwriters are interviewed. The writers that Flanagan interviewed express somewhat opposing views on the question of craft vs. inspiration. For some, songwriting is a workaday operation requiring time, effort, attention and re-writing. Others, like Van Morrison, adopt a more freewheeling approach, largely ignoring commercial considerations and viewing themselves almost as a vehicle to express ideas and feelings that are "in the air." Flanagan's book makes you want to go back and listen to many of the songs you may have taken for granted. More importantly it will inspire your own work with a broader perspective.

Meanwhile, following are a few more songwriting tips:

Melody Writing

Method	Advantages	Disadvantages
Play a series of chord progressions. Extract the melody notes from the structure of the chords.	Easy to get started.	Can the melody stand alone without the chords?
Write a melody in your head. Don't play it until the melody is completed.	Avoids any limitations caused by your lack of instrumental skill.	You may find the need for the rhythmic pulse that playing an instrument provides.
Write with a new instrument, in an unfamiliar key or rhythm, or in a different tuning on guitar.	Can take you to new musical terrain.	You may feel insecure because you have no idea where this process is going.
Explore new chord patterns through books or play-along records.	Avoids the deadening feeling that your songs "sound the same."	May not make musical sense to you.

Lyric Writing

Lyric Suggestions Method

1. Write a story song about an actual incident.

2. Write several songs that have absolutely nothing to do with your own experiences.

3. Write about something you have read or seen on TV.

4. Write several songs that relate to the same concept. If this seems productive, develop a complete concept album.

5. If you have a good melody but don't like the lyric, rewrite the lyric entirely, as though it were another song. (This will work if you have a good lyric but don't like the melody.)

CHAPTER 10 RESOURCES

If you are trying to polish your songwriting skills, there are some things that you can do without taking classes. There are a number of books about songwriting that explain how songs are written and merchandised. Michael Kosser's book, *How to Become a Successful Nashville Songwriter,* conveys a good sense of atmosphere as he takes you through the chronic writer's problems of rewrites, craft development, dry spells and intermittent successes.

Most of the other books about songwriting are concerned with the actual structure of popular song. A number of them are oriented toward the song forms of the 1930s and 1940s—forms of limited use today, except in the writing of Broadway shows. It is often difficult in popular music to separate the song from the production of that song on a recording.

A few of the better books are Kasha and Hirschorn's *If They Ask You, You Can Write a Song;* Stephan Citron's *Songwriting;* Mark and Cathy Liggett's *Songwriting: An Insider's Guide to the Music Industry;* and Sheila Davis' *The Craft of Lyric Writing.* (See Appendix D.)

For country writers, Tom T. Hall has a book called *The Songwriter's Handbook.* Although no two writers work in exactly the same way, it is interesting to see the way that Hall works. He sees himself as a sort of human tape recorder, and his antennae are always up for the right phrase or feeling that will lead to a song. Hall tells the reader that the title to one of his big hits, "Old Dogs, Children and Watermelon Wine" emerged from a conversation with a bartender in a dingy bar.

There are two other books about songwriting that every writer should have in his library. John Braheny's *The Craft and Business of Songwriting* covers virtually every area of songwriting. It is worthy of your attention for his discussions of the craft of lyric and melody writing—it has the best material in print about making demos and dealing with music business attorneys.

chapter 11

Making Inroads on the National and Regional Scene

In every group, there are specific questions of goals and responsibilities which should be resolved. It is best for all group members to share common goals and common work schedules outside the confines of the band. If two people in a quintet have 9 to 5 jobs and the others don't, the ability of the group to work late night jobs or jobs that involve extensive driving, is going to be a source of conflicts and compromises.

When groups stay together for long periods of time band members may develop a variety of commitments that go far beyond what they had at the age of twenty. Marriage may reduce a person's eagerness to work weekend evenings and persuading him to do so may result in compromising or destroying his marriage.

Any band seeking a national career needs to feel secure in its goals and identity. This cannot be accomplished if players wander in and out of the group whenever the mood suits them. One of the first areas a record company considers is whether a group will stay together long enough for the company to successfully promote and sell the group's albums.

Group members should be honest with each other and maintain regular communication about their goals. It may become necessary for a person to leave the group, if her day job makes regular rehearsals impossible or difficult. If this situation is handled directly and without equivocation, there shouldn't be any hard feelings. If it is ignored, it may result in the ultimate breakup of the group and lingering bitterness between the people involved. It is a reasonable idea for the group to actually have a legal agreement that details who owns the name of the group, along with the disposition of royalties and equipment if the group breaks up.

Keep a constant watch over the activities of the booking agent or agents who supply you with jobs. Sometimes, an agent becomes stale or complacent, becoming uninterested in doing the necessary legwork that will keep you working on a regular basis. Stay aware of who the new agents are in town, and what sort of acts they are seeking. Sometimes, breaking connections or old contacts is painful, but it must be done if your career is to grow. You may be moving in different and incompatible directions from your agent. An ambitious agent may have the connections that will catapult your group out of a local market into the national scene. If you are signing with a relatively large agency and are relying on one particular agent to work with you, it is a good idea to utilize a "keyman" clause in your contract with the agency. This clause enables you to leave the agency if your agent leaves the company. Since agents often leave to start their own agencies, this clause gives you an insurance policy against being tied up with an agency that doesn't know or care about your work.

Your own band may move in contradictory directions. Many musicians become dull or stop practicing. Sometimes, a member of the group experiences personal problems that make him impossible to tolerate. Often one person in a group may want to move the group in a musical direction that is not acceptable to the rest of the band.

Regional Geography

The geography of your home area make have a profound effect on the nature of the regional scene. In the Rocky Mountain States or most of Canada, for example, distances between cities are great. This can make it impractical for your band to pursue out-of-town weekend jobs—the travel involved may eat up more time than the job itself. It can also be a problem if you need to get to work on Monday morning or if you have to take off on mid-Friday afternoon to play a job that is 180 miles away.

As the core cities of the United States expand into sprawling suburbs, the length and breadth of a metropolitan scene can extend for scores of miles, or in the case of Los Angeles, hundreds of miles. Living in Trenton, New Jersey and working weekend gigs in Philadelphia is not a major problem because the two towns are only thirty miles apart. A city like Philadelphia has so many suburbs that, with careful planning, you could work in the many surrounding areas of New Jersey, Pennsylvania and Delaware for months without any anxiety about being over-exposed at a particular club or with a specific audience. If you live in a smaller town with a relatively small metropolitan area, you need to be careful not to play too often in a particular venue or section of town. Many local bands end up break-ing up because they never tour; people develop the feeling that if they don't see the band this week or this month they will be playing in the same place later anyway.

Making National Contacts As a Songwriter

Probably the most promising way to crash the national music scene without moving to a major music center is to try to break in as a songwriter. It is possi-ble to live in a secondary market and to make deals with big-city publishers who can push your material to major recording artists. How realistic is this scenario, and how can you make it happen?

The existing literature about the music business is often at odds on this issue. Some writers and lecturers maintain that if you are serious, you must move. Nashville writer Tom T. Hall suggests that you should stay where you are, and make occasional forays into the big city jungle. There are successful songwriters who have done it both ways and there are even major recording artists active on the national scene who deliberately live outside the major music centers. Dan Fogelberg has lived in Colorado for some time; John Mellencamp lives on a farm near Bloomington, Indiana; and successful "New Jack City" producer Teddy Riley headquarters in Virginia Beach. Bill Danoff, writer of "Afternoon Delight" and co-writer of "Take Me Home, Country Roads" has pursued a lengthy writ-ing and recording career from his base in Washington, D.C. Other successful writers (and artists) have joint residences in a major market and such cities as Aspen, Colorado.

If you have national ambitions, but want to stay in your hometown, you should be aware of what you may be sacrificing. You are not apt to get motion picture assignments if you live in Buffalo. If you are not on the scene, movie or televi-sion producers are not likely to think of you when an assignment comes up. On the other hand, if you have succeeded in developing a national reputation, you may get opportunities for work that would normally require you to live in New York or Hollywood. For example, Bill Danoff has done some writing for TV producer Norman Lear. However even someone with national credentials, like Danoff, will probably not get the call if there is a tight schedule for a project. The old cliché, "out of sight is out of mind", is apropos in such instances. Efficient communication can be pursued through phone calls, fax machines, E-mail and fiber optics which makes simultaneous recording in different cities possible. Still, there is much to be said for face-to-face communication and getting to know the people that you work with.

How can you make national contacts? One way that works is to have your business taken care of by a personal manager who lives in a major music business center, while you stay where you please. That is why I recommend your manager not be too "local." If your manager is "on the street," then she will know what TV shows are coming up, what publishing companies are hot, who is looking for staff writers, and what sort of dollars they are paying. This kind of information can be accessed from a secondary market, but requires much more diligence and hard work if your representative is not on the scene.

Most staff writers work out of offices in one of the major music centers, but there are a few examples of writers who are paid a weekly salary or "draw" and live in their hometowns. Staff writers are paid weekly salaries of $300-$500 and up, as an advance against future royalties. The only major music center where a writer might be able to exist on that kind of money is Nashville.

How to Access Artists from Your Home

Making inroads in the national scene while living at home is best accomplished in the area of songwriting. Many recording artists get deals because they write hit songs for other already established recording artists. The people who decide what songs get on recordings are the artists and their record producers. Occasionally an artist's manager or record company executive may suggest a song to an artist.

If you can gain access to an artist touring in your market, you can have a good chance of getting your songs cut. Bill Danoff had written a rough version of "Take Me Home, Country Roads" with Taffy Nivert when John Denver came to Washington to perform at a local club called the Cellar Door. Danoff was running the lights at the time, and he and Denver became friends. One night Bill played Denver the tune, which was originally about an artist who lived on a commune in West Virginia. Denver zeroed in on what he thought could make the song work commercially. His recording became a gigantic career-building hit. Danoff and Nivert then received a healthy taste of writers' money coming their way. This led to a recording deal on Denver's record label for their group, the Starland Vocal Band,

and their own major hit, "Afternoon Delight." The band was so loyal to Washington that they did a summer television show that was shot on the streets in the nation's capital.

On the other hand, a Denver writer once collared Waylon Jennings before a concert at Red Rocks Theater, and tried to hustle a song to him. Jennings wasn't in the mood, and simply told the writer to send the song to "Waylon Jennings, Nashville, Tennessee." The anxious writer asked if the song would really get to Jennings. He replied that everyone in Nashville knew him. This may have been true to a point, but the songwriter most likely got the message that Waylon was not in the mood to be pestered.

Sometimes, aggressiveness pays off. A writer who saw Melissa Manchester perform on the "Today Show" decided that she had the right tune for her. She promptly took a cab down to NBC, where she bribed the stage door guard to let her stay "in wait" for Manchester. When Manchester came out of the building the writer thrust a demo in her face and poof, the song got recorded.

For every story like the one about the "Today Show," there are at least fifty stories like the one about Jennings. You have to develop a sense of when an artist is receptive to hearing a song, and when they don't want their privacy disturbed. You also need to be lucky. Songwriter Tim O'Brien had his first top ten country hits while living in Boulder, Colorado. He got a tape to Kathy Mattea, and she happened to notice that he was originally from West Virginia. She also was raised in that state, and this made her curious about his song. The song, "Walk the Way the Wind Blows," became a Top 10 country hit, and broke open Tim's career as a songwriter.

Some other ways of getting a song to an artist who is appearing locally are through a club manager, a concert promoter, or a local disc jockey. Don't overdo it, though, and never try to get more than one song to the artist. Remember to supply a typed lyric sheet and to place your name and address on the tape box and on the tape itself. Make sure that your song is protected by copyright before submitting it to artists or producers, especially if you don't know them personally. Don't give up part of your writer's credit to someone making this sort of contact for you. The chances are heavily against the artist picking up any one song, and you may have given away a valuable asset that will later be recorded by someone else without obtaining any benefit at all.

Making Publishing Contacts by Mail

There is another way to delve further into the songwriting business. Pick up a current copy of the annual book *Songwriter's Market.* It lists music publishers, some record companies, songwriters, music print companies, advertising agencies, producers of slide shows and industrial films, managers and agents. Generally speaking, it is a good idea to stay away from the publishing companies with offices in rural Kansas. Their industry contacts are probably no broader than your own. The book's listings usually describe some songs that the publishing company has gotten recorded, and what sort of material they are looking for.

Small-time Publishers

The economics of songwriting are fairly simple: For every song recorded, there is a writer and a publisher. They share the current statutory mechanical royalty for each song, which should be split on a 50/50 basis. This royalty is the one that comes from sales of the record. Many record producers and recording artists own all or part of a music publishing company. One of the incentives you can offer them in return for recording your song is to give them the publishing rights. If you have already committed the song to a small publisher in Idaho, an artist may turn the song down because she can't own all or part of the publishing rights. This may sound unfair or callous, but is a reality of the business. Be sure there is a provision in your contract for the song's publishing rights to revert to you if the artist or producer doesn't actually get the song on the record. This is called a *reversion clause.* It is not unusual for an artist to record more songs than will actually appear on a finished album. They can then pick and choose the best songs and the best performances.

If you've never heard of a publisher, ask what songs they have had recorded in the last two or three years, and the names of the artists and the record labels. If you have never heard of the artists or the record companies, or if all the recorded cuts were written by the owners of the publishing company, it is safe to conclude that they are not a factor on the national scene.

Note that some of the major music publishers refuse to be listed in *Songwriter's Market.* This is because they are not interested in getting tons of unsolicited submissions. In order to be admitted through their doors, you will need to be able to drop the name of someone whom the publisher knows and respects, like a hit artist, songwriter, personal manager, prominent disc jockey or promoter.

Contacting Music Publishers in Person

If you have the time and are willing to spend the money, you can always head for a major music center to knock on the doors of publishers. You should pave the way by calling the publishers before you make the trip. Ask anyone in your town who has any possible contacts-record promotion people, disc jockeys, concert promoters and other songwriters. Call publishers listed in *Songwriter's Market* who seem to be possible prospects for your songs.

If you can, see the publisher in person. Some publishers will refuse to do this, because they feel they can concentrate better on the music when the writer is not around. They also are sometimes embarrassed because quite often they listen to only fragments of a song before turning it down. If it doesn't capture their attention, they fast forward the tape to the next tune. Some writers think that the publisher is being rude and don't understand that this is a custom in the industry. Never put more than three songs on a demo, because publishers usually will not want to spend too much time on a new, unknown writer. If they like your work, they'll ask for more.

If you do get to sit with a publisher (it is usually the professional manager or one of her assistants who will be screening your songs), listen carefully to what they have to say. Don't become defensive about your work. Remember that almost every major artist and songwriter has been rejected by some, often many, publishers and record companies. What you are looking for is some critical feedback that will place your songs in relation to that which is currently in the marketplace.

If the publisher will not see you, leave a tape with his secretary. It will probably take days or even weeks to get the tape heard. Be sure to make a note of the secretary's name. John Braheny calls secretaries and others who serve as screens to keep writers away from publishers "gatekeepers." If you want to get the gate to open for you at a future time, it's a good idea to become friendly with the gatekeeper.

Here's another little tip that can save you a lot of money. When you use the telephone, find the cheapest phone rates that you can get. The lowest rates are usually before 8 A.M. If you live on the West Coast, you're two hours earlier than Nashville time and three hours earlier than New York. If you live on the East Coast, try to call west after 5 P.M., when the middle tier of rates in effect. If you are serious about contacting publishers, you will be making dozens of long distance calls, so the amount of money involved can become considerable. Some high-level executives stay in their offices after their secretaries go home, and you can sometimes contact them directly by phone because they will take calls directly after hours. Other executives come in at amazingly early hours to try to catch up on their work. The more you know about the lifestyle of the person you are trying to reach, the better chance you can get through to her.

In general, it's somewhat easier to see music publishers than record company people. This is because music publishers are at a bit of a disadvantage today. Although the majority of songs recorded in Nashville are still written by people other than the recording artist, in New York and Los Angeles the opposite holds true. Because music publishers are having difficulty getting their songs cut, they are always looking for that magical writer amidst the sea of talent out there on the streets.

On your first trip, you probably won't place any songs with publishers, let alone get them recorded. What you will be able to accomplish, if your songs show promise, is that you will meet some publishers who will encourage you to keep writing and to submit new material to them. If a publisher seems encouraging, stay in touch with him. Remind him that you are the guy from Rawlins, Wyoming who visited him last month. Ask the secretary of the company for the best time to call.

If you leave a tape at a publisher's office, be sure your name, address and phone number are on the tape box and the tape itself. This procedure has already been mentioned, but it can't be stressed enough. Major publishers get hundreds of song submissions. Don't become a casualty of your (and their) carelessness.

Most music industry people prefer to have songs submitted on cassettes. They are the most convenient format, and also the format most commonly found in cars. Many publishers listen to songs during their commuting time in their cars.

If you are trying to establish a career as a songwriter, the publisher doesn't really care what you look like. A photo is of no importance, but any previous writing credits will make you look more like a professional. Send them along with a brief bio, but don't mention your hockey trophies or the fact that you were third clarinet in the all-state marching band.

Demos

When a music publisher picks up your songs, unless your tape is of excellent quality, they will want to make demonstration tapes (demos) of your songs. This entails hiring singers and musicians and renting a studio. The publisher should pay for these demos or the costs may be shared. Your share will usually be considered an advance against royalties.

If you can do demos in your hometown, the publisher should pay for your tape costs and the costs of hiring any additional musicians or singers. The publisher will want to be present at your initial demo sessions, if this is geographically feasible. Unless you have quite a bit of recording experience you may well find his presence helpful. It is a good idea to have worked out what sort of sound and style you and the publisher want on the demo before you enter the studio.

The need for quality demos is increasingly important. So many writers have excellent home studios that publishers have become more aware of the need for a demo that is virtually a finished product. It is no longer unusual for a producer or artist to copy (or even use) a rhythm track or a quality guitar lick from a demo on the actual record. A simple guitar or piano demo has a hard time holding its own in today's market, outside the country music genre. On the other hand, don't spend a great deal of money hiring musicians for demos. It's still the lyric, melody and essential groove that will best convey a song's message. Make sure these qualities are emphasized on your demos.

Tip Sheets

Small monthly periodicals called "tip sheets" are provide another source for matching your songs with artists or publishers. These publications list artists looking for songs, along with a description of what they want and a time frame for when the songs need to be submitted. Tip sheets are usually quit expensive. If you do want to send songs out to the artists or producers that they list, you may want to split the subscription cost with a fellow songwriter or persuade your local songwriters' organization to subscribe.

Performing Rights Organizations

ASCAP, BMI AND SESAC are performing rights societies that collect the royalties that come from the public performance of songs. The bulk of the money comes from airplay on radio or television. These rights can be quite lucrative, and often in country music, will bring much more income than the monies from the sale of recordings.

Which performing rights organization should you join and how can you contact the representatives? The addresses of these societies are in Appendix B. Generally, these people are interested in talking with you only when you have material that is close to being recordable. As a new writer, your best bet is to join the society where you have the greatest rapport with their Director of Artist Relations, or whatever title they are currently using for the person who sees new writers, or where they show an affinity to your style of music.

What good can these people do you? Marv Mattis, former West Coast Director of Artist Relations was instrumental in helping to build the music scene in Portland, Oregon and Denver. Ron Sobel, who holds a similar position at ASCAP, grasped the importance of the Seattle scene as it was evolving. He signed several key acts to ASCAP, and their photos with grateful inscriptions are on the wall of his office. These people are shrewd professionals, and they will only go out of their way to help the dedicated and talented few among the dozens of writers whom they meet.

The reasons for joining a performing rights society are:

1. To receive performing rights monies
2. To help make valuable contacts with writers and publishers
3. To participate in classes or seminars

Your choice of a performing rights society should include the following:

1. Are they responsive to your calls?
2. Do you have rapport with anyone in their office?
3. Have they provided you with any useful contacts?

ASCAP and BMI also offer classes for songwriters. They are usually small and intensive, and may focus on a particular aspect of songwriting, such as writing Broadway show material. It is not really possible to become involves in these classes unless you live or will stay in the town where they are offered.

All of the performing rights groups are involved in the major industry seminars and conferences, such as Austin's South By Southwest. Talk to their representatives, read their propaganda and make your choice.

Chapter 17 contains some information about the history of performing rights in America.

Accessing the Major Songwriters' Organizations

The Nashville Songwriters Association International can refer you to many of the publishers in town. They also hold large annual seminars that feature major writers and publishers. If you are headed to Nashville, try to attend one of these meetings, where you will hear writers and publishers talk about their craft and critique songs. If you attend the NSAI wing-ding, leave time afterwards for going around to publishers' offices. During the NSAI annual meetings, many of the publishers will be at the meetings-not in their offices.

Chapter 10 mentioned the weekly Songwriters' Showcase, sponsored by the National Association of Songwriters in Los Angeles. During these meetings, cassettes are placed in a roulette wheel, spun, chosen by chance, and played for publishers and producers. Only the writer knows that her song is playing. This avoids any favoritism on the part of the person doing the critiques. The song is only identified by a number. If a publisher wants to pick up the song, the moderator of the session connects them with the writer.

It is not realistic to go cold to NSAI or NAS and expect to blow everyone away. You are competing with highly-skilled professionals. What you will get is some valuable counseling, information, and eventually, some access to the sort of publishers and producers who are both reputable and apt to be receptive to your work. Both organizations have many out-of-town members, and NAS will even place your cassette in rotation from afar and send you a written copy of the publisher's critique.

NSAI, NAS and the previously-mentioned Songwriters Guild of America all charge membership fees to support their vastly overworked staffs. They are probably the best single investment a songwriter will ever make in the music business. Oddly, New York has no similar songwriting organization.

Music Print Publishers

Steady, sometimes surprisingly good income can be earned by writing instructional materials for the music print publishers who print instructional and artist's folios. Contact one of the companies, listed in Appendix D, and submit a table of contents and some sample pages. How does your work differ from material that is already available on the same subject? Don't be shy, but evaluate your strengths realistically and focus on the part of your approach that is innovative and may appeal to music teachers and musicians.

Publishers pay a royalty on each copy of these books that are sold. If you use copyrighted songs by other authors, you will have to share some of that royalty with the writers and publishers of that material. Consequently, many author use songs that are in the public domain (older than 75 years), or write their own original material. Not all music print publishers give advances, but those who do typically pay $500-$1,000. A portion of the advance is paid upon signing a contract, and the rest upon acceptance of a completed manuscript. A typical royalty is 10% of the retail selling price, but a music publisher may pay slightly more or less than that amount. It depends on their enthusiasm for your project, current market conditions and their normal business practices. The most popular instruments are keyboards and guitar, but these are also the instruments that have been covered in considerable depth by numerous authors.

It makes no difference where you live. The music print publishers are spread out all over the country. If you're an experienced arranger, there is also work available to write choral or band arrangements for school ensembles. There is also a great need for guitar transcribers who know tablature and have good ears. Arranging work includes no royalty payments, unless you include some original compositions in a folio. The publishers generally pay arrangers on a per page basis.

Summer Music Festivals

If you are a high school or college student and are free to travel during summers, there are numerous summer music festivals all over the United States and Canada. They provide instruction and performing opportunities in almost every imaginable type of music, and some them are held in wonderful scenic areas. The classical music world in particular offers some excellent summer music festivals.

The National Repertory Orchestra, located in Keystone, Colorado, is a major training ground for symphony musicians. Other such events are the Aspen, Banff and Tanglewood Music Festivals. The Hollywood Bowl Symphony also offers opportunities for young musicians to play chamber and symphonic music. There is a real lack of symphonic training orchestras—a graduate of a college music program will rarely have the opportunity to join a major orchestra fresh out of school. The stimulus of playing with other outstanding young musicians and under fine conductors can bring a young player to a higher level of performance.

Magazines like *Bluegrass Unlimited, Dirty Linen, Downbeat, Jazz Times* and *Sing Out* list summer blues, bluegrass, bluegrass and jazz festivals. At the annual Winnipeg and Vancouver Folk festivals held in July, musicians come from all over the world to play. Workshops and instructional sessions are featured in addition to the major evening concerts.

There are numerous opportunities available in local and regional music markets. Some artists will prefer to test the larger markets, and others will acquire business reputations in those markets but remain in then place where they prefer to live.

CHAPTER 11 RESOURCES

The annual *Songwriter's Market,* published by Writer's Digest Books in Cincinnati, is the best single source of information about music publishers. It is best to use the current edition, because companies and go in and out of business and change their names. Executives also often move from job to job. It is very embarrassing to write or call someone who hasn't worked for a company for two or three years.

chapter	**12**

The Urge for Going:

Staying or Leaving

]f you have ever played music professionally, somewhere, deep within you, you probably harbor the fantasy that you or your group could be the next major star. Should you wish to pursue such a goal, here are some of the roadblocks and detours that await you, as well as the possibility of making it in the big world but remaining or returning to your hometown.

To be straightforward—if you are after national exposure, hit records and the big bucks—the major music centers (see Chapter 1) are where you can find these things. It's where the major record companies have their headquarters, and where television, movies, commercials and music publishers are all present in profusion. (See the charts on the following pages.)

If you decide to go, there are a few recommendations which would be would be wise to follow: have enough money to live for six months before you have to worry about becoming a bag person. It's helpful to have or develop some non-music job skills, especially some that offer flexible hours of employment. Waiting on tables is something you can almost always do and word processing skills can usually get you a job with a temporary employment agency. My friend Ron Bergan, former National educator Director for NARAS, broke into the music industry through

Opportunity Chart

Major Music Market	Local Scene
National exposure	Local exposure
Heavyweight personal managers and music attorneys	Few or no full-time managers or music business attorneys
Record companies galore	A few small labels
Network television	Local news and talk show, perhaps a variety show (depending upon size of city)
Major concert halls and stadiums	Varies, depending upon size of market
Hundreds of studio musicians and songwriters	A small corps of professionals, often with a limited knowledge of musical styles
Major music publishers with worldwide contacts	A few music publishers; one or two may have some national access
Headquarters for music trade papers	Local correspondents for trades, maybe
Excellent music teachers of many kinds	A few select and experienced teachers
Major recording studios with state-of-the-art equipment	A few large studios; some competent studios with slightly-dated equipment
Access to a large pool of would-be band members, song collaborators	Easy access to a smaller talent pool

temping at music publishers and record companies. This gave him an opening wedge which ultimately resulted in his working for a music publisher.

Before you go to your city of choice, buy the Sunday newspaper. Check the want ads to see if it is feasible that you will find some employment once you move. Los Angeles and New York have a fairly constant demand for temporary office workers. It is also possible to find temporary manual labor jobs in large cities, or odd jobs, like giving out telephone directories.

The major music business towns all have entertainment papers or journals, like *Music City News* and *Music Row* in Nashville, the *Village Voice* in New York,

The Upside of Staying Where You Are

Major Music Market	Local Scene
Very expensive housing and high cost of living (less true of Nashville)	Relatively reasonable housing (you know where the best deals are because you live here)
Los Angeles: constant car expense, must drive great distances in heavy traffic; New York: impossible to keep car in the city because of incredible garage costs	Manageable transportation
You must make new contacts: you know virtually no one; hard to make new contacts: you always seem to be "on hold"	You know who is straight and who is jive; if you're not sure, you have the contacts to help you check it out; you have friends or peers to consult; you have friends and family there
Large and impersonal	Small and friendly (because you know the turf)
Jobs are hard to access	You know where the gigs are, or can find out
Not too friendly; you feel that you're lost in a maze of impersonal and complex business decisions	You know everyone; you feel comfortable

or the *LA Weekly, BAM* and the *Music Connection* in Los Angeles. These papers will give you a feel for what kind of live music is happening in town, and they may also help you to find an apartment, a songwriting collaborator, or even a job with a record company. Some of these newspapers will even be available in your hometown. Check with the largest newsstand or book store in town.

Let's assume that you took your two week tour, and now with or without your band you've move to The Big Apple, LA-LA Land or Music City. Where do you go from here? It's going to be apparent to you within a matter of weeks that you're not likely to crash the big time without any help. If you want to try to find a record deal, there are three possible directions in which to look.

Personal Managers with National Clout

The first and likeliest method to break through the big city-barriers is to enlist the services of a personal manager. Of course the personal manager that you want may prefer to represent an act that already has a record deal. (See more on this subject in my book *The Music Business: Career Opportunities & Self Defense.*)

In the book *Entertainers and Their Professional Advisers* by Egon Dumler and Robert F. Cushman, there's an excellent article by Dee Anthony about personal management. Anthony has managed a broad range of talented and successful musicians and entertainers, from Tony Bennett to Emerson, Lake and Palmer. He points out that a manager not only obtains a record deal, but works with a music business lawyer to negotiate it. Later on, she must exercise gentle or forceful persuasion in order to convince the record company to spend money on publicizing the artist, funding videos and offering tour support.

A manager should not represent too many clients, nor should he choose to represent clients who have skills that are directly competitive with one another. A big-time manager may be able to offer an immediate set of bookings to a new client alongside a better-known act that the manager also represents.

An experienced manager can also help a group with matters such as pacing a set or establishing a lighting chart. She can get professional help in these areas if she doesn't have that sort of expertise.

Be careful when signing a management agreement that includes the manager handling your publishing and producing your records. Check that he is not also simultaneously taking commission on your earnings as a writer or recording artist. Try to build in some performance guarantees in your agreement, such as getting your group a recording contract.

The contract should clearly state how much of the artist's monies the manager will be allowed to spend on the group's development. These include travel and entertainment expenses. If the monies owed to the group go directly to the manager, a special account should be set up to disburse this income. It should not be co-mingled with the manager's other income or expenses. There also needs to be some understanding of what continuing royalty income the manager may receive in the event that the group and the manager agree to separate.

Finding a Manager

It is difficult to find an honest and tireless manager. *Billboard* and *Performance* list managers in annual directories. There is a guild of managers called The Conference of Personal Managers, that has branches in New York and Los Angeles. Membership in this group is not a seal of approval, but at least it indicates that a manager is part of a peer network of professionals.

To check out a manager, ask her for a client list of current acts that she has handled. Check out these credentials with these clients, as carefully as you can. Ask how many people work in her office, and how many clients she represents. If the office has other managers working with the one who has signed you, consider the "Key Man Clause," the one that stipulates that if she leaves the office you can break your contract without penalty or payment of additional monies.

Most management deals run from three (optimum) to five years, although a manager might try to sign you to a seven year agreement. Never sign a managerial contract without consulting a good music business attorney to read it. Don't use the same attorney that the manager has (or recommends) to insure that your own interests are properly represented.

Agents

Unlike the situation that prevails in local markets, a nationally-oriented booking agency will insist on an exclusive agreement with an artist or group before booking them into clubs or concerts. The choice of the booking agency can critically affect the group's finances—and the choice of venues that the group plays will have a profound influence on the possible sale of the group's records. The actual choice of bookings can also have a positive or negative influence on how the artists feel about their music. Some issues that are apt to surface include the amount of attention the band is apt to receive from a particular audience that, in all likelihood has come to see a well-known headline performer.

Other Paths to a Record Deal

If you cannot locate a competent manager, it is still possible to get a record deal through a music business attorney. Music business attorneys know many record people. They often have social relationships with them that include attending or participating in sports events and hanging out together. A lawyer can get you to the proper person at a record company, and he can also suggest an appropriate personal manager. If a record company is genuinely excited about an act, they can also provide leads to managers. Generally speaking, record companies prefer not to do business with acts directly, because in often leads to hard feelings on the part of the artist.

Music publishers sometimes will front the money for high-quality demos, and even produce entire albums. They then will try to market the records to record labels. Any active publisher has a wide circle of record company acquaintances through his normal song-plugging activities.

Another path to a record deal is through an independent record producer. If a producer has a good track record, that alone may be enough to convince a record company to take a chance on your act. Occasionally a record company likes a group, but not the person who produced the demos. If you are under contract to the producer, this may destroy not only your chances of getting a deal, but of getting a true story out of the jilted producer.

Music Business Attorneys

Skilled music business attorneys are expensive. In a major music market fees of $200-$500 an hour are not unusual. Sometimes, the payments can be spread out, or based on your income. It is best not to give a lawyer a percentage of your income, because she will then earn money whenever you perform as well as record. If you have to give up a percentage to a lawyer, it is preferable to restrict that payment to the record deal itself. Some lawyers are willing to place a cap on a specific contract. This means that there is a maximum fee that you will be charged for the negotiation, regardless of the exact number of hours that the lawyer spends.

In a number of cities, there are organizations of lawyers who perform legal services for artists at minimal cost. Whether this is really a good deal for the artist depends on the lawyer's experience and his negotiating skills. I certainly would not hesitate to show a single song songwriter's agreement to such an attorney, or a local deal with an agent. I would be somewhat less comfortable at showing him a 120 page Polygram Records contract that covers merchandising rights, publishing, producer royalties, etc. It is a good idea to see if your lawyer has ever negotiated contracts that are roughly similar to the one you are looking at. The national organization of these lawyers is called Volunteer Lawyers for the Arts, but each city has a somewhat different localized name for the group. (See Appendix B for more sources.)

Staying or Going Summary

You may want to make yourself a circular life diagram and figure out where you fit into the picture before you head for the major music market. (See the chart on the next page.)

Question marks are placed next to "aesthetic satisfaction" and "income" because for some people, these drives lead them to the national market. For example, if you want to compose feature film scores, it's hard to work that out when you live in southern Kansas. Others might do quite well at home without the additional pressures and expenses of big-city living.

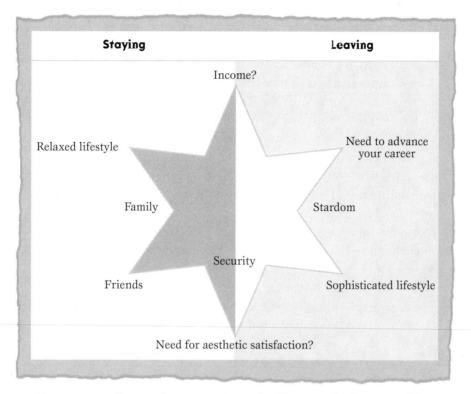

Staying	Leaving
	Income?
Relaxed lifestyle	Need to advance your career
Family	Stardom
	Security
Friends	Sophisticated lifestyle
	Need for aesthetic satisfaction?

No one can tell you what you want to do. You must look at your life, your goals and your dreams, and evaluate them in terms of your own needs, talent and personality.

Going, But Coming Back

It is possible to strive for success on the national scene while maintaining a goal of eventually returning to your hometown. Once you have secured big city representation, you can return to your original home base.

In any case, you're going to need a couple of years just to know where to go and what to do. If you're totally on your own and are moving in order to join up with other musicians, it's likely to take you three to five years.

You can try to get help by networking through the Union or local music or songwriters' organizations, music stores or entertainment publications, but you're essentially involved in a trial and error process. You are apt to audition for bands that you won't like, meet people who are flakes, encounter styles that are unfamiliar, and in general, try to figure out what in the world is going on. You will hear endless horror stories from songwriters who had songs "stolen" from them, band members who were fleeced by record companies, records that came out without any promotional effort behind them, producers who were hype artists, and managers who didn't do anything for their clients.

Consider the source of this information. Many people who are not successful are always able to find an external reason for their lack of success. Invariably, that reason has to do with someone else who let them down. How many people have you met in the record business who told you, "The record company did a good job, but I blew it. I wasn't ready." Or, "Our manager was cool, but so many people in the band were drunk that we never did consistent shows." Or, "I had a good publisher, but I just couldn't deliver hit songs consistently because I was too young and inexperienced."

Anyone who always blames other people for her own lack of success is probably deluding herself. There are bad record companies, crooked managers and thieving lawyers. But you are also responsible for your own actions. You weren't forced to sign a contract. Remember, most people who get recording contracts don't become stars, and most people don't get recording contracts at all. Most songwriters don't write hits, and most don't even get publishing deals.

Desiring success is undoubtedly one part of making it. Having some form of talent, whether it's singing or dancing well, or writing wonderful songs is another. Finding a good manager is a combination of thorough searching and luck. Getting a hit record involves luck and talent. There are artists who get their fair shot at success, but the public simply won't buy whatever they do.

Money Isn't Everything

Success can be defined any way one chooses. Selling millions of records doesn't make a group musically profound, it just means that the public bought what the group had to sell. You may find that you are happiest doing something that is outside the mainstream of popular taste. It may be that your musical interests are esoteric or unusual, that you are musically ahead of what the public wants to hear or that the public is simply not interested in what you have to offer. Popular music often revolves around fads that bear no particular relationship to anything tangible. Take the accordion. There used to be thousands of accordion players and teachers throughout North America. Every time you turned around, there was somebody on a TV variety show playing "Lady of Spain." During the 1960s the guitar took over. Suddenly the only accordions in sight were found in polka bands or oom-pah groups. The accordion didn't change—it simply took on the connotation of being square and old-fashioned.

Then lo and behold, the accordion became "in" again. All sorts of hot zydeco groups featured it, as did the group Los Lobos in the movie *La Bamba*. The late '80s adolescents never knew it was corny, so it outgrew its negative connotations. A similar thing has happened to the mandolin, once seen as kind of a parlor instrument, or one associated with Italian music. The popularity of David Grisman, and the use of mandolin on Shaun Colvin's hit, "Sunny Came Home," has made people see the mandolin in a different light as a contemporary instrument.

You need to identify the essential qualities of your music and to locate the marketplace where there are buyers for your musical wares. What you cannot do is to assume massive success will come from following such a path.

Some of the record labels that specialize in music that is not necessarily designed to appeal to the mass market are located in secondary music markets. There is a good deal of New Age music coming out of Boulder, Milwaukee and San Francisco, and specialty jazz labels are quite active in the San Francisco area. There are some important traditional jazz labels in the New Orleans area and blues labels in Chicago. Country and folk music labels are also found in such places as Boston and the southern part of the United States. Sometimes, a label starts in a particular place because the owner lives there, or a strong regional musical style, like Cajun music, leads to the founding of a regional label that later expands into the national market.

There are several books that list dozens of record companies all over the United States. If you contact one of these labels, invest in a phone call or query letter before sending your tape to make sure that you know who to send your tape to. In general these sorts of companies are friendlier to new talent than the major labels, who are besieged by submissions.

Small record companies offer an artist more personal service and access than a large label can provide. It is possible to remain in direct contact with the decision makers at the label and to get a "yes" or "no" answer without having to wait for a series of committee meetings to consider your project. You are not apt to get any large cash advances from small labels, nor should you be surprised that your record will not necessarily be stocked by the massive chain stores that are spread across the shopping malls of North America. Many of these stores avoid minor label records because their stock doesn't turn over often enough.

Living outside the Mainstream

There is no reason why a successful artist can't live outside the major music markets once her career has taken off, as long as someone in the major markets is taking care of her business affairs. If a musical group wishes to relocate outside the major markets, it is best if they all live in reasonable proximity to one another. If the bass player lives in Florida and the lead singer is in Iowa, there are going to be problems in establishing regular rehearsals and routing the band to and from jobs. This highlights the needs for people working in groups to continue to communicate as their careers build. It is a bit different when a group simply re-creates their own (or other people's) hits. If there is no new repertoire to learn or record, the need for regular rehearsals diminishes.

Groups need to retain a common sense of the musical direction that brought them together in he first place. Of course, there is room for personal and musical variations and explorations, but there should be some solid common ground for the group to continue.

Assuming that you do have the same general goals, that you still enjoy hanging out and playing together, it is indeed quite possible to live almost anywhere you choose. You may even be able to record your product locally, which can prove to be a great idea or a poor one. You should know one another well enough by this time to be aware of what constitutes a valuable support group, and what provides disturbing distractions. Some people work better when their families are nearby, and some, like boxers, seem to require an isolated environment.

Of course, other factors may come into play. If you want to work with a hot production team like Jimmy Jam and Terry Lewis, you may find yourself freezing to death in their wintry home of Minneapolis, rather than sunning yourself in Phoenix while recording at a studio of your choice.

A new scene can be a stimulus to the creative process, and that is why some artists make a point of going to another town or even a foreign country each time they record. Some artists run through producers in a similar fashion.

You know who you are and what works for you. If you don't, it's up to your manager to discuss it with you. Major groups tour most of the time, and they can live anywhere. It is different if the basis of your attempt to scale the heights of the music business is daily work on a TV show in Los Angeles, or if you're an established country star whose fans expect you to appear every Saturday night on the Grand Ole Opry. If you feel strongly about living outside the major music centers, then you and your manager should develop a plan that will enable you to realize that goal.

Developing Local and Regional Music Scenes

Consider a final possibility. You may want to leave the area where you grew up or went to school and go to a secondary music market in another part of the country. Portland (Oregon), Austin (Texas) and Minneapolis are all appealing cities and each of them has a growing music scene.

Your choice of what town to live in could be governed by factors such as contacts, climate, lifestyle, family considerations, or a chance to visit a new locale. You may also change your mind about such matters as what sort of climate, lifestyle and musical work you prefer.

Shifting opportunities occur as different areas become larger population centers, with increasing employment possibilities.

CHAPTER 12 RESOURCES

There are a number of resources that can help to access independent labels. Musician publishes an annual *Musician's Guide To Touring & Promotion* that lists labels and includes the names of contacts. Rising Star Music Publishers of Atlanta also publishes an annual book entitled *National Directory of Record Labels & Music Publishers.*

If you use these books, be sure that you have the most recent edition available. People change jobs and labels change names and sometimes go out of business. Writing or calling someone who has not worked at a label for over a year marks you as an amateur.

Playing Music Part-Time

An overwhelming majority of people in North America who call them-selves professional musicians do not attempt to pursue a career in music on a full-time basis. Past surveys have shown that 80% of musicians who belong to the American Federation of Musicians work at music on a part-time basis.[1] No survey has ever been taken that indicates what percentage of these people have made this choice because they can't make a living in music, and how many prefer the security of another more stable or lucrative profession.

There are a number of positive aspects that accompany playing music part-time rather than on a regular basis. First of all, you're less likely to become bored or cynical about music if you don't have to do it all the time. Many full-time musicians do not have the luxury of rejecting work, but take whatever playing jobs they are offered. Some must ignore the question of finding a job that fulfills their musical interests, and take the best-paying jobs that are available.

In all fairness, sometimes taking a musical job that you would never choose for reasons of your own stylistic preferences or prejudices can turn out to be a good experience. It can lead to the mastering new styles, change your approach

1. Weissman, Dick. *Making Music in America.*

to a particular instrument, and even lead to the development of new musical tastes and knowledge.

Most full-time musicians are forced to do some traveling, whether it may be a weekend commute to a ski resort or a club gig in a suburban location miles away from town. Traveling is expensive and if weather conditions are unfavorable or the driver is tired, it can be dangerous as well. It tends to upset many marital relationships, because the spouse who is a home may feel abandoned for so-called "fun," while the musician feels that he is misunderstood.

When full-time musicians embark on a national touring career, the situation is even more difficult. Tours can last for months at a time and the traveling musician is subject to temptations of drug, sex and alcohol, none of which tend to reinforce a marriage or improve the attitude of the touring musician. Long and tiring travel, working late at night, and the necessity of living for weeks in hotels with little human contact outside the members of your own band can be very disruptive and bring on loneliness and depression.

The part-time musician has the opportunity to operate at maximal musical efficiency by turning down jobs that are of no musical interest. Many full-time musicians refuse to do this, feeling that if they refuse one job, they may stop getting any musical opportunities at all. To be released from financial dependency on unwelcome gigs can be an incredibly liberating experience. It means that you can direct your musical energies toward practicing and playing the music of your choice, rather than the music that a club owner, band leader or other employer may require.

There are a surprising number of really fine musicians who make a living at some other profession. Ron Aldridge, a noted periodontist in New York, is equally well-known to New York jazz connoisseurs as a superb clarinet player. Denny Zeitlin is a psychiatrist and piano soloist of renown in the San Francisco area. Other musicians play part-time until they retire. Armed with a comfortable pension they then play primarily because they enjoy doing so.

Full-time musicians have a difficult time wresting with the demons of night work, keeping a practice and rehearsal schedule, and family responsibilities. For many talented people, this makes a career as a full-time musician incompatible with raising a family. Part-time playing can provide a welcome respite from the demands of child care, although it requires the presence of a cooperative spouse who will make evening commitments to child care.

Freelance dance band musicians often play dances just on weekends. They may be tea dances or singles mixers, which occur more often in larger cities. The average young musician may be totally unaware of such gigs. The repertoire is usually material that dates back to the '30s or '40s, and the players usually work for union minimum or even less. These are not show groups, but musicians who play for dancing. If the band plays well and the leader has some good charts, these jobs provide an enjoyable outlet for local musicians who do little or no performing during the week.

Some musicians satisfy their need for security by accepting jobs as school music teachers, or occasionally as teachers of other subjects. This leaves weekends, summer vacations and holidays free to accept playing jobs.

It is up to you to determine what will make you happy and to decide what options are realistic. Some musicians prefer to stop playing if they can't play at the level that they wish to attain.

The quality of musical life that a musician can sustain over the years is largely a function of his willingness to practice. There is the occasional brilliant player who doesn't practice at all. Usually these people have a regular club job, or do so much studio work that they are able to do their practicing on the job. I knew a superb New York percussionist who recorded constantly but didn't keep a musical instrument in his house for over twenty years. He literally got his practice on the gig.

Some musicians who are part-time players make a conscious choice only to play music that appeals to them. They use their other profession as a way of securing regular income and only play jobs that they know will be enjoyable. This group of musicians may be among the happiest and most fulfilled of musicians. They don't have to compromise their musical tastes or work with undesirable people, because they never allow themselves to get into a situation where compromise is necessary.

This is not to imply that full-time musicians are unhappy people or that it is impossible to make a living playing music. These are only some of the many compelling reasons that cause some musicians to turn to music as a part-time profession.

As a part-timer, you can assume an independent freelancer attitude. Since no particular job is essential to your security, you can turn down anything that isn't worth doing. Full-time musicians are often confronted by contractors that make unreasonable demands. The implication, felt or stated, is that if you don't take this job, they will not hire you again. A part-timer can simply laugh at such demands.

A very close friend of mine had a variety of reasons for dropping music as a regular source of employment. He found that when he tried to work as a full-time musician, he was unable to resist the temptations of hard drugs and alcohol. After he saw some very talented musician-friends destroy their lives by taking drugs, he elected to quit both drugs and music. He moved to another town and got a job cleaning airplanes.

He never cared for his job, but the discipline that it required inspired him to pursue a part-time musical career as a disc jockey, songwriter and arranger for a local gospel group. Since his bills were paid through a regular job and he had flying privileges, he was able to spend the bulk of his free time in one musical pursuit or another. He was able to get some of his songs recorded by The Staple Singers by pitching them in-person, courtesy of the airline. He was also able to sustain family relationships, which he knew would have been destroyed had he continued his junkie life in New York as a would-be bebop trumpet player.

The Life of the Symphony Player

Playing in a major symphony orchestra is probably the most stable job a musician can find. In the top orchestras, the minimum wage scale is as high as $2,000 a week, with medical, dental and pension benefits, instrument insurance, and extra income available through freelance work, teaching and recording sessions. For some one thousand musicians who play in the top North American orchestras, their career as musicians has attained the stability, respectability and income level that more traditional professions enjoy. The more typical symphony player works in a ten-to-forty week season and earns from $5,000 to $30,000 a year.

Symphonic musicians are hired on the basis of auditions. It is not unusual to find fifty or more players competing for a single job in a minor orchestra. Naturally, the competition gets tougher when an orchestra like the Chicago Symphony or Philadelphia Orchestra is hiring. If you are interested in these jobs, the *International Musician,* the monthly publication of the American Federation of Musicians, has several pages of classified jobs each month advertising vacancies in various orchestras.

Other opportunities for classical musicians include playing in chamber music groups on a regular or informal basis. Some chamber groups become artists in residence at a particular college or music school, and often perform regular concerts together with teaching a relatively light load. Some of these groups, like the Juilliard String Quartet, do extensive recording work.

Major cities usually have some sort of opera and ballet companies. They provide further employment for classical players. In the largest cities, these playing opportunities actually provide regular employment.

A very small number of classical musicians make handsome livings as solo recitalists. In Los Angeles they play on film scores, and in New York may find work on commercials. In the largest cities there is a pool of freelance players who go from one sort of job to another. The pay is good, but the competition is fierce. In secondary markets these opportunities are more limited. Columbia Artists Management sponsors a Community Concert series that provides extensive performance opportunities in smaller cities for musicians whose careers are in the middle stages of development.

Because of the limited number of opportunities available in performance, many classical musicians and composers take teaching jobs at universities or colleges. For a composer, a school job offers several fringe benefits. Graduate students are available to assist with lengthy orchestration or the operation of MIDI equipment, and the college orchestras offer virtually guaranteed outlets for performances of new music. Moreover this work can provide valuable experience for the student, as well as being useful to the composer. There is relatively little new music performed by professional symphonies, and when a composer is fortunate enough to have a new work performed, the orchestra often allots insufficient rehearsal time to learn a piece. It is far usually more difficult for an orchestra to perform a new piece than something that is a staple in the repertoire. When a composer is teaching at a college, she can rehearse a piece until she feels the college orchestra has reached a reasonable performance level.

There are virtually no full-time composers who don't moonlight as college professors—the bulk of whom can be found composing music for films. Many colleges offer internal grant programs that encourage musicians and composers to write or perform music. As the budgets for state and national arts councils shrink, these opportunities become increasingly important. Grants can assist composers not only with money, but by providing a formal or informal public relations support group.

Specialized Performing Groups

In certain cities such as Boston or San Francisco, there is considerable interest in "early music," ensembles that play music going back as far as the twelfth or thirteenth century. These ensembles provide a steady living for a small number of musicians who have mastered these styles and who usually perform on authentic instruments of the period.

Songwriting

Songwriting, though still a longshot, offers attractive options for the part-time musician. Songs may be submitted to publishers, record producers, or artists through the mail, or through some of the songwriting groups already mentioned. It takes a great deal of persistence to continue developing one's craft and to continue to keep making demos and submitting tunes. If a part-time writer has access to a local performing group, then at least the writer can have the satisfaction of hearing his work performed in a professional manner.

Some part-time performing musicians even form groups that are outlets for their own original music. Other full-time musicians may be members of several groups or accept solo gigs, but have another performing group where they play original music. Often such groups self-produce their own CDs and sell them wherever they perform. The danger of this sort of arrangement is that a musician can't play at two venues at the same time. Consequently, a musician may find herself honoring a prior commitment to play music she doesn't particularly like, rather than pursuing the music that she prefers.

Performing Full Time, Part of the Time

Some bands perform music on a full-time basis part of the year, but devote a portion of their time to other musical projects. This can be because some of the group have family or teaching commitments, or that certain members of the band are interested in and perform music that other members of the group don't particularly like. There are numerous summer jobs at outdoor venues and music festivals that may make it attractive for a band to play together in the summer, and to perform little or not at all during the rest of the year. Certain holidays like St. Patrick's Day, Christmas or July 4th may provide playing opportunities that are not available at other times of the year. A friend of mine from Denver named Charley Provenza played three winter ski seasons with a duo in Steamboat Springs, Colorado, but pursued other musical options when he returned to Denver each spring.

Dedicated Amateurs and Semi-Professionals

For dedicated amateur or semi-professional musicians, music is their principal hobby. Many such musicians devote many hours of practicing and listening in an effort to enhance their skills. Earning money from music is at most, only a remote consideration to someone with this sort of orientation.

The dedicated amateur has one great advantage over the full-time musician—since money is not a factor in the creation or performance of her music—she is free to do whatever she likes with her music. This may mean playing music for a church group, for family, friends, schools or whoever she chooses. These enthusiasts often make the best students, because they continue their studies with full-time professionals. They put in long hours and spend a good deal of time researching the way music is created and how it should be performed. There have been times, to be honest, when I was jealous of this luxury, because I was accepting musical jobs that were boring or stupid.

Many of these amateurs constitute the best audience for full-time musicians. They listen to and react to subtle musical nuances. They are the ones that ask a performer intelligent questions after a performance, as opposed to being concerned about hair styles, hobbies, etc. There are dedicated amateurs in every form of music, from the weekend chamber music players, to the parking-lot pickers at bluegrass festivals, or the jazz fans who organize local jazz appreciation societies. Sometimes, they offer financial support by helping a group to produce a record or tape, or serve as a formal or informal public relations group. Folk music fans may even provide their living rooms for informal house concerts for traveling artists.

Technology, the Composer and the Schools

Electronic music technology, the proliferation of music software programs for computers, sampling devices that enable one musician to imitate the sounds of an entire orchestra or to create new sounds and colors, make it possible for a composer to write and perform music in his own home studio. As the 21st century dawns, many full-time and part-time musicians will be able to devote long hours to realizing their musical compositions with the aid of these tools. Other musicians are terrified at this prospect, because they feel that it threatens the tradition of acoustic instruments that have dominated Western music for the last four hundred years.

More and more school music programs are acquiring equipment that offer the individual student useful information about the various aspects of orchestration. Self-programmed software frees the band director to concentrate on other matters as the individual player learns and rehearses her parts. Many schools are already combining acoustic and electric instruments to produce rich orchestral sounds. In a small town, synthesizers and sequencers can be utilized to fill in parts left out because of a lack or orchestral players.

It's important for school music programs to spend more time teaching children to listen, and to experiment with the new musical tools that technology has developed. This could greatly expand the prospects for music-making in our society.

Musical Literacy

A friend of mine named Bruce Ronkin, who teaches at Northeastern University, has developed a re-definition of the term "musical literacy." He defines it as an awareness and understanding of all musical styles, instead of concentrating on the technical aspects of music. I think this is a very useful concept because it places the emphasis on the student and teacher being open to many musical styles. The truth is that most of us are fixated on specific musical styles and techniques, and many of us don't listen to a variety of musical styles.

Bruce's notion also re-focuses the notion of literacy, removing it from the sheer ability to read and write music in notation. It isn't that these are not useful skills, it is rather that they don't necessarily define musicality. Many rock and country music players, and some jazz musicians are extremely musical and have developed advanced technical skills on their instruments. Such musicians should be encouraged to read music, but this encouragement is best presented as the development of additional tools, rather than presented in a condescending way. Many teachers would also benefit from a more open attitude towards a variety of musical styles. Invariably, when I hear someone say they don't like a specific form of music, like country music, I have found that they in fact have listened to very little of that music. They are not aware that country swing, country rock, and bluegrass, for example are distinctly different musical styles.

Where Do You Fit In?

Now that we've looked at the various categories of professional and amateur musicians, locate yourself in these pictures. Determine what you want, what you dream about, and what it is that you find gratifying. Mix into this recipe the question of what is practical in your particular circumstance. What sort of stress fires you up, and what level of of anxiety makes you incapable of functioning as an intelligent human being?

Evaluate how much music means to you, in what musical direction you want to go, how much effort you are capable of putting into your music, and how the demands or desires for a home and family life, economic security, and decent income fit into your personal crystal ball.

Place your life in an overall time frame. How much does music mean in your life now, and how much do you expect it to mean in fifteen years? Do you have career goals that can be fulfilled in a specific and realistic way, or are your musical aspirations simply unresolved fantasies?

These are difficult questions to answer, and the answers may lead to some tough decisions. One person may become totally dedicated to improving her craft, and another may set up a timetable for success with an alternate career option at the end of the experimental period. A third person may walk away from a musical career because it is too much of a longshot.

The purpose of this chapter, and to a certain extent of this whole book, is to help you to clarify your choices, not to give you pat answers. Take a long-term view of your career, and in that context, evaluate your choice of residence and answer the question of full-time vs. part-time vs. amateur musical career. Whatever you do, orient yourself towards realizing your goals in a creative and fulfilling way.

CHAPTER 13 RESOURCES

Very little has been written about music as a part-time profession. I wrote one chapter about it in my out-of-print book, *Music Making in America,* published by Frederick Ungar in 1981. Books about careers in classical music are also scarce, one good, if somewhat dated book is Ann Summers-Dossena's *Getting It All Together,* published by The Scarecrow Press in 1985. A useful more recent resource is Nancy Uscher's *Your Own Way in Music: A Career and Resource Guide,* published by St. Martin's Press in 1990. Randy Poe's *Music Publishing: A Songwriter's Guide,* published by Writer's Digest in 1990 is a reasonable guide to the business of songwriting.

| chapter | 14 |

The History and Development of Regional Music Markets

From time to time in the music business, a number of secondary music markets have exploded, usually lit up by one or a few major talents. Some of these artists were able to build long-term careers. Many of them disappeared, and most of the music scenes that spawned them (or was it the other way around?) have not shown the staying power over the years that characterizes the four major music markets of North America.

Detroit

One of the most spectacular and most consistent of all the regional scenes developed in the early 1960s around Motown Records in Detroit. Prior to Berry Gordy's efforts, the musical cachet that Detroit possessed came from the presence of such sterling jazz players as Kenny Burrell and Louis Hayes. Most of the jazzmen left at the first opportunity to go to New York, where the jazz scene was "really happening."

Motown records was built around the songwriting and production talents of Holland, Dozier and Holland, Mickey Stephenson, Smoky Robinson, and such artists as The Supremes, Martha and the Vandellas, the Temptations, the Miracles,

Marvin Gaye and Stevie Wonder. All of the work was supervised by the energetic business and creative perfectionism of Berry Gordy. There was a small but select group of studio musicians involved, especially the legendary bassist James Jamerson and drummer Bennie Benjamin.

Motown also had a talent management division that even schooled its artists to behave as ladies and gentlemen at any social occasion. The bulk of the hits were published through Jobete Music, the publishing wing of Motown. The management wing of Motown was responsible for the career advancement of its artists. All divisions of the company brought in revenues to keep Motown prospering. The company also employed choreographers to ensure that each act was carefully staged.

It seemed the success of the company would never end. The Jackson Five and The Commodores were signed, and the solo careers of Michael Jackson and Lionel Ritchie were also piloted by Motown. It is possible Berry Gordy simply became bored. He moved the company to Los Angeles so he could become involved in the motion picture business. At the same time, he invested the company's money in Broadway shows. The star Detroit rhythm players were eventually replaced by Los Angeles studio players. When Motown left, the music business in Detroit vanished into thin air.

A few years ago, I was in Detroit and saw an ad in the local paper advertising that the "Motown All Stars" were performing at a local Holiday Inn. It was a sad commentary on the exodus of Motown. If there is a lesson here, it is that there needs to be more than one game in town for a local scene to develop and prosper. When Motown left Detroit, the music scene folded because Motown was the pop music scene there.

The Philly Sound

In the late '50s and early '60s Jamie/Guyden Records was born in Philadelphia. It developed around the talents of rockabilly idol and guitar hero Duane Eddy. Swan Records started at about the same time. Its most dramatic success occurred when Swan picked up the rights to a couple of English 45s by a little-known act called The Beatles.

The first major music scene in Philly was built around Cameo Parkway Records, the production and writing skills of Dave Appell and Kal Mann, and such acts as Chubby Checker, Bobby Rydell and the Dovells.

Cameo's decline was caused partially by the success of the English rock groups and by the inability of the company to continue to come up with new acts to sustain their reign on the charts. Another factor in its demise was its attempt to expand into other areas of music, such as MOR and even folk rock. The founders of the company never really had a feel for these idioms.

The decline of Cameo was followed by the success of the Philly Sound of writers-musicians-producers Gamble and Huff. They reigned supreme on the soul and pop charts in the '70s, producing such acts as the O'Jays, the Spinners, Harold Melvin and the Blue Notes, Billy Paul and others. Much of the Philly Sound involved complex orchestral arrangements by the gifted arranger-composer-producer Thom Bell, who also wrote songs with lyricist Linda Creed. By the end of the '70s the Philly Sound had run its course. However, Gamble and Huff continued to make records and experienced intermittent success.

Since the glory days, the town has experienced some success in the rap and alternative rock fields. Since Philadelphia is only 90 miles away from New York, this means musicians and songwriters in the New York area are readily accessible to Philadelphia producers. However, the same proximity means that a large percentage of Philly-based talent heads for New York. It's also too close to New York to develop an independent corps of big-time managers, booking agents, or music business attorneys. It's too easy to get on the New Jersey Turnpike or hop on a train and head over to Manhattan.

New Orleans

New Orleans was the incubator for hit after hit in the '50s. Fats Domino was the single most consistent hit-maker, but there were also hits by Ernie K. Doe, Huey Smith, Aaron Nevillle, Lloyd Price, and others. Many of these records involved the songwriting and arranging talents of Dave Bartholomew, and later on, the arranging, composing and production talents of the legendary Allen Toussaint. Many of these hits were engineered in a thrown-together studio by ace engineer Cossimo Matassa, but it didn't seem to translate into the modern multi-track world of white rock and roll. New Orleans lost its preeminence in rock, although the occasional superstar, like Paul McCartney, would go down to the Crescent City to work with Toussaint in his Sea Saint Studios. In recent years Rounder Records, an important independent label, has recorded quite a few blues and Cajun records in New Orleans. These records have a modest but consistent sale, and do well in Europe. The Canadian producer Daniel Lanois has a studio in New Orleans, and has produced some successful records with Bob Dylan, R.E.M. and Pearl Jam, among others. The city retains its reputation as the home of traditional jazz, and the

Marsalis brothers began their careers here. Rock acts Better Than Ezra, and Cowboy Mouth are among a half dozen acts with major label deals.

Memphis and Points South

Memphis has its own story to tell. The first important pop records cut in Memphis were produced in a makeshift studio by Sam Phillips. Phillips started out recording black bluesmen in the early 1950s, but had in his mind the sound of a white man who would sing the blues and popularize it to the American teenager. He finally found that man in Elvis Presley. During the early Presley years, Phillips also successfully recorded Johnny Cash, Jerry Lee Lewis, Carl Perkins and others. Phillips sold Presley's contract to RCA for $35,000, which he used to expand his recording operation. Presley went on to become an authentic superstar, and the early "Sun Session" recordings are still prized items among Presley fans. They were re-released by RCA (now known as BMG.) Phillips had hoped Carl Perkins would succeed Presley, and the Perkins recording of Blue Suede Shoes was a big hit. Unfortunately, Perkins got into a serious auto accident, and his career languished during his long recovery. Phillips drifted out of the record business and became one of the early founders of the Holiday Inn.

Just as there were two generations of Philadelphia pop success, Sam Phillips' exit from the record business was followed by the meteoric rise of Stax and Volt Records. Throughout the 1960s and 1970s, a group of studio musicians who recorded under the name Booker T. and the MG's. turned out numerous hits for themselves and other Stax artists. The same group was hired by producer Jerry Wexler to play for many Atlantic Records sessions. Successful Stax artists included Rufus and Irma Thomas; Sam and Dave; Otis Redding; Isaac Hayes; and the Markeys.

The company had a long and involved artistic and business history, much of it detailed in Peter Gurlanick's excellent book *Sweet Soul Music: Rhythm and Blues and the Southern Dream of Freedom.* A brilliant study of the company by Rob Bowman called *Soulsville. U.S.A.: The Story of Stax Records* offers a detailed view of the company's rise, evolution and decline. Bowman points out that by 1973 the music industry was generating about $185 million a year, making it the third-largest commercial activity in the town, and the fourth largest recording center in the world.

During this time, Willie Mitchell, a competing producer with his own record label, had considerable success with an instrumental group called the Bill Black Combo, but hit even richer paydirt with soul superstar Al Green. Green turned to gospel music, and although he's been quite successful in that field and at time worked again with Mitchell, the glory days are long gone.

All of Stax's success wasn't enough to nourish a permanent music scene, despite Memphis' long musical roots in the W.C. Handy blues tradition, and its role as a focal point for the bluesmen of the Mississippi delta. After Stax folded, most of the scene went with it. However, Ardent Recording Studios hosted a number of the successful ZZ Top sessions, and there are other up-to-date studios in operation. Beale Street was considered one of the key centers for blues and is currently experiencing a sort of blues revival.

The legendary Chips Moman also played a considerable role in the success of the Memphis sound. He cut some 120 pop, rock and rhythm and blues hits at his American studios in Memphis. Many of these records were cut with co-writer Dan Penn. Both were also involved in the music scene in Muscle Shoals, Alabama.

Memphis developed into a regional jingle center, but nothing has replaced the preeminence of Stax. The town remains an active music community with a healthy, deep-rooted respect for roots music. Memphis State University even has a record label that specializes in gospel and blues music. Some Stax artists like Memphis Horns trumpeter Wayne Jackson still live here, as do producer Jim Dickinson and songwriter Keith Sykes. It's just that the glorious past was so dramatic that it all pales by comparison.

Another "happening" music area in the 1970s was in Muscle Shoals, Alabama. The town exists around a population base of about 100,000 in four neighboring cities in Northern Alabama. In its heyday, the scene featured three thriving recording operations: Rick Hall's Fame Studios; Muscle Shoals Sound, formed by a group of rhythm players who left Hall to go out on their own; and the neighboring Wishbone Sound.

The Muscle Shoals rhythm players were considered among the best in the nation. They recorded hit after hit with such artists as Paul Simon, the Starland Vocal Band, and a long list of rhythm and blues-oriented acts including Aretha Franklin. According to Charlie Gillette, writing in his book *Making Tracks,* the Muscle Shoals players were willing to consider one song a single union recording session, whether it took ten minutes or ten hours to record. Jerry Wexler was one of the prime users of the Muscle Shoals rhythm section. When he moved to Miami he offered them a regular job as his rhythm section. They refused the opportunity and the Muscle Shoals scene started to dissipate. Barry Beckett, the ace keyboard player of the section, moved to Nashville and started playing on and producing country and western records. Some of the other players followed him to Nashville or to Memphis, and Wexler found himself another rhythm section.

More recently, Muscle Shoals has experienced an odd revival. Country artists like Sawyer Brown and Earl Thomas Conley have cut records at Rick Hall's fame or Muscle Shoals Sound. There is a certain irony in the changeover from funk to country music. Many of the Muscle Shoals musicians enjoyed financial success by refining what are essentially black musical styles, yet they themselves are white.

Miami

Even before Jerry Wexler moved to Miami, a music scene was developing there. An excellent studio complex, Criteria, had already recorded Crosby, Stills, Nash and Young. Other records were being cut by producer/engineer Bill Szymczyk. Henry Stone, a music business veteran active in record distribution and production experienced great initial success in the disco years. His act, K.C. and the Sunshine Band didn't last, nor did the several successive hits by The Cornelius Brothers and Sister Rose lead to a long-term career. Another local group, Gloria Estefan and the Miami Sound Machine, was able to establish itself as a major recording act, with a string of hits and nationwide support.

Miami is a major importer and exporter to all of Latin America. In recent years all of the major labels have established branches in the area that are primarily aimed at jumping into the expanding Latin American music market. Chris Blackwell, former CEO of Island Records, has a studio here, and is reportedly going to start a new label. It seems certain that Miami will be the major center for Spanish language recording. As the population base of the United States becomes increasingly Spanish-speaking, Miami will probably become a significant. if not a major music market in the 21st century. Miami has a large population of Cuban immigrants, but is also home to people coming to the United States from virtually every country in Latin America.

Atlanta, Macon and Athens

For years, Bill Lowry has run a significant publishing and recording operation in Atlanta. Over the years, he has produced hit records by such artists as Tommy Roe, Joe South, and the Atlanta Rhythm Section. He remains active today, primarily as a music publisher. Atlanta is also an important regional jingle center, and a significant city for post-production work for television. Ted Turner's television networks have their headquarters in Atlanta.

In the 1990s Atlanta has developed into one of the centers of black pop music. La Face Records is located in town, and there are a number of other successful producers and label owners. An article in the March 8th the *New York Times Arts & Leisure* section by Kevin Sacks referred to the music scene as "an heir to Motown." Sacks listed Dallas Austin of Rowdy Records, Jermaine Dupri of So So Def Recordings and Rico Wade of the Organized Noize production group as being among the prime movers and shakers. The town has a strong black music radio scene and some major black colleges. La Face Records provides a major recording label outlet for local productions. Founded by L.A. Reid and Babyface Edmonds, it has survived a split between the two principals. Though Edmonds returned to Los Angeles and Reid remains in Atlanta with the company, the two remain business partners. In the Sacks article, Reid estimates that the company had a value of $100 million in 1998.

Capricorn Records made Macon, Georgia shine via the success of the Allman Brothers and the outstanding soul artist Otis Redding. The company was revived in the 1990s, and continues to record new music and to re-issue leased product on CD. Athens is a thriving college town, home of the University of Georgia. The B-52's and R.E.M emerged from the live music scene in Athens to achieve national fame.

San Francisco and the Bay Area

Another rich regional music scene was the fabled San Francisco sound, epitomized by such bands as the Jefferson Airplane, Moby Grape, the Grateful Dead and Quicksilver Messenger Service. San Francisco was one of the centers of pop-folk music in the later '50s and early '60s, serving as the incubation center for the Kingston Trio and the Smothers Brothers. It has a long history as a good jazz town, and Fantasy Records has had its offices here for years.

It is an unusual town, characterized by charm, diversity and sophistication. The area has a large student population, with several universities in close proximity. San Francisco itself boasts an ethnically mixed and diversified population. The area directly south of the city is Silicon Valley, the computer heart of the world.

In the '60s, the town became one of the centers of the hippie movement, with its flower power, use of psychedelic drugs and love-ins. Record companies jumped on the avant-garde image and found themselves in a bidding war to sign the hot San Francisco rock acts. These groups were drawing thousands of people at clubs with unique light shows. There were also massive audiences at love-ins and open air concerts in the park. Promoter and sometimes-manager Bill Graham was a sparkplug of the local music scene. Modern FM radio was born here, with the freeform efforts of KSAN. Prior to the birth of the rock format on this station, FM was the sort of radio wasteland that we find on AM radio today. KSAN featured a high degree of community involvement, live music on the radio, and disc jockeys who saw their work as being artistic rather than simply commercial.

All of the San Francisco bands noted above were signed by major record labels and all did quite well, with the exception of Moby Grape, a brief shooting star for Columbia. The Grateful Dead had a long-lasting career that was distinguished by lengthy and successful concert appearances, supported by a fanatical group of fans called "Deadheads." The band's career ended in the mid-'90s with the death of guitarist Jerry Garcia.

Janis Joplin also burst on the San Francisco scene, and after a brief career with Mainstream Records, was a major artist for Columbia. Sly and the Family Stone also stemmed from the Bay Area. Ultimately, the season of love ended, as did the San Francisco sound; other subsequent popular groups were grounded in the San Francisco scene, such as Huey Lewis & The News, Metallica and jazz guitarist Charley Hunter.

There are certain parallels to the dilemma of Philadelphia. San Francisco is 450 miles away from Los Angeles-about an hour by plane. Many of the local people gravitated south. The acid-rock style also became passé as we moved into the funk era of the 1970s.

Engineer-producer Fred Catero started a record label called Catero records in San Francisco. David Rubinson and Narada Michael Walden are Bay Area producers with successful track records. The late 1970s saw the re-emergence of San Francisco on the national scene with the birth and success of the Windham Hill record label. The label began its life in Palo Alto, achieving great success with "New Age" music. Windham Hill started with acoustic guitar and piano music, but has spilled over into more of a jazz and world music orientation. Today it is owned by BMG.

There is a strong local music scene in San Francisco in jazz, classical music, and to some extent in folk and new age music. There are also dozens of small "alternative rock" labels in Berkeley and San Francisco. Many musicians are supported through the active club scene. Radio stations and some strong independent record stores, like Amoeba Music, make a point of featuring local music. The popularity of relatively esoteric music, such as classical or world music can be attributed to the sophistication of the San Francisco population and the presence of so many colleges. The annual NARAS-sponsored San Francisco Music Fair also fuels the local scene. George Lucas' Luke Skywalker Ranch has an excellent audio facility, and there are some opportunities for musicians to play on film scores. The late Bill Graham may be gone, but his promotional activities continue through his company, Bill Graham Presents. The main problem is, once again, the comparison to past glories and the easy proximity of that old devil Los Angeles.

Boston

The San Francisco sound exposed some authentic musical talents to the national music scene; this was not the case with the MGM Records-promoted "Bosstown" (Boston) Sound. Apparently, MGM realized that Boston was a college town too, and had its own share of crazed hippies in the late '60s. So MGM signed a group of forgettable Boston bands and under the guiding hand of producer Alan Lorber, dumped thousands of dollars into what proved to be a vacuum. Nothing came of the Boston sound except a large tax loss for MGM and discouragement for a group of unhappy bands.

Boston is home to an extraordinary number of colleges, including the Berklee College of Music and the New England Conservatory. There are local jingles, and fairly lucrative opportunities for local musicians to play in shows that are trying out in Boston before heading for the Big Apple. During the '80s Maurice Starr found and produced the archetypal teenybopper band New Kids on the Block, but he has left town without further comparable successes. The world is still waiting for a "Boston sound." The lesson to be drawn from the Boston debacle is that a regional music style must have some integrity. Simply selling artists on the basis that they are from Des Moines is not going to induce thousands of record buyers to flock to the stores to support the Iowa sound!

Austin

Austin, Texas represents a different sort of musical atmosphere. The nightclub scene has always been a significant part of the Austin musical canvas. When the Texas Music Conference sponsored its first South By Southwest musical gathering in 1986, it flew in dozens of music industry folks from both coasts to view 200 bands playing in clubs during a four-day period. At that conference, twenty record company offers were tendered to the bands and soloists who performed during the festivities.

Austin has always been a center for young, single people who have the energy and interest to go out at night. There is the huge University of Texas campus, and also the state government, with its large number of employees. A variety of musical interests groups are present in this varied population. It is interesting that many college towns, such as Athens (Georgia), Bloomington (Indiana), Ann Arbor (Michigan), Madison (Wisconsin), and Durham and Chapel Hill (North Carolina), all have some sort of active music scene. Many of these scenes are derivative folk-influenced scenes, not necessarily ones that reflect mainstream pop music values.

Part of Austin's appeal for musicians has to do with its role as a sort of cultural refuge for the person who doesn't feel at home in Dallas, Houston or El Paso. By the end of the 1960s into the early 1970s, Austin experienced a great influx of musical talent. There was Steve Fromholz, a consummate writer and entertainer who achieved local and regional fame; Rusty Weir, the ultimate bar musician; B. W. Stephenson, with his one big hit "My Man" for RCA; Jerry Jeff Walker, the transplanted New Yorker who wrote "Mr. Bojangles"; the sardonic rock madness of Kinky Friedman and his Texas Jewboys; and there was Michael Martin Murphy, with his hit, "Wildfire." Murphy invented the Cosmic Cowboy and then drifted north to Colorado to escape his image, and south to Taos, New Mexico to become a pioneer in the revival of "western" music. Most of all, there was Willie Nelson.

More than any of the other Austin performers, Willie Nelson had the ability to bring the entire music scene together. Everybody was a Nelson fan, from ladies with beehive hairdos to truckdrivers, ropers, freaks of all descriptions, as well as the university crowd.

In the same way, Nelson brought different aspects of the music together as well. His band was a mixture of old and new. He could play old-time country songs, his own ballads, or the uptempo honky-tonk style of music that could bring a bar crowd to its feet. Nelson had his beard and pony tail, and he looked more like a hippie than a cowboy, but he talked more like a cowboy than a hippie. His performances at the famous club, Armadillo World Headquarters, became legendary, as did his 4th of July picnics, where every social class in Austin got together to drink beer and party in the hot Texas summer.

Musically Nelson was the original "outlaw." He and Waylon Jennings defied the Nashville establishment with their long hair and their insistence on retaining control over the artistic components of their records. Nelson eventually built a studio called Lone Star, where he sometimes recorded and where other local musicians cut sessions. He also befriended some of his local buddies by recording their songs, probably earning these writers far more money than their years of nightclub performances had reaped.

Austin was not a racially mixed music scene in the sense that Stax Records had been. Its obvious country roots were represented by Kenneth Threadgill. He was a "hillbilly" singer who ran a bar in the early '60s that provided, among other things, welcome and shelter for a young and troubled Janis Joplin. However, the Austin scene did cover plenty of ground outside of country music. It drew on such Texas bluesmen as Mance Lipscomb and Lightnin' Hopkins.

From the mid-'70s, Antone's became the home of live blues music in Austin. The Fabulous Thunderbirds with Jimmy Vaughan were the house band and Jimmy's brother, guitar idol Stevie Ray Vaughan, cut a lot of his musical eyeteeth there. Blues singers Marcia Ball and Angela Strehli were other local favorites. Not content with his night club and record store, Clifford Antone started a record label that enabled some of his artists to achieve some national recognition.

In 1976, the Austin City Limits television show appeared for the first time. The show was nationally syndicated and became one of the most popular shows on public television. The first season showcased only local Austin performers, but over the years there has been a mix of the Austin fixtures, along with visitors like Chet Atkins, Jimmy Buffett and Merle Haggard. For the most part, the show has been country-oriented, and this probably fueled the general public notion that Austin is a country and western music scene.

What the Austin music scene has that so many local music scenes lack is the ability to constantly re-invent itself with new talent that feeds and extends the music. Singer-songwriters have always comprised the heart of the Austin music scene. Willis Alan Ramsey, author of "Muskrat Love," and the late Townes Van Zandt, who wrote "Pancho And Lefty", were important participants in the '60s. More recent singer-songwriters include Nanci Griffith, who wrote "Love At The Five and Dime," and the talented and quirky Lyle Lovett. Though neither record in Austin, the town is an important aspect of their musical and psychological roots.

The city of Austin has lent its support to the music scene by hiring a liaison to the music community who works on such prosaic but real problems as creating proper Loading Zones in the congested 6th Street night club area, so that musicians don't have to trek for blocks carrying amplifiers and P.A. equipment. In general Austin seems to want to promote itself as a music town, just as Nashville calls itself Music City, USA.

Because Austin has a warm climate, and because virtually all pop musicians know about the South By Southwest music conference and the 6th Street club scene, musicians have been visiting Austin for thirty years now. They often they end up staying there. By virtue of this longevity, the Austin music scene has proven itself in a more significant way than virtually any of the other local or regional scenes. Other music communities may have started out bigger, or peaked higher, but they also suffered precipitous declines.

In order for Austin to sustain its musical scene, there needs to be an emphasis on more locally recorded product. Watermelon Records has provided some of that impetus, and Arista-Texas has its headquarters in Austin. San Antonio, less than a hundred miles south, has a major Tejano music scene—Austin would probably benefit by more direct interaction with that community. There is a music business program at Austin Community College, but the University of Texas Music Department has no direct connection with the music community. The university media programs have been more generous. Austin City Limits is televised at the university and there is a significant college radio station. There is clearly a need for more of an overall infrastructure to build the local community-personal managers, agents, music industry attorneys, record producers, engineers and recording studios. There is a thriving advertising community here.

One of the keys to Austin's future is whether the major writers and artists who come out of this scene can be induced to stay there to record, and to invest their dollars in the local music community. As long as the talented writers and recording artists are going to Nashville and Los Angeles to record, and even to live, they are making a statement that something is missing in the local scene.

Austin plays a unique role in terms of the overall Texas scene. Texas is a huge land mass dotted by cities in different sections of the state that vary from being rather typical, suburbanite mall-infested areas to cities whose basic function is to provide a business center for a particular geographic and cultural area. It was acceptable to have long hair and a beard in Austin when there were parts of the state where doing so would subject the bearer to abuse or physical harm.

Since rock and roll, "outlaw" country, and contemporary folk music have always had a rather thin alliance with society's "straight" values, Austin became a refuge for musicians and other artists seeking to escape an oppressive cultural climate. the Austin country writers followed Nelson's lead in the sense that they envisaged themselves outside of the Nashville mill that so efficiently organizes the composition, manufacture and distribution of country and western music.

Minneapolis

Bob Dylan was probably the first pop superstar to come from Minnesota. However, because all his recordings took place in the major music business towns, his emergence was more of a general spiritual encouragement than anything else. During the late '50s and early '60s, Minneapolis was a regional jingle center and also played a prominent role in the folk music revival. Koerner, Ray and Glover were among the leading white blues singers on the coffeehouse circuit who helped to bring about the re-awakening of consciousness in America's blues roots.

Minneapolis has always been an important center for the sale and distribution of records. Target Stores are headquartered here with their own internal rack jobber division. This differs from most other department and discount stores who usually order from outside rack jobbers. Rack jobbers stock and service these outlets for a percentage of the store's record sales. They are, in effect, renting space in the stores K-Tel, the record oldies television outlet, and Pickwick International, another major record manufacturer and distributor, are headquartered here.

In the 1980s two significant developments influenced the Minneapolis music scene. First came the astounding success of (the artist formerly known as) Prince. He put together bands, arrangers and a production team and opened a massive studio facility called Paisley Park. Other producers and arrangers, like David Z. (Rivkin) and his brother Bobby, soon emerged from projects that involved Prince, his band members, or acts he signed to the WEA-distributed Paisley Park label.

Secondly, there was the brilliant and consistent record production team of Jimmy Jam and Terry Lewis. Originally associated with a Prince-controlled band from which they were fired, Jam and Lewis have won dozens of writing, and publishing awards to go with their 1986 Grammy Producers of the Year award. The Minneapolis scene includes other musical idioms as well. Michael Johnson, who has achieved success in the pop and country-pop field, lives there and has done some recording in the area. So does semi-legendary guitar guru Leo Kottke. Garrison Keillor has returned to broadcast the "Prairie Home Companion" radio show, after a brief hiatus in New York. This program provides a key forum for folk, country and occasional jazz musicians in the area.

Since Prince's record label did not achieve their hoped-for success with the WEA group, neither the label nor Prince himself are connected with WEA any longer. There are many live outlets for music in the Minneapolis-St. Paul area, and Red House has emerged as a leading folk music record company. A thriving booking agency called The Good Music Agency has emerged as an important force on the local music scene.

Minneapolis also has a symphony orchestra, as well as a unique group called the St. Paul Chamber Orchestra, perhaps the most outstanding ensemble of its kind in North America. The presence of these ensembles makes quality string and woodwind players available for recording sessions. This makes it possible to do the sort of feature film and television work that requires good orchestras. The Tyrone Guthrie Theater is a strong regional theater with a repertory company. It contributes to and is a reflection of the health of the cultural scene in the twin Cities area. The advertising business has always been strong here, and the state film commission promotes the music community as well as seeking to induce Hollywood productions to shoot here.

The problem with developing an extensive music business mechanism in the Twin Cities is that the power centers of the music industry remain on both coasts. For a major talent management operation to work, the people involved would have to be willing to become virtual bi-coastal commuters. Perhaps a better possibility is the establishment of Twin City offices for companies that headquarter in Los Angeles or New York. This is more likely to occur in Chicago. As long as Jimmy Jam and Terry Lewis remain factors in the music marketplace, Minneapolis will retain some importance on the American popular music scene.

Chicago

The Chicago music scene has had a long and interesting story of its own. At one time, all of the major record companies had staff offices in Chicago, and the corporate offices of Mercury, now part of Polygram, was headquartered here. Chicago had a hot rhythm and blues scene in the '50s, sparked by producer Carl Davis. In the late '50s and '60s, Jerry Butler had periodic success as an artist, and other major success was enjoyed by Curtis Mayfield and his group The Impressions. Chess and Vee Jay Records were important producers of blues and rhythm and blues records through the 1960s.

Today the major labels have gone, but there are several important blues labels based in Chicago. Alligator, Blind Pig and Delmark remain in the Windy City. Chicago remains an important center for jingles, with the giant Leo Burnett Advertising Agency based here. In recent years Chicago has slipped behind Los Angeles as the #2 advertising center for jingles, with New York remaining the heavy player.

There are several major recording studios here that do recording work for CDs, film and television. Chicago had a big hand in the folk music revival and spawned the talents of numerous folk revivalists and singer-songwriters, including Steve Goodman and John Prine. There was also an important gospel music community, with T.J. Dorsey and Mahalia Jackson bringing notoriety and attention to the gospel music scene. Recently, there has been an upsurge of successful recording artists operating out of Chicago, including Liz Phair and Smashing Pumpkins. At the moment Chicago lacks a distinct musical identity, outside the blues clubs and record labels.

Portland, Oregon

The Portland music scene has never had a single artist or musical style that has galvanized the musical scene there. It has been more like a steady proliferation of mainstream rock (with a touch of the blues) bands and acts, like Robert Cray, Quarterflash, Jeff Lorber, the Dandy Warhols, Cherry Poppin' Daddies and Meredith Brooks making their way into the major record companies and larger music communities.

Portland talent has also enjoyed support from local radio stations. Although this may not make a major difference in the big picture of national music exposure, it has provided a basic part of nurturing and developing for the northwest music community. Quarterflash's record "Harden My Heart" sold 10,000 copies in Portland and Seattle before Geffin Records picked it up and helped it go platinum.

In downtown Portland, there is an unusual record store called Locals Only. It only stocks records recorded in the northwest. The last time I was there, about a year ago, owner Dan Sauce told me that there were about 1500 CDs in the store. Recently they have also opened a branch in Seattle. The stock includes records by major label artists, independent label artists, and people who have produced their own albums. All genres of music are represented. There are also posters, T shirts and various locally-produced items. The artists represented come from Seattle and Portland, Eugene, Corvallis, Olympia and other, smaller towns. By visiting this shop, one can get a brief snapshot of the music scene in the northwest in an afternoon. It is an amazingly simple idea—one that would benefit any regional music center of some size.

Another focus of the Portland music scene is an annual rock and roll charity ball. The proceeds go to charities and some fifty bands perform throughout the evening. Bud Clark, the former mayor or Porland, was a big supporter of this event, formerly called The Mayor's Ball. The current mayor appears to be uninterested in the event.

So far, Portland is yet to produce a musical superstar. Nevertheless, there is a steady stream of bands forming, maturing, performing and getting recording deals and local airplay. Many of these bands have been able to tour nationally, and have sustained relatively successful careers without enjoying hit records.

Other music-related enterprises have also begun to prosper. Weiden and Kennedy is a local advertising agency that created the Nike "Just Do It" campaign, and has recently won much of the Microsoft advertising account. *Williamette Week* is the local weekly paper and it provides good music coverage, in a generally well-written paper. Other music papers, including the *Two Louies* deal specifically with local music.

Other Scenes

If you read the national music trades like *Billboard* or *Radio and Records*, and look for the local music and entertainment magazines, like the *Rocket* in Seattle or *BAM (Bay Area Music)* in San Francisco, you can follow the development of regional music markets. Tower Records and Sam Goody/Musicland publish monthlies that also contain reports from various cities.

There are always some music scenes developing in the most unlikely parts of North America. New Jack City musical guru Teddy Riley has his studio in Virginia Beach; rap producer Jay King continues to work in Sacramento; and John Cougar Mellencamp records in a home studio on a farm near Bloomington, Indiana. Albuquerque has an interesting fusion of American Indian and Chicano music, and Tom Bee has created a sort of Indian Motown there. The other leading producer of Native American music is Canyon Records, located in Phoenix. San Antonio is the major center for the recording of Tejano music. Recently Vancouver and Toronto have developed into major television and film production centers, not just for Canadian productions, but for numerous American films and television shows.

There are always certain fundamental ingredients behind the evolution of American popular music, at least in the rock and roll era. Rock music is a fusion of elements drawn from the roots of the blues, country and gospel music. On the country music side are old fiddle tunes, Appalachian Mountain ballads, and the sort of vocal style that Alan Lomax refers to as "closed-throat singing." This vocal style is an anguished nasal, pinched cry. The black or Afro-American tradition includes field hollers, work songs, call and response chants, an "open-throat" vocal style, and adaptations of European culture mixed with African elements, like bottleneck blues guitar style. Blues employs the "metronome sense" of the African drummer. Bluegrass, by contrast, is notorious for its high lonesome vocal sounds and the frequently-used device of speeding up tempos during a performance.

Most of these regional scenes contain interesting fusions of black and white musical style, such as the peculiarity of Muscle Shoals with its all-white but funk-oriented rhythm players. Memphis was unique in that the Booker T. and the MG's rhythm section was a racially integrated group.

The Philly and Motown sounds were derived from black musical styles that were laundered with white musical mannerisms, such as string sections on the Philly records, and Motown's simplified four-beats-to-the-bar that Motown devised to appeal to the white teenager.

Local Markets Ebb and Flow

In looking at the way that scenes start, grow and change, there are a few similarities that emerge from these creative and business explosions:

1. **Over-dependency on a single account or producer:**
   Since the average career of a record producer has been estimated to last five years, clearly a single producer cannot sustain a music scene's long-term growth. Even the most successful producers are apt to move to another locale to use a different group of musicians, studios or arrangers or simply because they want to sample another "scene."

2. **Focus on a single musical style:**
   American popular music is distinguished mostly by its unpredictability. No one knows what the next successful musical innovation will be or where it may originate. Reliance on specific musical styles to the exclusion of experimentation and growth is almost a certain invitation to a scene cresting and meeting its demise, as the musical style goes through the stages of innovation, success, imitation, rust and neglect.

3. **Lack of overall music business development in conjunction with successful records:**
   Many of the towns discussed, like New Orleans, didn't have a full-time music business apparatus. These towns lacked a jingle, film, music publishing, or television business that could provide additional work for studio musicians, composers, and arrangers. The absence of music publishers inhibits the growth of a vital songwriting community. There also needs to be a music business community of lawyers, personal and business managers and accountants that can service the business of the music community.

4. **Financial ability to keep up with the latest technology:**

Purchasing and exploring the latest recording paraphernalia and electronic musical instruments is an expensive and time-consuming process. many regional scenes cannot support this aspect of development. As each new format appears, it may be necessary for a studio to totally abandon its existing equipment, or to create another recording room to house the new gear. In the same way that musical scenes rise and fall, recording studios become the talk of the business, and then may be forgotten.

5. **Presence of a vital live music scene:**

There has to be some place for talent to emerge, polish its skills, get audience feedback, and develop a following. Some towns, like Philadelphia, historically had restrictive liquor laws that discouraged nightclubs. When the laws were finally changed, the scene had moved to surrounding suburban areas in another county or state.

6. **Government support:**

Although government support cannot create a scene, it can assist in sustaining and expanding it. This support can be tied in to each state's film commission, but very few states have chosen to follow this path.

7. **Media support:**

Media support includes music papers, better music coverage in daily papers, the presence of a college radio station that plays different styles of music outside the mainstream, and assistance from local record stores, unions and the creation of viable local and regional music organizations. It is also important to try to convince existing privately-owned radio stations to feature a local music show.

8. **Music education:**

There are an increasing number of colleges teaching classes that discuss the music business, and hands-on classes in music engineering. It is logical that some of the graduates of these programs will be the future sparkplugs of their local music scenes. A number of these schools have even started their own record labels, a good way to provide hands-on experience.

To evaluate all of these factors, take a look at the chart on the following page. Clearly, the first ingredient for a healthy music scene is the presence of local talent that is worth recording. Next, there has to be a local studio that is good enough to get that sound on tape. This, in turn, requires the presence of musicians, engineers and producers.

Ingredients for a Successful Local Music Scene

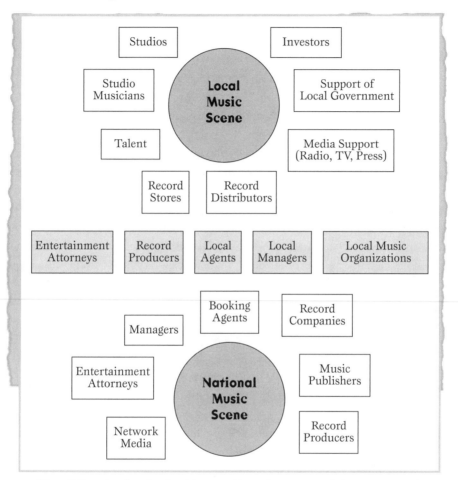

(The middle section shows local entities networking or interacting with the national scene.)

None of this can happen unless someone or some group of investors provide financial backing. The investors can be the band itself, a recording studio, a manager, family or friends, bankers lending money based on proven equity from a music publishing company, or a group of investors who buy shares in a recording project. To pare it down to the essentials there must be:

1. Talent to be recorded.
2. Money to complete the recording.
3. Talent in the studio capable of carrying out the production.

4. A manager to sell the product to a record company or the group must have an alternate plan to put the record out themselves.
5. The local music scene needs to nurture the act, by providing local radio play and reviews from the local music press.
6. Local music stores who carry and display the record.
7. Publicity apparatus in place to create excitement about the group.
8. Managers to help build careers and agents to get work for the artists.

A key ingredient to the longevity of music scenes is the development of musical variety. Of all the major music scenes, only Nashville is still predominantly identified with a single musical style. Although this may be an unjust label in the sense that there really is a great variety of music available in Nashville, in the mind of the public and most of the music industry, Nashville is a country music town. It is country music that brings in the artists, the fans, the songwriters and the dollars. Nashville has survived because country music itself has gone through numerous trends and fads, while retaining a core base of fans.

Nashville is an exception to the rule. The identification of Memphis and Muscle Shoals with rhythm and blues music may have made these towns' reputations, but it also led to their eclipse. The same goes for the Philly Sound. Motown is probably the other exception to the rule, but they left Detroit and some of their artists, like Marvin Gaye and Stevie Wonder, evolved in new musical directions far beyond the scope of the original Motown sound.

This has been a brief survey of how a music scene develops, the ingredients that reinforce the music, and where the process leads. It is my hope that this has given you some encouragement for helping to build a viable music scene wherever you may live.

Note: there are many other meaningful regional music scenes, such as the one surrounding King Records in Cincinnati; The C.W. McCall and Mannheim Steamroller product from Omaha; and the story of Peacock Records in Houston. Other product has emerged from Jackson, Mississippi, Cleveland, Ohio, Sacramento, California, and the beach music scene of Virginia and South Carolina. We shouldn't overlook the "alternative" product coming out of Chapel Hill, North Carolina from Mammoth and Merge Records, or artist Ani DiFranco's successes with her Righteous Babe label in Buffalo.

CHAPTER 14 RESOURCES

There are many books available on the music scenes in the towns discussed in this chapter. They are listed in Appendix D of this book. There is really no detailed general discussion of regional music in any other books that I have seen.

Seattle & Denver:

A Tale of Two Cities

N ow that we've mapped the fundamentals of how regional music scenes operate, let's take a look at two very different regional music scenes.

Part One: Seattle

The history of the Seattle music scene includes some early hits by a vocal group called the Fleetwoods. Their first hit, "Come Softly to Me," hit the charts in 1959. Shortly thereafter, the rock instrumental combo, the Ventures, achieved national success with their recording of "Walk, Don't Run." In the late '60s and early '70s, Paul Revere and the Raiders, dressing in Revolutionary-War-styled costumes, made a number of hit records.

The first edition of this book was written in 1989. At that point, Queensryche was the best known Seattle band. It was a sort of progressive heavy metal band pushing the aesthetic borders of that style of music. Subsequently, a series of events occurred that evolved into the sound explosion dubbed "the Seattle Sound."

A local label called Sub Pop began its life as a fan magazine in 1979. By 1986 it had turned into a record company. It then released a series of albums by several (then) obscure bands—Soundgarden, Nirvana and a band called Mother Love Bone that later evolved into Pearl Jam.

Sub Pop was founded by two young punk-oriented fans named Bruce Pavitt and Jonathan Poneman. From the first, it was their intention to create a regional music scene. Lacking the money that MGM had dumped into the ill-fated Boston Sound, the two partners proceeded along somewhat different lines. They enlisted photographer Charles Peterson and producer-engineer Jack Endino to work on virtually all of the Sub Pop products. The idea was to create a somewhat uniform look and sound, even though the bands signed were rather different from one another. They invested some money to fly in Everett True, a writer for the English music magazine *Melody Maker.* True wrote a series of profiles and stories that established the credibility of the Seattle music scene. It worked beyond anyone's wildest dreams. By the mid 1990s there were some thirty bands in Seattle with national recording deals, plus many, many more on the dozens of local labels that emerged with the success of the so-called "grunge" bands.

Sony even hired a local A&R rep to live in Seattle and provide the company with leads to the newest hot bands. By the mid-'90s, Sub Pop had sold 49% of the company to the huge Warner Brothers-WEA organization. This enabled the company to obtain substantial financing to sign acts, expand their catalog and promote their product.

Initially most of the record companies believed that Seattle's success was simply a temporary boom based on the sound of Soundgarden, the first of the '90s bands to hit big. When Alice in Chains, Nirvana and Pearl Jam all became major acts in quick succession, the boom hit epidemic proportions. New bands were created by the minute, and existing bands and unemployed musicians flocked to Seattle to inhale the magic elixir of grunge.

In fact there was a stronger foundation to Seattle's music scene than these bands. Sir Mix-A-Lot achieved some major success in the area of rap music, Kenny G. is a long-term local resident, and for years Seattle has had an important folk scene centered around two massive music festivals that occur during the Memorial Day and Labor Day weekends. In fact, Douglas Mays, a local booking agent quoted in Clark Humphrey's book, *Loser: The Seattle Music Story,* has said that "Seattle has more different kinds of bands and more studios per capita, than maybe any other city in America. We still need a pressing plant, but we have just about all the other elements to become a major music center."

One of the major catalysts for local music is a music paper called the *Rocket,* which appears every two weeks. Browsing through its pages reveals an active recording scene, and a passionate involvement with music. The paper started as a monthly insert to the *Seattle Sun,* in 1979. the *Sun* was an alternative paper in Seattle during this period, in the style pioneered by the *Village Voice* in New York.

Recording Studios

Like a number of other cities, Seattle has experienced some attempts to turn it into a major center for film work and recording. This included a studio called Smith-Kaye and a temporary move to the area by Hollywood director Stanley Kramer.

Neither of these experiments worked out, but Seattle hit the media jackpot with the opening of Bad Animals Recording Studio. Bad Animals was a partnership between long-time Seattle residents the Wilson sisters, lead singers of the band Heart, and multi-media producer Steve Lawson. The association with Lawson virtually guaranteed activity in the areas of film, television and commercials, while the cachet of the Wilson Sisters brought in the rock 'n' rollers and the record projects.[1]

Bear Creek is another large studio operation that is more of a CD project studio, with a rural farmhouse location. It tends to be blocked out for long time periods for bands who are recording album projects. Soundgarden recorded their *Superunknown* project at Bear Creek.

A student of mine named Scott Liss did a survey of Seattle studios in the mid -'90s. He uncovered twelve relatively inexpensive studio operations that had recording capabilities ranging from 16–32 tracks, and rental rates of $20–$35 an hour. Certainly, the range of studios is adequate to service the needs of everyone from garage bands who intend to produce their own records, to world-class bands recording with big budgets for major labels.

Personal Managers, Agents, Etc.

Part of the support system that builds major music scenes is the presence of a major music business infrastructure. This includes the various aspects of the business not apparent to the general public, such as management companies, booking agencies, and entertainment attorneys. Although Susan Silver Management handled Soundgarden and Alice in Chains, there is nothing here comparable to what is in Los Angeles. A single entertainment attorney, Neil Sussman, seems to be well-known in the Seattle area, and he advertises regularly in the *Rocket.*

---

1. The partnership is now dissolved and Steve Lawson has a multi-media studio. He is not connected with the music recording studio located next door.

Live Music

During the mid '90s Clark Humphrey reported almost two dozen "over-21" clubs and bars that featured original live music in Seattle, Tacoma, Olympia and Bellingham. As long as the Seattle economy, jointly fueled by Microsoft and Boeing, continues to boom, this trend will almost certainly continue. Downtown Seattle is extremely congested and offers limited parking. This will certainly be a deterrent to the expansion and even continuation of an active live music scene in the downtown area. Another negative is that the city seems disinterested in the local music scene, except for its attempts to ban concert posters. The state offers even less support. Local musicians have had to fight to keep the state legislature from passing offensive censorship bills. On the other hand, the presence of a number of college and universities in the area, especially the giant University of Washington in Seattle, provide a built-in audience for live music.

Other Aspects of Seattle Music

Paul Allen, the multi-millionaire co-founder of Microsoft, has announced plans to build a museum to honor Seattle native Jimi Hendrix. The consequent influx of tourists will almost certainly have a positive long-term effect on the government's attitude towards the rock music scene.

An odd side-bar to the Seattle music universe is the presence of background music giant Muzak. This resulted from a merger of the New York Muzak Company with the Seattle Yesco Foreground Music Company. All operations were moved to Seattle. Although the company has little relevance to the Seattle rock music scene as such, it does provide employment for programmers, engineers and music editors. Among the ex-employees are Sub-Pop founders Pavitt and Poneman.

Record Companies

Clark Humphreys lists almost eighty active local record companies in the appendix of *Loser*. This does not include labels that are really a single band putting out their own album. This is a very large number of companies for a city with less than three quarters of a million people. Naturally, many of these companies have primarily local distribution. As the scene has developed, more possibilities exist for distribution deals with larger companies or even the purchase of these labels. The Seattle branch of the Locals Only record store should provide a good outlet for local artists.

General Ambiance

Seattle is definitely one of the "magic" cities in the United States. It is a place where people like to come and visit; fall in love with the general atmosphere and quality of life; and decide to stay. There is the ocean, the mountain views, the houseboats, and a generally cosmopolitan feeling about the area that is a bit reminiscent of San Francisco.

Another part of the lifestyle is the ever-present coffee and espresso houses, the colorful Pike Street Market, and the rain. The nearby presence of Vancouver (British Columbia), itself quite a thriving and attractive city, with such neighboring or nearby towns as Tacoma, Olympia, Bellingham and Portland, not all that far away, contribute to the notion that the Northwest has a unique and unusual identity. Every one of these towns has a large college community, which provides an ideal audience for new and regional music styles.

Can It Continue?

As the end of the twentieth century dawns, the Seattle music scene is no longer the flavor of the week. Soundgarden has broken up, Nirvana is no more, and although Pearl Jam continues it is no longer the super-group of the early '90s. Nevertheless, new bands seem to continually emerge from the rain. Built to Spill and Tuatara are on Warner Brothers; Sub Pop has a bunch of new groups; and several other bands enjoy major label deals. Dave Grohl has merged from the wreckage of Nirvana with the Foo Fighters. Who knows how many other groups are woodshedding in garages and basements?

In 1993, the Christian label, Tooth and Nail, moved to Seattle to add yet another ingredient to this eclectic scene. Certainly, what Seattle does have is a viable music community that raises some interesting questions about the growth and longevity of a regional music scene.

Part Two: Denver— Some Would Rather Be in Colorado

I moved to Colorado from the New York area in 1972. After ten years of studio work, songwriting and record production it was quite a shock. At the time, it seemed everyone was moving here. Oil companies were booming at the time and Western Colorado was supposed to become the oil shale capitol of the United States. John Denver was singing songs about the Rocky Mountain High. People thronged into the state from California, Texas, New York and other places. The band Firefall was headquartered in Boulder, and they and Dan Fogelberg did some recording at a studio called North Star. Jim Guercio build a studio at his Caribou Ranch north of Boulder, and all sorts of major artists recorded there, including the Beach Boys, Elton John and Chicago. Successful New York producer Bill Szymczyk moved here and started Tumbleweed Records. Barry Fey had already established himself as a major league promoter, and was putting on concerts not only in Denver and Boulder but in adjoining states. Recording studios opened and the Denver Center for the Performing Arts soon emerged as Denver's version of the Guthrie Theater. The population grew and the music community was primed for the start of a major music community.

By the early 1980s things started to slow down. Oil prices dropped and the oil companies started to leave Denver. They concluded that it was not viable to pursue oil shale as a natural resource. A regional music organization called the Rocky Mountain Music Association was formed and in the mid-'80s held several regional conferences that attracted music publishers and A&R representatives from major labels. In the period of about a year, local attorney Ed Pierson made a deal with MCA Records, made two major publishing deals for bands and writers, signed Jill Sobule to MCA, and after witnessing (and promoting) a bidding war, signed the Subdudes to Atlantic Records.

By the end of the 1980s the economy had declined. It had gotten so bad that the large buildings which had changed the skyline of downtown Denver were like ghost towns. Space was available for $1 a square foot for the first year of a three year lease, and other, similarly extreme deals were being made to rent at anyone at virtually any price they chose. Six multi-track studios in the Denver-Boulder area were out of business by this time. Firefall was long gone. John Denver had become old news. It seemed that everyone was moving to California. That included me, and I lived in the Los Angeles area from 1987-1988, working for NARAS, the National Academy of Recording Arts & Sciences, the organization that created the Grammy Show. I was their National Education Coordinator; it was during this time that I began to write the first edition of this book.

After one year in California, I decided that I would rather be in Colorado. I came back to the Denver area just at the point when California suffered a series of catastrophes. The riots resulting from the arrest of Rodney King were followed by the closure of many military bases in California and some disastrous fires and rock slides. It seemed that everyone was leaving California—thousands were headed to Colorado. Meanwhile, the studio business had quietly resumed, but this time, the studios seemed to position themselves into different niches. Several mutlitrack rooms added automated mixing, the A-DAT format came in, and it seemed as though all the studios were reasonably busy. Barry Fey continued to be an active promoter, but MCA opened a huge outdoor facility south of Denver that held close to 20,000 people. Several independent promoters emerged that specialized in rap, hard rock, folk music and women's music. A couple of theaters in Denver became entertainment venues, as well as two in Boulder.

Colorado is the corporate headquarters for TCI and several other major players in the cable television business. Unfortunately for the local community, little actual production is done here. Every year one or two feature films are cranked out, but so far none of them has proved to be a major success. Dan Fogelberg has moved to the western part of the state and has a home studio. John Denver, who never did record in Colorado, died in a tragic airplane accident. Several of the Eagles have residences in Aspen, and Glenn Frey has a home studio there. Caribou Studios burned down, but Pat Leonard, who has produced Madonna, among others, has a small home studio operation at Caribou, and in a quiet way there are at least four acts with major label deals. The most successful has been Big Head Todd & the Monsters, with one gold album to their name so far. They initially recorded on their own label. Through extensive touring, they were selling some 30,000 units of their self-produced CDs, before picking up a management deal with Morris/Bliesener Associates. This in turn led to their record deal with Irving Azoff's Warner-distributed Giant Records, now re-named Revolution Records.

The area also is the home of Silver Wave Records, which started out as a New Age label, and has now added more of a world music profile. W.A.R. Records moved to Boulder from New York, and they are the home label of The Samples, another act that tours nationally. The Samples have been in and out of major label deals with Arista and MCA, but seem happier as independent artists.

Denver doesn't have a strong, regularly published entertainment paper, although new ones seem to sprout up or disappear each year. *Westword* is the local alternative paper, and they devote quite a bit of (sometimes controversial) coverage to music. Each issue usually includes a couple of articles about local bands. The Rocky Mountain Music Association still exists, but it no longer holds an annual conference. Barry Fey has sold his business to Universal. MCA remains along with some further possible competition from an alliance between manager Chuck Morris and Bill Graham Presents. Contrary to the opinion of most local musicians, there is a fairly active live music scene. No one is getting rich, but the clubs do at least pay people. There is also a large convention business here. Other work is available at the state's various ski resorts, at least during the winter months. There are regional jingles here and some musical work is available on local industrial or tourist films. A couple of people write jingles full time, but a large percentage of their work is done with samplers and synthesizers.

The Denver Symphony went under, but was quickly replaced by a co-operative orchestra called The Colorado Symphony. Various players function as both labor and management. A local chamber music orchestra is a distant memory.

Denver is truly a sports-crazy town—there is a new downtown baseball field, with restaurants and clubs all around it which usually have some live music during the season. A new basketball arena is also under construction, which will supposedly feature a full sound stage and the capability of doing film and recording. A new football stadium will probably follow, depending upon the voters' generosity.

One of the problems of building a music scene in Denver is that the city is like an island in the Rockies. Salt Lake City is 500 miles to the west; Omaha and Kansas City are 600 miles to the east; Albuquerque is about 350 miles south, but it is a much smaller city; Colorado Springs is only 65 miles south of Denver, and it is a growing city, with a population of 300,000. It's a tough trip in the winter months, and Colorado Springs is a rather conservative town between the large military presence and its role as the headquarters for a number of right-wing religious organizations.

It's difficult for musicians to tour efficiently with such large distances involved. The Morris-Bliesener management firm and another manager named Ted Guggenheim seem to have positive record company interactions, but since Ed Pierson left to go to California in 1988, there are no "deal-maker" attorneys who have good record company access. There are no local booking agencies who book on a national level, other than Scott O'Malley in Colorado Springs, who focuses on cowboy poets and country-folk music.

Colorado has a fairly active folk and country music community. The Swallow Hill Music Association in Denver books concerts by touring artists, and has a very successful acoustic music school, and there are several large country music clubs. The Boulder-Nederland area has an active coffeehouse scene for acoustic music. In the mid-'80s through the early '90s there were a number of soft jazz or jazz fusion bands with national deals. Nelson Rangell still records for GRP Records. A band called Images has gone through several major deals before recording for a local jazz label called Fahrenheit. Another local band on the label that tours extensively is Dotsero.

One of the biggest problems for Denver musicians is that local radio has become extremely corporate. Two companies own the larger stations here and there is no college radio station that can be heard outside college dormitories. There are occasional local music shows that drift in and out of the airwaves, and even several of the NPR stations are tightly formatted. Several stations regularly play folk rock or soft rock, but they don't extensively program local artists. There are a number of strong independent record stores, but a number of them have gone out of business since Tower Records moved in.

The school where I teach, the University of Colorado at Denver, is going through a significant expansion in its School of the Arts. The Professional Studies department has an active music and recording engineering program. It is an open question whether a college program can play a major role in creating a music scene, as opposed to reacting to an already existing scene. It certainly should be goal of such programs to relate to the local music community in a dynamic and useful way.

In my opinion, it will be difficult for Denver to become a major regional music market. There is relatively little infrastructure, the local film commission is almost entirely ignorant of the presence of a music community, and Denver's location makes mounting touring clumsy. The best bet for Denver would be for a superstar artist or producer to decide to want to open up shop here. The few that have done so, have not had any relationship to speak of with the local music community. Denver also lacks a specific musical style that it could represent to record company people. If a Pavitt or Poneman were here, they possibly could invent that. The question remains, however, if there is enough significant local talent to follow the hype. Possibly, Denver is better off assuming the role of a Portland, rather than a Seattle. There is plenty of music in and around the area, and there are good studios and competent engineers. Without a larger population base, and closer large cities, it is hard to sell records in quantity.

CHAPTER 15 RESOURCES

The most useful book about the Seattle music scene that I have found is Clark Humphreys *Loser: The Seattle Music Story*, published by Ferral Books, in Portland in 1995. Other books are listed in Appendix D.

The information about the Denver music scene comes from my 25 years of living here and input from my friends and colleagues Frank Jermance, Jim Mason and Harry Tuft.

The Music Business in Canada

C anada is the uncharted northern neighbor of the United States. The average statesider probably knows more about his local football team than he knows about Canada. So this chapter is as much for statesiders who are curious about music in Canada as it is for Canadians.

Although Canada is geographically larger than the United States, the population is about 10% of that of the U.S. The nation is divided into provinces instead of states, each province has one or two major cities. There are four national political parties, plus one that operates only in Quebec. Canada is the leading importer of American goods and Canadians usually pay a higher price for most of these products than statesiders do. The Canadian dollar is worth less than the U.S. greenback. For the last few years, the American dollar has been worth between $1.25 and $1.35 Canadian.

The Canadian music scene parallels the one found in the States, but is different in some respects. Radio and TV are divided into the government and private sectors. The government portion is operated by CBC, the Canadian Broadcasting Company. Most of the major Canadian cities are fairly close to the United States border, so that many Canadians can readily watch American TV or listen to U.S., radio stations.

In comparing the two music scenes, there is some good news and some bad news for Canadians. The good news is that the Canadian government is friendlier to the arts than is the United States government. The Canada Council offers quite a few grant programs that offer support to the artist. Provincial programs are also available. To some extent, CBC provides an outlet for local musicians that few U.S. stations can match, and which goes beyond what support NET. or NPR offer in the United States.

In the "bad news department," for a number of years Canada has had much higher unemployment than is found stateside. The large distances between cities also make it much more difficult to tour in the United States. There is nothing that resembles the Boston-New York-Philadelphia-Baltimore-Washington, D.C. corridor of cities to support touring musicians.

Staying or Going

Canadian musical artists can follow four possible geographical scenarios in pursuing a professional music career. They are:

1. **Stay in Canada, rely on local support, and don't worry about exporting your music.** Try to play performances in the United States only if it makes geographic sense. In other words it's easy for a Toronto act to play in Buffalo, not so easy for any Canadian act to play in Florida or California.

2. **Move to the United States.** This is also known as "giving it up." In this plan the musician decides that since the big bucks are not available in Canada, it's easier to just pack up and leave.

3. **Go stateside to tour and perhaps, to record.** Take the money home and live in Canada.

4. **Stay in the U.S. long enough to establish a career.** Find someone to handle your business in the United States, build a reputation in the U.S., and then return home as an established act who expects to tour and record periodically in the United States.

Few Americans are apt to be familiar with artists who have adopted plan one, because these artists are rarely heard in the States. As in the United States, there are many local musicians who play bars, square dances, weddings, etc. The artist who stays home is in friendly territory and is able to build a stable base of support, and to add new territories with a minimum of discomfort. For example, such a musician might add a teaching or freelance playing opportunity to her normal gigs.

A small number of successful artists have relocated to the United States. Neil Young, Joni Mitchell and Shania Twain are conspicuous examples. There are also a few musicians who moved from the United States to Canada. Sometimes, this was an accident, sometimes a conscious choice. In the late 1960s, quite a few draft-age Americans fled to Canada to avoid military service in Viet Nam. Some of the Canadian musical artists who originally came from the U.S. include long-time rock-abilly star Ronnie Hawkins and children's artist Eric Nagler.

Some Canadians, like Ian Tyson and Sylvia Fricker, seem to have pursued a sort of dual residency before returning home to Canada.

The third group of musicians, the ones who have stayed in Canada but who aggressively pursued bi-national careers, include Anne Murray, Bryan Adams, Bruce Cockburn, Gordon Lightfoot, Rush, the Bare Naked Ladies and Sarah McLachlan. These artists use Canada as a base of support, but have been able to chalk up extensive record sales and to make considerable income from stateside tours. It is probably also true that their success in the states has validated these artists in Canada, and actually aided their Canadian careers.

There are three drawbacks for Canadian musicians who try to make it by moving to the States. First of all, the U.S. dollar is worth about $1.35 Canadian (it varies from day to day.) In other words, a Canadian musician who comes south with $1,000 Canadian that she has saved would find that she really only had about $650 in U.S. funds.

Both the U.S. and the Canadian Musicians' Unions make it a bit tough to work in each other's country—the U.S. Government has passed some odd and restrictive rulings that insist that a foreign musical artist needs to be "distinguished." What this usually translate to is that the group must have sufficient notoriety that the immigration people have heard of them.

Anyone who works in both the United States and Canada on a fairly regular basis is in the unfortunate position of having to pay double income tax. In other words, they must pay taxes in both countries.

What brings Canadian musicians south is the lure of a much larger pot of gold at the end of the rainbow. 100,000 albums represent a platinum sale in Canada, whereas 1,000,000 are required to achieve similar recognition in the States. Another lure is that most major Canadian labels won't sign an act unless their

American counterpart expresses interest. It's too difficult to make big money out of strictly Canadian sales—it's so much easier to make large sums of money by selling records in both countries. Under these circumstances, it is natural for Canadians to feel that if an American record company is really going to make the decision about their recording career, why not contact the companion at its home office, rather than through its Canadian affiliate?

It is not only artists that face these problems, but song-writers and record producers as well. Canadian writers Eddy Schwartz and Dan Hill live in Canada, but have achieved success through developing American publishing contacts. There are also several well-known Canadian record producers. Bruce Fairborn, who produced Loverboy and Bon Jovi lives in Canada; arranger-composer-producer David Foster lives in Los Angeles; and Daniel Lanois in New Orleans.

Government Aid

In addition to grant programs, there are several other government programs that are available to help Canadian artists and record companies. It all started with the Canadian Content Law, or CANCON. This rule requires that 30% of radio programming in Canada must go to records that have at least two out of four components that are Canadian. The components are the recording artist, the lyricist, the music composer and where the record was produced. In Quebec a similar rule requires that 65% of airplay be devoted to songs sung in French.

There is some controversy as to the real effects of CANCON. There are record companies that believe that any locally-produced Canadian record will almost automatically succeed because of CANCON. Since airplay does not guarantee sales and there are records, after all, that are competing for the 30% quota, this attitude seems to be highly exaggerated. Broadcasters sometimes complain that there aren't enough quality Canadian recordings to enable them to meet the quota, so they periodically request a reduction in a specific area of music, such as country music. In general, the government is reluctant to accept reduced quotas; it does on only on rare occasions.

Some of the Canadian record companies, particularly the smaller ones, openly admit that they would not be in business were it not for the stimulus supplied by CANCON. It has certainly made it easier to compete with product coming out of the United States.

FACTOR Awards

In 1981, the Canadian radio broadcast industry pooled its money in order to set up a fund designed to boost the recording of music in Canada. The funds are administered by the Canadian Independent Record Production Association (CIRPA). In 1987, the government announced that it would contribute $25,000,000 to the fund over the next five years. These contributions are made in each province and information about contacting FACTOR is available in the Resources Section at the end of this chapter. The budget varies from year to year.

There are a number of programs available through FACTOR. It funnels various monies through CIRPA, including a loan program for bands that want to make a CD. The band submits a demo and a precise budget that is judged by a group of music industry processionals. The funding may comprise up to 50% of the record's total budget and the loan must be paid back if the record makes money. If the album stiffs, the CIRPA writes off the loan.

Other programs assist artists in making demos. These grants pay for studio time and recording tape. Studio prices are standardized in this program, so that a band may get an unusually large amount of recording time from a high-class studio.

The costs of these FACTOR programs are split between the broadcasters and the government. The government also sponsors music videos, loans, and a Foreign Tour Loan program. The latter is designed for new groups going abroad who actually anticipate losing money on such a tour.

In her useful book, *Marketing Your Songs,* Valerie Mahonin points out that another government regulation in Canada provides that most radio stations are obligated to spend a certain amount of money on promoting Canadian talent. Some stations produce local entertainment or talent shows, and some sponsor compilation albums that feature local performers. If you are a Canadian, it is worth contacting local radio stations to see if they are involved in this program.

There is a regional agency in Vancouver assisting in the process of record distribution. The rationale is that the center of power, population and expertise is in Toronto, which is too far away to be of any help to the west coast province.

Telefilm is a federal fund set up to promote film production in Canada. The funds must be matched by other investors. The program requires a certain amount of Canadian creative involvement in the project, or the government will not offer support.

Currently, there is a large amount of "runaway" American television and film production in Toronto and Vancouver. The main reason for this is the favorable currency exchange. American TV producer-writer Stephen J. Cannell has a large facility in Vancouver and his company has trained a half dozen crews in Vancouver to do every aspect of television production. "The X-Files" is just one of a number of American television series shot in Vancouver.

The Canadian Record Market

Most of the music business mechanism in Canada is in Toronto, with Montreal providing the headquarters for music recorded in French. Since the province of Quebec is mostly French-speaking, the country is divided into two separate musical communities, despite its legislated bilingualism. The effect of the two cultures is that an already small market is further fragmented through linguistic and cultural differences.

This bilingual market marks the most obvious difference between the U.S. and Canadian music scenes. Rhythm and blues and black dance music represent a smaller market share in Canada, because of the smaller percentage of black population. Nevertheless Toronto does have an urban contemporary record scene.

One rather unusual and odd aspect of the record business in Canada is the success of the Canadian children's record market. The United States has a children's record market that falls into four general areas. One is TV programs like Sesame Street which features combinations of real people or cartoon characters or puppets; another is the MOR Disneyland sort of recordings that are old-style Hollywood film scores addressed as much to parents as to children. Another genre is a sort of Disney-ish version of rock and roll songs. These songs contain the same sort of musical and lyric hooks found in pop rock songs. The difference is that these tunes represent cartoon characters or television situations. Essentially they are simplified rock songs for younger audiences. The fourth style of American children's songs are recordings targeted primarily to teachers and music educators. Such artists and writers as Steve and Greg, Hap Palmer and Ella Jenkins sell mostly in the schools rather than directly to consumers

The Canadian children's market, on the other hand, is dominated by folksingers. Some of the popular artists include Raffi, a veritable Pied Piper of children's music; Sharon, Lois and Bram; and Fred Penner. Raffi has also achieved extraordinary success in the U.S. Consequently a number of American major and minor labels have tried their hand, with varying results, at children's music. The success of the Canadian artists has encouraged a sort of folk American children's genre, featuring artists like Cathy Fink and Marcy Marxer; Joe Scruggs; Tom Chapin and others.

Many of the successful Canadian performers have fueled their record sales by developing their own television shows. The Nickelodeon TV Network has picked up some of these shows in the United States.

Festivals

Another part of the Canadian music scene is the incredible summer festival circuit, which includes, Winnipeg, Vancouver and Edmonton, among many other, smaller venues. These giant folk festivals bring in talent from all over the world, as well as featuring local and Canadian artists. Thousands attend the performances, which include workshops on specific musical instruments and styles, craft displays, and folklife-oriented events. The Vancouver Folk Festival has even spawned its own record label and record distribution outlet, called Festival.

Performing Rights

Canada's performing rights organization is called SOCAN, the Society of, Composers, Authors and Music Publishers of Canada. It operates similarly to the way ASCAP and BMI work in the United States.

Canada has only about 600 radio stations, so that performance rights in Canada generate only a small percentage of what airplay produces in the United States. Canadian writers receive performance royalties for Canadian movie performances, a right that composers in the United States do not enjoy.

More Aspects of the Music Business in Canada

CARAS (Canadian Academy of Recording Arts & Sciences) is the Canadian equivalent of NARAS; the Juneau Awards correspond to the Grammy awards in the United States. Canadian Music week is an annual event help each March in Toronto, where A&R personnel, music publishers and other industry luminaries hold seminars and go to the local clubs to view performances of hundreds of Canadian artists and bands. Vancouver holds a similar event each year.

There are three cable TV music networks in Canada. "Music, Music" parallels MTV; "Musique Plus" is the French music television network in Quebec; and "CMT Canada" deals with country music. Quebecois music tends to be more MOR than the music found in the rest of Canada. The language barrier limits sales and prevents most of these records from crossing over to the English-speaking market. Celine Dion, who sings in English, is an international superstar.

We have already mentioned the phenomenal growth in the Canadian film and television business, largely an artifact of the cheaper (than U.S.) Canadian dollar.

Toronto and Vancouver have a number of trained film and television crews and post-production facilities. Because Vancouver has both mountain and ocean locations, it is particularly attractive to Hollywood producers. Besides the savings in dollars, producer Stephen J. Cannell, in an 1996 interview in the magazine *Variety on Production,* has pointed out that the Canadian unions are more willing to be flexible in re-working rules to fit the needs of a particular shoot. The dollar savings include everything from wages to hotel and food expenses. Cannell's facility in Vancouver was partly financed through loans from the Canadian government.

The Canadian music business has several pluses when compared to the scene in the States. First, there is government support through the CANCON laws, and government participation with the broadcasters in the FACTOR program. Secondly, there is an awareness of alternative music forms, and the willingness of the Canadian people to buy independently-produced albums in such areas as children's music. The big money is not readily available in Canada; which possibly accounts for a somewhat more open musical attitude in the music business itself.

CHAPTER 16 RESOURCES

A number of books, organizations and tradepapers are listed in the Appendices, but the single best resource on the Canadian music business is the biennial *Music Directory Canada,* published by Norris-Whitney Communications in Ontario. It has extensive lists of Canadian music business organizations, government agencies, radio stations, record companies, and virtually everything else you would want to know in researching the Canadian music business.

chapter 17

Songwriting Income

Every song that is recorded brings in income from a variety of sources. These revenue sources are usually called a "bundle of rights." Prior to 1914, songwriters and composers in the United States were not compensated for the performance of their music in public. They received most of their income from the sale of sheet music. At that time, records existed in the form of cylinders and generated relatively little income to writers or performers.

Composers and publishers became increasingly aware that although their music was performed in public, they did not receive any compensation for these performances. A group of composers and publishers established the American Society of Composers, Authors and Publishers, ASCAP, to collect these monies. This was done by licensing the performance of music in public places. Establishments using music paid flat fees to ASCAP, based upon the size of the venue and the annual budget for entertainment. When radio stations began to be licensed for the performance of music, they paid an annual fee based on the gross of their yearly advertising income.

Towards the end of the 1930s, ASCAP tried to raise these fees whereupon the broadcasters organized their own performing rights society, BMI (Broadcast

Music Incorporated), to compete with ASCAP. When BMI was formed, ASCAP was almost totally controlled by "Tin Pan Alley" songwriters and the people who wrote music for Broadway shows and films, as well as classical composers. BMI deliberately sought out country and blues writers, partly because they were denied entrance to ASCAP. When rock 'n' roll became a significant factor in the middle 1950s, BMI became a viable competitor to ASCAP. By this time SESAC, the Society for European Stage Authors and Composers, another much smaller performing rights organization had entered the picture. Unlike the other, non-profit organizations, SESAC was a privately held company.

Over the years, broadcasters fought with the performing rights organizations over the fees that they had to pay for performing rights. This percentage has varied from approximately 1% to 2% of the station's advertising gross. The broadcasters accused ASCAP and BMI of violating federal anti-trust regulations. As a result of many lawsuits ASCAP and BMI now operate under federal judicial decrees. The rates that they charge are adjusted in lengthy negotiations between the societies and the broadcasters, with the courts mediating or adjudicating the resulting fees.

Although the local broadcasters technically own BMI, it is a non-profit organization which in reality operates in a similar manner to ASCAP. Thus, BMI has found itself in court fighting against some of the very broadcasters who nominally own it.

Blanket and per Program Licenses

Most radio and television stations have blanket licenses, which means that they can play any songs they wish as often as they may choose. Stations that rarely play music buy per program licenses, which are proportionately more expensive, but still economically feasible if the station rarely programs music.

Legal Controversies

For years the media have been fighting to reduce or eliminate the system of blanket licensing. These fights have taken place in court, and in the U.S. Congress. It seems as though there is always legislation in Congress to change the licensing system. These attempts have varied from the broadcasters' seeking to license music directly from the composer to eliminating licensing fees for certain venues, such as small restaurants or beauty parlors. Currently any establishment that uses two speakers and broadcasts music for the entertainment of its customers must pay these fees. The single exception is record stores, which clearly aid in the sale of records and therefore bring in income to composers and music publishers.

Every time a new medium of transmission arises, such as cable TV or the Internet, new negotiations must take place to establish the rights of composers and publishers to their intellectual property. The broadcasters often use the new technologies to re-open the arguments as to the necessary payments for these rights. It is difficult to understand why anyone can rationally argue that intellectual property differs from any other sort of invention, trademark or copyright. The problem is that the media can enjoy substantial income from reducing or eliminating these fees.

Some Tips to Local Composers

If your music is used on local television or for commercials, you are entitled to synchronization fees. These are not set fees, as is the case for royalties on the sale of records (currently 6.95 cents per song, or 1.3 cents a minute, whichever is greater.) If you are writing music that is intended for local use only, it is advantageous for you to have your own music publishing company. Generally publishers and writers split income on a 50/50 basis. If you are seeking to get recordings of your songs by major artists, music publishers have the contacts and the ability to access these people. They can also license you songs for movies, TV shows, commercials, and sheet music.[1]

Common Fallacies

In the twenty some years I have been teaching and writing about the music business, I have constantly encountered several common, incorrect notions. First of all, there is some sort of word-of-mouth fantasy that has convinced musicians that they can copy up to four bars of music without penalty. There is nothing in the copyright law that says that you can copy *anything* without penalty. The law restricts "substantial similarity," and that word is defined in a court proceeding. It is a bad idea to assume that you can borrow *anything.* Another common error is the notion that you can mail a song to yourself and that that constitutes a valid copyright. Courts are unlikely to agree. An envelope could be steamed open, and changed to one with an earlier postmark. The cheapest way to copyright your songs is to make a tape of up to ten songs, and announce each title. Use form SR and send it to the Register of Copyrights at the Library of Congress. The cost is $20,

1. For further information, see my book *The Music Business: Career Opportunities & Self Defense, 2nd Revised Edition,* Three Rivers Press, 1997.

and the address is in the appendix. You will get a receipt back, and now there is a copy of your tape you can call on if anyone copies your song. The Copyright Office has a dated receipt that proves when that song was received. Now your songs are indeed safe. The SR form copyrights both the song and your performance of it. If you prefer to copyright songs individually, use form PA and write out a lead-sheet that contains the melody line, chorus and all lyrics.

In copyright suits, there are two fundamental elements which must be proved: similarity of the song in question, your song; and that author's ability to access your work. In most instances you must be able to prove that the author of the new work a some point heard your song.

CHAPTER 17 RESOURCES

An invaluable resource for accessing publishers is the annual *Songwriter's Market*, published by Writer's Digest. There are many books about songwriting and music publishing that are listed, along with comments about them, in Appendix D of this book.

chapter ▮18▮

Music and Technology Futures

NOTE: This chapter, until noted, was written by Ron Sobel, Vice President of ASCAP, Los Angeles, and an Adjunct Professor at California State/Pomona and the University of Colorado at Denver. From his vantage point in Los Angeles, Ron is in an ideal position to comment on the way that music will be transmitted in the 21st century.

The recent advances in computer, multimedia and internet technology, although revolutionizing most businesses, may be most profoundly felt in the entertainment industry. The changes that are radically and irrevocably altering the film, television and publishing industries are having a startling impact on the music business. New technologies are exploding old entertainment models, and transforming all aspects of music-from how works are written, financed, produced and distributed, to their ultimate enjoyment by the consumer.

We live in a highly evolutionary world-one where digitalization, deregulation and globalization are profoundly re-shaping the creative landscape. The transition from analog to digital, together with the popularity of the internet, has created a next-generation multimedia marketplace. Current technology allows for the master quality digital transmission and download of music over the Internet. For composers, musicians, and consumers of all genres of music from classical music to rap, we stand at an unprecedented threshold: the door is open for music to become the first major packaged product to make the legendary transition from atoms to bits. That's a scary concept to those with a heavy investment in atom-based technology. But for those of us who choose to embrace new technology, the next millennium can bring limitless opportunity. Whether you are a composer, teacher, player or listener, the tools and resources available to you today simply did not exist ten years ago. As we peer into the future, however, the next ten years promise to be even more dazzling and inventive. The opportunities available to the music community will stem not only from technology, but from innovation, creativity and perseverance. In a few years the Internet may have the same impact for emerging artists that radio and major record companies have today. Beyond the Internet, sheer ingenuity and inventiveness will create new opportunities for writers and artists in fields ranging from film to retail to urban architecture. Making demos at home and transmitting them around the world will be commonplace. Roll over Beethoven and tell Tchaikovsky he's being digitally downloaded, and cybercast to Uzbeckistan.

Short Term Technological Hurdles

Before we take the futurist plunge, there are three short-term technological hurdles that need to be addressed. Although there are significant promises and pitfalls to each of these innovations, the only remaining doubts about these no-brainers revolve around when they will be implemented, as opposed to whether they will be implemented.

Copyright Protection

The fundamental concern with the creative community is the protection and safeguarding of intellectual property in the digital world. Significant progress has been made in digital watermark technology-the process of placing an imperceptible, embedded fingerprint containing copyright information within the song or film itself. The watermark ensures royalty and licensing agreements are upheld by allowing decoders to monitor any broadcast of the song, whether on the Internet or the radio.[1] In addition to passive watermark safeguards, the industry has very recently cleared a major obstacle to the delivery of digital movies and music into consumers' homes, by agreeing on technology designed to protect content from illegal copying. The encryption technology will require a "digital handshake," or

---

1. SESAC has announced that it is currently implementing watermark technology. (DW)

"key," to be used between one device and another before a protected piece of work can be transferred.

Estimated time of implementation: 1–4 years

Electronic Commerce/E-Cash

In 1997, electric commerce accounted for $7 billion in business-to-business sales, and that number is expected to rise to $171 billion by the year 2000. On the business-to-consumer side, nearly $2.75 billion was transacted in 1997, and it is projected that by the year 2000, the number will be increase to about $10 billion.[2] Although the revenues for music sales on the Internet are only a fraction of these numbers, $40 million in sales in 1997, online sales are expected to hit $1.6 billion in four years, or 8% of total music sales.[3]

To make sure that these numbers rise as predict, companies need to assure their customers that no harm will come to them if they choose to make electronic purchases. Companies and online retailers will soothe jittery consumers by installing some basic security precautions such as forewalls and secure servers. To convince consumers, companies can use technologies that meet the Secure Electronic Transaction (SET) standard set in May, 1997. The SET mark, like a Good Housekeeping Seal of Approval for electronic commerce software-assures users that software on the site meets SET specifications and is therefore safe for online transactions.

Estimated time of implementation and acceptance: 1–3 years

Bandwidth

Much of the content that can be transmitted over the Internet, or any computer connection, is conditioned by the capacity of the connectors and the delivery systems. The larger the delivery "pipeline," the larger the amount of information that can flow through it per second. Together with the dramatic improvement in computing power of PCs, music and multimedia content is rapidly diffusing across a wide range of products available at affordable prices, and the pace of change is accelerating. Indeed, today's high-end PCs boast gains of nearly 40% in capacity and memory over last year's models. The transition to large capacity T-1 lines, and the eventual wireless transmission of multimedia content, will allow

---

2. The Yankee Group in Boston, an internet research group.
3. Jupiter Communications, an internet research group.

for routine real-time delivery of master quality digital music and video to desktop screens.

Estimated time of implementation: 2–4 years

Music on the Internet

Perhaps no greater tool exists to enhance the exposure, promotion and marketing of music than the Internet. Virtually all of the traditional barriers to new writers and new bands are eliminated through the various opportunities that are available on the Net.

Online Retailing

The near-impossible challenge of securing shelf space for an unsigned or indie label band at a traditional "brick and mortar" retail record store takes on wholly manageable proportions when dealing with online retailers. Without the need to physically carry CDs in stock-the inventory is owned and warehoused by third parties. Often the bands themselves hold the CD inventory until a sale is generated through the site. On-line sites are able to offer audio samples, simple search mechanisms, bio info on the artists, articles, and a much larger inventory than traditional record stores. CDNOW (CDNOW.COM) offers 250,000 CD titles, while N2K (MUSICBLVD.COM) offers 300,000 titles. Sales of CDs from N2K, CDNOW and TOWERRECORDS. COM averaged between $5 million and $12 million each in 1997.[4]

Web Pages

The World Wide Web—that section of the Internet that offers easy access to text, graphics, sound and other multimedia resources—can also be the source of worldwide exposure for a local or major recording act. Whether on a home-made Web page created for a single band or as part of a larger web site featuring many different bands, Web pages have grown to be an affordable means of promoting a music project. Sites such as IUMA.COM include band photos, bios and audio samples for hundreds of local bands. TOURDATES.COM lists upcoming tour schedules for local bands according to geographical location, genre of music., biographical information or the music itself, all with simple searches of any of the several web sites now available that provide such listings. Other recommended sites includes

---

3. Jupiter Communications, an internet research group.

ARTISTDIRECT.COM, The Ultimate Band List (UBL.COM), Kaleidospace (KSPACE.COM) and BILLBOARD TALENT.COM.

Internet Cybercasts

Whether live or pre-recorded, the Net is increasingly being used to broadcast music concerts and interviews of well-known and unknown artists. Many traditional radio stations are now simulcasting their programming on the Net, while many of the 2800 new internet "radio stations" (SONICNET.COM, JAMTV.COM, THEDJ.COM) can deliver multiple channel options of various kinds of music. Internet radio can display song and artist information as music is played, provide links enabling online purchases of songs being played, and allow for real-time listener feedback and chats. Other recommended sites include AUDIONET.COM.

Greenhouse Channels

As the graphics, sound and video elements of the Net move towards convergence with television, the drive to create a new genre of entertainment programming on the Internet is emerging. The notion that interactive, online variety shows featuring a mix of movie reviews, celebrity interviews, stand-up comedy and music can evolve into major leisure time attractions is fueling the creation of hundreds of show-business-oriented web sites. established entertainment sites such as Mr. Showbiz (MRSHOWBIZ.COM) and E!Online (EONLINE.COM) are facing competition from next-generation "greenhouse channels," such as ASYLUM.COM, and MUSICOSM.COM. These channels add enhanced personality, with news from local music scenes, performances of demo tapes by unsigned bands, and opportunities to participate and interact with music industry executives. The increasing emergence of these Internet channels will provide yet another vehicle for regional bands and composers to promote their music.

The Evolution of Traditional Music Distribution

The fact that the Net is rapidly becoming a visible means of ordering CDs and promoting new music is only half of the Internet story.

The potential of the Net to deliver digital copies of musical works, downloadable to your own hard drive or recordable CD, represents the most significant change in the manufacturing and distribution of recorded music. Indeed, once the short-term technological hurdles have been overcome, we are only a few small audio tweaks away from routinely ordering and receiving instantaneous digital copies of music works in our homes. We will be able to download the music to whatever source we choose, and access it on demand. This phenomenon, whereby the physical atom-based packaged product called CDs can be replaced by the bit-based download of "data," harbors enormous implications for those businesses who manufacture traditional CDs and ship them to retail stores. Ultimately, the retail stores themselves will be dramatically effected. The transition means, simply, that we will need fewer manufacturing plants, use less natural resources, need fewer trucks and less fuel to ship product, and we will need fewer and smaller "brick and mortar" retail record stores to warehouse and display CDs. The cost savings to consumers can be significant. Fully 65% of the price of today's CDs are attributed to costs that disappear with a digital download. Some folks may prefer, in 2004, to take the time to drive to their local record store and pay $15.99 for a CD. Others, I assume, will prefer to stay at home and download the same music for $5.[5]

Beyond the Internet

Notwithstanding the breadth of opportunity that the Internet presents for the music community, there are equally diverse innovations occurring in music beyond the Net. For both the established and emerging musician, the retail, leisure and film industries are in a process of revolutionizing their retailing concepts, and are embracing broader and deeper uses of music to attract and retain customers.

The Store Strikes Back: Retail's Revenge

The retail store, facing competitive challenges from catalogs, the Home Shopping Network, and the Internet was expected to roll over and play dead. What happened? Instead of convenience, retail had to give shoppers the one element that technology could not replace-a grander, bigger, more exhilarating experience, beyond mere service. It needed to provide services that the customer could not get at home. Indeed, inventive retailers have come to embrace the very tools of audio-visual, multimedia technology that nearly threatened their existence. From Times Square to Niketown, the music and entertainment have become the touchstone of new retailing. From wide-screen music videos to pre-recorded background

---

5. In July of 1997, N2K started selling digital download of singles for 99 cents. The music can be downloaded from Liquid Audio, encryption keys and watermark technology from Solana Technology Development.

music to live bands and performers, the entertainment/experiential component of retailing has never been more important. The opportunities for inventive musicians will grow.

Themed Environments

Themed restaurants—those that mix food with music and entertainment—are attracting more visitors and tend to be more profitable than non-theme dining establishments. According to a 1998 *Los Angeles Times* article, the average restaurant generates annual revenue of $500,000 to $1 million. Annual sales at theme restaurants range from $4 million to $14 million.

Hard Rock Cafe, Planet Hollywood, Marvelmania and Quark's Bar & Restaurant at "Star Trek: The Experience" in Las Vegas, are the pioneers of restaurant ventures that have brought music from the background to the foreground. The trend to utilize entertainment and music-driven multimedia in restaurants will continue to provide new outlets for the innovative music maker.

Desktop Filmmaking

In an era of monstrous feature film budgets and costly post-production, today's desktop PC allows for the use of affordable graphics programs, including over-the-counter editing and image processing software, to create finished films for less than $25,000. These more affordable methods of making films will generate not only more films, but the need for more music in films. In much the same way that indie record labels and grassroots distribution allowed more bands to make records, the desktop PC will allow for more films and music to lead a grassroots film distribution market into tours of colleges and small art theaters.

Architectural Entertainment

In the drive to give people more reason to leave their homes, city planners, developers and architects are embracing a new discipline: experiential design. The Fremont Street Experience, for example, in downtown Las Vegas, attracts 25,000 visitors nightly to a computer-generated animation and music show projected on a screen topping the four acre complex. Two million lights and 540,000 watts of sound make up the world's largest graphics display system. Coupled with projects that are taking cinema out of the theater and into "entertainment environments"—projecting movies outdoors on the side of 10 story buildings, in theme parks, warehouses, casinos and 360 degree circular theaters—music will be an integral part of next-millennium urban culture.

Final Thoughts by Dick Weissman

In the first portion of this chapter, Ron Sobel has presented a sketch of how the future will look to aspiring musicians, composers, record companies, retail stores and consumers. A single issue of *Billboard,* on February 28, 1998, had stories about an Internet label called J-Bird, and Putamayo, a world music label, adopting innovative marketing techniques by tie-ins with a coffee retailer. A friend of mine had his ATM machine ask if he wanted to order any CDs. These things are happening *now.*

The purpose of this book is to provide a practical guide to working in local and regional music scenes. If you have read through the book, then you have developed a reasonably good idea of the differences between working in a major music market and pursuing a career in a secondary market, or even one that hasn't yet developed. This means that you should learn as much as you can about what goes on in every aspect of the music and music-related community. Investigate freelance work, recording studios, booking agents, songwriters' organizations, music schools and stores, and any available grant programs. Even if the bulk of your musical time and energy is taken up with a specific performing group, it is important for you to do some freelancing.

Look at your musical talent as being in a state of evolution, no matter what your age. Whatever you are doing now, you should be able to look forward to improving and polishing your musical skills, as well as expanding the sort of music that you can perform and understand. This may mean studying with a local teacher, or on your own. If you do take classes or lessons, approach your teachers with enthusiasm, but don't hesitate to question or challenge them.

Try to approach long-range commitments to jobs or performing groups by projecting the situation five years into the future. How will accepting this particular opportunity advance your musical goals? We all go through phases where we take musical jobs that may not fulfill our deepest desires or talents, but if this keeps happening to you, there is either something wrong with the breadth of your music business contacts, or, frankly, you are allowing yourself to settle into a musical rut. If you lock yourself into a very specific musical style or approach, your employment opportunities may evaporate when that music loses favor with the public. You need to do what you want, but you also need to be realistic about your professional opportunities. This sort of approach may make you move to a different town, but it shouldn't necessarily be one of the North American "Big 4" music markets.

Remember, this is the music *business.* Treat it like a business endeavor. Buy the type of musical instrument that will assist in advancing your career and your musical skills. Keep adequate tax records in order to avoid unpleasant surprises from your friends at Internal Revenue. If you make a long term commitment to a musical group, make sure there's room for musical give-and-take from all the people involved.

By this time, you should have a good understanding of the basics. You need a good demo and a press kit. You need some good pictures of your group, and a demo that looks and sounds good. With these tools at your command, you should be able to find a decent local agent, or, if need be, do the booking yourself.

Unless you know how to get excited about selling your act in the same way that music excites you, you will need to find one or more booking agents. If they can't get you more money than you can get yourself, you should not utilize their services.

Investigate working in more than one group, or both as a soloist and in a group. This will expand your possibilities of employment. It is much easier to get a grant if you work alone, because grant monies are generally limited. Try your hand at songwriting, arranging, composing, and developing a home studio. With today's technology a home studio has become increasingly affordable. Learn how to play new instruments, or develop new techniques on the instruments that you are already playing.

Consider supplementing your income by teaching. Balance your teaching hours with your writing and playing time, unless you find that teaching is the most fulfilling area of music for you.

Contact your local recording studios and try to get work as a studio musician or singer. Developing good studio skills will help you in your own songwriting and arranging, and can provide an excellent source of income, irregular as it may be.

Get involved in any music organizations that you can. Your Union Local can assist you in getting jobs; it can help with instrument insurance; and can assist you in joining a medical plan. Get involved in your Union Local—go to meetings and make your voice heard. Vote in elections and stand up for what you believe in.

The same holds true if there is a songwriters' organization in your community. You can use it to find collaborators, and to get feedback on your work.

If you set up a home studio, try to get some work writing jingles or background scores for local industrial films or slide shows. If the studio develops a reputation, consider renting it out to other musicians or composers. If you start to do much jingle or film work, be sure to be paid creative fees and to file union contracts. Contact local advertising agencies, film producers and editors to find additional work.

If your band wants to make a CD, develop a mailing list to build a solid base of local support. Consider making and distributing your own record, and use your existing fans as a starting point. Look into developing a web page and selling your product on the Internet. If your recording gets some reviews, add them to your press kit. Raise your performance price, as the demand for your group grows. While you're at it, consider making a video, particularly if your union local, local college or cable TV outlet provides you with the possibility of doing one free of charge.

If your goal is to build a national reputation, pursue the possibility of finding a personal manager in a major music market. You can develop songwriting contacts by making an occasional trip to a major city, and establishing an on-going relationship that builds through mail, faxes and phone calls. Don't get discouraged by rejection. Stay in there and keep pitching. A career is measured in years, not months. Every record company in England turned down the Beatles, until they met George Martin. Behind most overnight successes are long-term struggles.

If you are truly serious about developing a national career, you will need to spend some time in a major music center in order to find a heavyweight personal manager, a national booking agent, a big-time entertainment lawyer and a recording deal. You may, at that time, want to consider the possibility of staying there. Be aware of the trade-offs. The competition is much stiffer, and you will probably face several really tough years of establishing yourself in a new and often strange place. Remember, you can always go to a major market and return home at a later time. The important thing is to honestly evaluate your career in terms of the way your musical and business goals are unfolding.

Another alternative may be to move in the opposite direction and channel your musical activities into part-time work. Many part-time musicians are content with playing occasional jobs, without the full-time commitment or the insecurity that a full-time musical career may bring. You may possess extraordinary musical skills, but they may be unsuited for the sort of music that is lucrative where you happen to live. The issues of staying or going, and working part-time or full-time are all choices that you must make for yourself. It's your life, and you have the ability to change it.

Get involved in developing your regional music scene into a powerful one. Use the examples cited in this book, and apply them to your locale. Encourage your Union Local, your city government, local songwriting organization, and even business groups to participate in developing a local music scene through their financial support and media coverage. The more musical opportunities that develop in your market, the better your chance at getting a piece of the musical and financial pie. Don't bad-mouth other musical groups: try to support them in their own struggles. If anyone experiences success in your musical community, it can only help the other people in the community.

Above all, avoid whining. Musicians have many opportunities to support themselves through their music. Imagine being a dancer whose low-paying career is about over at the age of 35. For every Tom Cruise or Julia Roberts there are thousands of unemployed actors. Artists pay 40–50% of their gross to galleries, and are responsible for their own framing costs and the cost of materials.[6] I have known many, many musicians who are unknown to the general public, but are able to generate reasonable incomes and long-term careers. It isn't easy, but there are probably more musicians leading a "middle class" lifestyle than can be found in any of the other art-related professions.

If you live in Canada, you have many of the same choices. Staying or going may mean staying in Canada or going to the States to access the more lucrative opportunities. Whatever you do, become aware of the governmental grants available and the FACTOR programs that provide a source of assistance to Canadian musicians.

If you write songs or instrumental music, you will need to join a performing rights organization. Join the one where you feel the most rapport and support in terms of developing contacts with publishers and record companies.

There is much promise in the new musical technologies and delivery systems for music. Keep up with technology, but try to make it work for you, not the other way around. Before you buy equipment, decide what fit your musical style and preference, what is economically feasible for you to purchase, and what will be outmoded in six months.

---

6. Some New York galleries are now demanding 60% of the gross!

The Appendices of this book are designed to serve as a tour guide for your trip through the world of the music industry. Consult it from time to time as your goals and needs shift.

Whatever happens, don't lose your enthusiasm or your sense of humor. Retain some objectivity while looking at the business and your own career. You'll need all of these qualities, plus some luck to survive and get what you want. Keep your ears open. I wish you the best of luck.

CHAPTER 18 RESOURCES

The best way to keep up with current and future developments is to read as many music-related periodicals as you can. The Sunday editions of the *New York Times* and the *Los Angeles Times* often have articles about new developments in the entertainment industry.

Books necessarily become dated very quickly in a world of rapid change. Remember that it takes six months to a year to produce a book. Often a writer has done the research over a much longer period of time. You may be reading a 1999 book that contains information researched in 1992!

Books about music on the Internet started to appear in the mid-'90s. One reference is Brad Hill's *The Virtual Musician: A Complete Guide to Online Resources and Services.* Published by Schirmer Books in 1996, it contains a CD-ROM.

Afterword:

The Global Marketplace

I n November 1997, I did a one week teaching residency at the Liverpool Institute For Performing Arts in England. This is a school of performing arts that was literally built in Paul McCartney's primary school, with McCartney himself providing some seed money and enlisting some of his friends and associates to assist in establishing a school for the 21st century. The students come from all over the world, but particularly from various countries of Europe. The technical facilities are marvelous, and go far beyond what any college could afford. To me, that isn't what the school is all about. The atmosphere is somewhat chaotic, but dynamic and interesting. Everywhere there are dancers, singers, musicians, actors, and would-be entrepreneurs learning and practicing their craft in a college setting, but not the sort of college setting that typically governs a college performing arts program. Yet this *is* a college, with three sets of programs. There is a college degree program (three years in England), a one year certificate program, and an evening program. The evening program is designed for local residents, most of them in bands. It isn't so hard to imagine a young, possibly wiser, McCartney emerging from this program.

During the last ten to twenty years, we have seen the American share of the world record market go from about 60% to 30%. This is not because record sales are down in the United States, but because Asia, South America, and other territories are starting to sell CDs in quantity. Imagine what will happen as China and India become important factors in the world record market. It isn't difficult to see the American share of the record business become half of what it is today by the middle of the 21st century.

While this process has been going on, the ownership of the major record and film countries has become increasingly international. As we discussed early in this book, the Warner Record Group is now the only American-owned record company. How will this shift of ownership and market share transform the world record business?

America is one of the few countries in the world where young people don't quickly learn one, two or three foreign languages. For years, the entertainment business has been rooted in the English language. In most other parts of the world, a large portion of the population is reasonably fluent in two or three languages.

Sooner or later there will be a super-group made up of representatives from three or four continents. They will speak and sing in four or more languages, and the demand for them will truly be global. They will be welcomed in all parts of the world because they are representative of people from all over the world. They will from different cultures and be of different colors. Once a group like this exists, there will be many others that will copy this approach.

Other seemingly inevitable developments in the music industry will involve a much more creative utilization of music video. The music and the video will complement one another and yet may lead artistically in different directions. This will overcome the typical over-simplification of music videos, which often fall into dull stereotypes.

Just as Ron Sobel has explained how music retailing and distribution will change dramatically, so will the art of performance. As the world of technology shrinks the geographic world, the art and style of performance will inevitably change. If it doesn't, people will have no more desire to go to live performances than they will to go to retail record stores. The art of performance must evolve as dramatically as the methods of music merchandising, or there will be no reason for people to buy tickets.

Part of this change will be the integration of regional and territorial music styles into the overall universe of popular music. Another part will be the integration of dance, theater and music into what we have historically called music performance. More than ever, people will be seeking meaningful if broader-based experiences when they listen to music. It's a difficult time, an evolutionary time, but an exciting time. With vision and planning it can be *your* time.

appendix  a

Organizations

State Arts Councils

Alabama State Council on the Arts
1 Dexter Ave.
Montgomery, AL 36150-1800
334/242-4076

Alaska State Council on the Arts
411 W. 4th Ave., Suite 1E
Anchorage, AK 99501
907/269-6610

American Samoa Arts Council
PO Box 1540
Pago, Pago AS 96799
0116846334347

Arizona Commission on the Arts
411 W. Roosevelt Ave.
Phoenix, AZ 85003
602/255-5882

Arkansas Arts Council
1500 Tower Bldg. 323 Center Street
Little Rock, AK 72001
501/324-9766

California Arts Council
1300 I St., Suite 930
Sacramento, CA 95814
916/322-6555

Colorado Council on the Arts
750 Pennsylvania St.
Denver, CO 80203-3699
303/894-2617

Connecticut Commission on the Arts
755 Main St.
Hartford, CT 06103
860/566-4770

Delaware Division of the Arts
820 N. French St.
Wilmington, DE 19801
302/577-3540

District of Columbia Commission on the Arts and Humanities
410 8th St. NW, 5th Floor
Washington, DC 20004
202/724-5613

Florida Division of Cultural Affairs
Dept. of State, The Capitol
Tallahasse, FL 32399-0250
904/484-2980

Guam Council on the Arts & Humanities
PO Box 2950
Agana, GU 96910
0116716472242

Hawaii State Foundation
44 Merchant St.
Honolulu, HI 96813
808/586-0306

Idaho Commission on the Arts
PO Box 83720
Boise, ID 93720-0008
208/334-2119

Illinois Arts Council
State of Illinois Center
100 W. Randolph St., #10-500
Chicago, IL 60601
312/814-6750

Indiana Arts Commission
402 W. Washington St., #072
Indianapolis, IN 46204
317/232-1268

Iowa Arts Council
State Capitol Complex
600 E. Locust St.
Des Moines, IA 50319
515/281-4451

Kansas Arts Commission
700 SW Jackson, Suite 1004
Topeka, KS 66603
913/296-3335

Kentucky Arts Council
31 Fountain Place
Frankfort, KY 40601
502/564-3757

Louisiana Division of the Arts
PO Box 44247
Baton Rouge, LA 70804
504/342-8180

Maine Arts Commission
55 Capitol St.
State House, Station 25
Augusta, ME 04333
207/287-2724

Maryland State Arts Council
601 N. Howard St., 1st Floor
Baltimore, MD 21201
410/333-8232

Massachusetts Cultural Council
120 Boylston St., 2nd Floor
Boston, MA 02116-4600
800/232-0960

Michigan Council for the Arts
1200 6th Ave., Executive Plaza
Detroit, MI 48226-2461
313/256-3731

Minnesota State Arts Board
Park Square Court
400 Sibley S., Suite 200
Saint Paul, MN 55101-1949
800/866-2787

Mississippi Arts Commission
239 N. Lamar St., 2nd Floor
Jackson, MS 39201
601/359-6030

Missouri Arts Council
111 N. 7th St., Suite 105
St. Louis, MO 63101
314/340-6845

Montana Arts Council
PO Box 202201
316 North Park Ave., Rm. 252
Helena, MT 59620
406/444-6430

Nebraska Arts Council
3838 Davenport
Omaha, NE 68131-2329
402/595-2122

Nevada State Council on the Arts
602 N. Curry St.
Carson City, NV 89710
702/687-6680

New Hampshire State Council on the Arts
40 N. Main St., Phenix Hall
Concord, NH 03301
603/271-2789

New Jersey State Council on the Arts
20 W. State St., 3rd Floor, CN 306
Trenton, NJ 08625-0306
609/292-6130

New Mexico Arts Division
228 E. Palace Ave.
Santa Fe, NM 87501
505/827-6490

New York State Council on the Arts
915 Broadway
New York, NY 10010
212/387-7000
North Carolina Arts Council
Dept. of Cultural Resources
Raleigh, NC 27611
919/733-2821

North Dakota Council on the Arts
418 E. Broadway, Suite 70
Bismarck, ND 58501-4086
701/328-3954

Commonwealth Council for Arts Northern Mariana Islands
PO Box 5553 CHRB
0116703229982

Ohio Arts Council
722 E. Main St.
Columbus, OH 43205
614/466-2613

State Arts Council of Oklahoma
PO Box 52001-2002, Jim Thorpe Bldg.
Oklahoma City, OK 73152-2001
405/521-2931

Oregon Arts Commission
775 Summer St. NE
Salem, OR 97310
503/986-0082

Pennsylvania Council on the Arts
216 Finance Bldg.
Harrisburg, PA 17120
717/787-6883

Institute of Puerto Rican Culture, Arts
PO Box 4184
San Juan, PR 00905-4184
809/723-2115

Rhode Island State Council. on the Arts
95 Cedar St., D Suite 103
Providence, RI 02903-1024
401/277-3880

South Carolina Arts Commission
1800 Gervais St.
Columbia, SC 29201
803/734-8696

South Dakota Arts Council
Office of Arts, 800 Governor Drive
Pierre, SD 57101-2294
605/773-3131

Tennesse Arts Commission
404 James Robertson Parkway, Ste. 160
Nashville, TN 37243-0708
615/741-1701

Texas Commission on the Arts
PO Box 13406, Capitol Station
Austin, TX 78711
512/463-5535

Utah Arts Council
617 E. South Temple St.
Salt Lake City, UT 84102
801/533-5895

Vermont Council on the Arts
136 State St., Drawer 33
Montpelier, VT 05633-6001
802/828-3291

Virgin Islands Council on the Arts
PO Box 103, 41-42 Norre Gade
St. Thomas, VI 00804
802/774-5984

Virginia Commission for the Arts
223 Governor St.
Richmond, VA 23219
804/225-3132

Washington State Arts Commission
P.O. Box 42675, 234 E. 8th Ave.
Olympia, WA. 98504-2775
360/753-3860

West Virginia Department of Culture & History
1900 Kanawha Blvd. East
Cultural Center
Charleston, WV 23303
304/558-0240

Wisconsin Arts Board
101 E. Wilson St., 1st Floor
Madison, WI 53702
608/266-0190

Wyoming Arts Council
320 Capitol Ave.
Cheyenne., WY 82002
307/777-7742

Regional Arts Councils

Arts Midwest
101 E. Wilson St., 1st Floor
Madison, WI 53702
608/266-0190

Consortium for Pacific Arts & Cultures
2141-C Atherton Rd.
Honolulu, HI 96822
808/946-7381

Mid America Arts Alliance
912 Baltimore Ave., Ste. 700
Kansas City, MO 64105
816/421-1388

Mid Atlantic Arts Foundation
11 E. Chase St., Ste. 2A
Baltimore, MD 21202
410/539-6656

New England Foundation for the Arts
330 Congress St., 6th Floor
Boston, MA 02139
617/951-0010

Southern Arts Federation
81 14th St., NE, Ste. 400
Atlanta, GA 30309-7603
404/874-7244

Western States Arts Foundation
236 Montezuma Ave.
Santa Fe, NM 87501
505/988-1166

Canadian Arts Councils

Alberta Provincial Government
1004 104th Ave., 11th Floor, CN Tower
Edmonton, Alb. T5J OK5

B.C. Touring
Council for the Performing Arts
518 Beatty St., #103
Vancouver, BC V8B 2L3

British Columbia Ministry of Tourism, Recreation and Culture
Cultural Services Branch
Legislative Bldgs.
Victoria, BC V8V 1X4

Manitoba Arts Council
525-93 Lombard Ave.
Winnipeg, MN R3B 3B1

New Brunswick Department of Tourism, Recreation and Culture
Cultural Developent Branch
P.O. Box 12345
Frederickton, NB E3B 5C3

Newfoundland Department of Culture, Recreation and Youth
Project Grants
P.O. Box 5011
For sound recording loans, new talent demo awards and international tour support:

Nova Scotia Performing Arts Policies
Dept. of Culture, Recreation and Fitness
P.O. Box 864
Halifax, NS B3J 2V2

Ontario Arts Council
151 Bloor St. W., #500
Toronto, ON M5S 1T6

Prince Edward Island Council for the Arts
P.O. Box 2234
Charlottetown, PE C1A 8B9

Saskatchewan Arts Board
2240 Broad St.
Regina, SK S4P 3V7

Organization of Saskatchewan Arts Councils
4000 Pasqua St., #600
Regina, SK S4A 2H7

Foundation to Assist Canadian Talent on Record (Factor)
146 Front St., W., #355
Toronto, ON M5J 2L7
For sound recording loans, new talent demo awards and international tour support.

Video FACT Video Foundation to Assist Canadian Talent
151 John St., #301
Toronto, ON M5B 2T2
For similar video project support

State Humanities Councils

Alabama Humanities Foundation
2217 Tenth Court South
Birmingham, AL 35205
205/930-0540

Alaska Humanities Forum
421 W. 1st Ave., Ste. 210
Anchorage, AK 99501
907/272-5341

Arizona Humanities Council
Ellis-Shackelford House
242 N. Central Ave.
Phoenix, AZ 85004
602/257-0335

California Council for the Humanities
312 Sutter, Ste. 601
San Francisco, CA 94108
415/391-1474

and 315 W. 9th St., Ste. 702
Los Angeles, CA 90015
213/623-5993
and 614 Fifth St., Ste. C
San Diego, CA 92101
619/232-4020

Colorado Endowment for the Humanities
1623 Blake St., Ste. 200
Denver, CO 80202
303/573-7733

Connecticut Humanities Council
41 Lawn St., Wesleyan Station
Middletown, CT 06457
203/685-2260

Delaware Humanities Forum
1812 Newport Gap Pike
Wilmington, DE 19808-6179
302/633-2400

D.C. Community Humanities Council
1331 H St., NW Ste. 902
Washington, DC 20005
202/347-1732

Florida Humanities Council
1514 1/2 East Eighth Ave.
Tampa, FL 33605-3708
813/272-3473

Georgia Humanities Council
50 Hurt Plaza, SE, Se. 440
Atlanta, GA 30303-2936
404/523-6220

Guam Humanities Council
Renaissance Plaza, Ste. 2A
272 West Route 8
Barrigada, Guam 96913
011-671-734-1713/4

Hawaii Comm. for the Humanities.
First Hawaiian Bank Bldg.
3599 Wai'alae Ave., Rm. 23
Honolulu, HI 96816
808/732-5402

Idaho Humanities Council
217 West State St.
Boise, ID 83702
208/345-5346

Illinois Humanities Council
203 N. Wabash Ave., Ste. 2020
Chicago, IL 60601-2417
312/422-5580

Indiana Humanities Council
1500 N. Delaware St.
Indianapolis, IN 46202
317/638-1500

Iowa Humanities Board
100 Oakdale Campus, N210 OH
Iowa City, IA 52242-5000
319/335-4153

Kansas Humanities Council
112 West Sixth St., Ste. 210
Topeka, KS 66603
913/357-0359

Kentucky Humanities Council
P.O. Box 4449
Lexington, KY 40544-4449
606/257-5932

Louisiana Endowment for the Humanities
The Ten-O-One Bldg.
1001 Howard Ave., Ste. 3110
New Orleans, LA 70113
504/523-4352

Maine Humanities Council
P.O. Box 7202
Portland, ME 04112
207/773-5051

Maryland Humanities Council
601 N. Howard St.
Baltimore, MD 21201-4585
410/625-4830

Massachusetts Foundation for the Humanities
6 Temple Place, 4th Floor
Boston, MA 02111-1366
617/451-9021

Michigan Humanities Council
119 Pere Marquette Dr., Ste. 3B
Lansing, MI 48912-1270
517/372-7770

and c/o Detroit Public Library
5201 Woodward Ave., Fourth Floor
Detroit, MI 48202-4093
313/993-7770
and E4624 Highway, M-35
19 Pillsbury St., PO Box 2228
Escanaba, MI 49829
906/789-9471

Minnesota Humanities Commission
26 E. Exchange St.
St. Paul, MN 55101
612/224-5739

Mississippi Humanities Council
3825 Ridgewood Rd., Rm. 311
Jackson, MS 39211-6453
1001 Howard Ave., Ste. 3110
601/982-6752

Missouri Humanities Council
922 Washington Ave., Ste. 215
St. Louis, MO 63101-1208
 314/621-7705

**Montana Commission for the
Humanities**
P.O. Box 8036, Hellgate Station
Missoula, MT 59807
406/243-6022

Nebraska Humanities Council
Lincoln Center Bldg., #225
215 Centennial Mall South
Lincoln, NE 68508
402/474-2131

Nevada Humanities Committee
1034 N. Sierra St.
Reno, NV 89503
702/787-6587, 800/382-5023

**New England Foundation for
Humanities**
46 Temple Place, 4th Flr.
Boston, MA 02111-1306

New Hampshire Humanities Council
19 Pillsbury St.
P.O. Box 2228
Concord, NH 03302-2228
603/224-4071

**New Jersey Council for the
Humanities**
28 W. State St., Sixth Floor
Trenton, NJ 08608
609/695-4838

**New Mexico Endowment for the
Humanities**
209 Onate Hall
Corner of Campus & Girard NE
Albuqerque, NM 87131
505/277-3705

New York Council for the Humanities
198 Broadway, 10th Floor
New York, NY 10038
212/233-1131

North Carolina Humanities Council
425 Spring Garden St.
Greensboro, NC 27401
910/334-5325

North Dakota Humanities Council
P.O. Box 2191
Bismarck, ND 58502
701/255-3360

Commonwealth of the Northern Mariana Islands Council. for the Humanities
AAA 3394 Box 10001
Saipan, MP 96950
670/235-4785

Ohio Humanities Council
695 Bryden Rd, P.O.Box 06354
Columbus, OH 43206-0354
614/461-7802

Oklahoma Foundation for the Humanities
Festival Plaza, 428 California St., Ste. 270
Oklahoma City, OK. 73102
405/2365-0280

Oregon Council for the Humanities
812 SW Washington, Ste. 225
Portland, OR 97205
503/241-0543

Pennsylvania Humanities Council
320 Walnut St., #305
Philadelphia, PA 19106
215/925-1005

Fundacion Puerto Riquena de las Humanidades
Apartado Postal S-4307
San Juan de Puerto Rico 00902
809/721-2087
and Bacon House Mews
606 18th St., NW, 2nd Floor
Washington, DC 20006
202/371-8111

Rhode Island Commission for the Humanities
60 Ship St.
Providence, RI 02903
401/273-2250

South Carolina Humanities Council
P.O. Box 5287, 1200
Catawba St., Columbia, SC 29250
803/771-8864

South Dakota Humanities Council
Box 7050, University Station
Brookings, SD 67007
605/688-6113

Tennessee Humanities Council
1003 18th Ave. South
Nashville, TN 37212
615/320-7001

Texas Commission for the Humanities
3809 S. Second St.
Austin, TX 78704
512/440-1991

Utah Humanities Council
350 South 400 East, Ste. 110
Salt Lake City, UT 84111-2946
801/359-9670

Vermont Council on the Humanities
17 Park St., R.R. 1 Box
7285, Morrisivlle, VT 0566
802/888-3183

Virgin Islands Humanities Council
P.O.Box 1829
St. Thomas, VI 00803
809/776-4044

Virginia Foundation for the Humanities
145 Ednam Drive
Charlottesville, VA 22903
804/924-3296

Washington Commission for the Humanities
615 Second Ave., Ste. 300
Seattle, WA 98104
206/682-1770

Wisconsin Humanities Council
802 Regent St.
Madison, EWI 53715-2610
608/262-0706

West Virginia Humanities Council
723 Kanawha Blvd., Se. 800
Charleston, WV 25301
304/346-8500

Wyoming Council. for the Humanities
P.O. Box 3643
Laramie, WY 82071-3643
307/766-6496

Young Audiences

Nat'l. Office-Young Audiences, Inc.
115 E. 92nd St.
New York, NY 10128
212/831-8110

Santa Cruz County
190 E. Adams St.
Nogales, AZ 85621

Southern Arizona
P.O. Box 43606
Tucson, AZ 85733

Kern County
P.O. Box 9983
Bakersfield, CA 93389

San Diego
1549 El Prado St., Ste. 14
Balboa Park
San Diego, CA 92101

Bay Area
1182 Market St., Ste. 310
San Francisco, CA 94102

San Jose
1211 Park Ave., Ste. 203
San Jose, CA 95126

Colorado
P.O. Box 205, Loretta Station
3001 South Federal Blvd.
Denver, CO 80236-2711

Connecticut
254 College St., Ste. 406
New Haven, CT 06510-2403

District of Columbia
1200 29th St. NW, Lower Level
Washington, DC 20007

Georgia
P.O. Box 420195
Atlanta, GA 30342

Indiana
3050 North Meridian St.
Indianapolis, IN 46208

Louisiana
234 Loyola St., Ste. 302
New Orleans, LA 70112

Maryland
927 North Calvert
Baltimore, MD 21202

Massachusetts
One Kendall Sq., Bldg. 200
Cambridge, MA 02139

Michigan
Historic Fort Wayne
P.O. Box 32-1014
Detroit, MI 48232

Minnesota
514 Nicollet Mall, Ste. 540
Minneapolis, MN 55402

Missouri
4601 Madison Ave.
Kansas City, MO 64112

St. Louis
5615 Pershing, Ste. 27
St. Louis, MO 63112

Western Montana
P.O. Box 9096, 221 E. Front
Missoula, MT 59807

Northern Nevada
P.O. Box 471
Reno, NV 89504

New Jersey
245 Nassau St.
Princeton, NJ 08540

Buffalo
16 Linwood Ave.
Buffalo, NY 14209

New York City
One East 53rd St.
New York, NY 10022

Rochester
935 East Ave.
Rochester, NY 14607

North Carolina
VP Resource, Mgmt., Arts & Science Cncil.
Charlotte, NC 29202

Ohio
Greater Cleveland
4614 Prospect Ave., Ste. 533
Cleveland, OH 44103-4314

Oregon
418 SW Washington, Ste. 400
Portland, OR 97204-2208

Eastern Pennsylvania
2400 Chestnut St., #1410
Philadelphia, PA 19103

Texas
Abilene
T & P Depot, 1101 N. 1st
Abilenbe, TX 79601

Beaumont
P.O.Box 5346
Beaumont, TX 77726-5346

Greater Dallas
145 Travis St., Ste. 201
Dallas, TX 75204-1809

Houston
2515 W. Main & Kirby, Ste. 500
Houston, TX 77098

Utah
9361 South 300 East
Sandy, UT 84070-2998

Virginia
#5 Koger Center, Ste. 216
Norfolk, VA 23502

National Arts and Humanities Councils

Don't overlook the more generous grant programs offered by the following:

National Endowment for the Arts
100 Pennsylvania Avenue, NW
Washington, DC 20506

National Endowment for the Humanities
Washington, DC 20506

Canada Council
P.O. 1047, 99 Metcalf St.
Ottawa, ON, Canada, K1P 5V8

In addition to government grants, there are numerous private foundations and organizations that have grant programs. For information in your state, check with the local arts and humanities councils, or the reference librarian at your local library. There are numerous books about grants that describe available grants, and offer tips about how to write successful proposals. Check into the latest publications of the *Washington International Arts Letter,* 1321 4th St., SW, Washington, DC, 20204, and the materials available from the Foundation Center, 888 Seventh Ave., New York, NY 10019. The Foundation Center also sells computer printouts that list specific grant areas, such as grants for composers.

University libraries are a good place to look for information about grants. Many universities have extensive grant programs that support as substantial amount of their research. The librarians in these facilities are quite familiar with grant programs.

Art Organziations Dealing with Special Populations

Artreach
Dept. of the Arts, UCLA Extension
Los Angeles, CA 90024
213/825-9493

Performing Tree
Los Angeles Unified School District
1320 W. Third St.
Los Angeles, CA 90017
213/482-8830

Artreach
3400 W. 38th Ave.
Denver, CO 80212
303/3433-2882

Hai-Hawaii
330 Wilder Ave., #209
Honolulu, HI 16822
808/537-3111

Audiences Unlimited
Foelinger Ctr., 227 E. Washington Blvd.
Fort Wayne, IN 46802
219/422-1336

Hospital Audiences, Inc.
220 W. 42nd St.
New York, NY 10036
212-575-7676

Access
Durham Arts Council
120 Morris St.
Durham, NC
919/682-5519

Artreach-Dallas, Inc.
P.O. Box 191277
Dallas, TX 75219
214/526-3513

Cultural Experiences Unlimited
P.O. Box 808
Norfolk, VA 23501
804/625-7857

Artreach
152 W. Wisconsin Ave., #434
Milwaukee, WI 53203
414/271-4704

Volunteer Lawyers for the Arts Groups

In deference to the fact that many artists and musicians cannot afford adequate representation, a number of lawyers contribute their time at little or no costs to aid artists in obtaining this help. Volunteer Lawyers for the Arts is a national organization that compiles an annual direcory that lists each of the organizations that offer such help, along with their criteria for eligibility, and what costs they may require for this service. You can purchase this directory by writing to the Volunteer Lawyers for the Arts, 1 East 53rd St., Sixth Floor, New York, NY 10022-4201, 212/319-ARTS. The list printed below is printed with the kind permission of the Volunteer Lawyers for the Arts, without the detailed information about costs and service that appears in their directory.

Cahill, Sutton & Thomas
2141 E. Highland Ave., #5
Phoenix, AZ 85016
602/956-7000

Beverly Hills Bar Association Barristers Committee For The Arts
300 S. Beverly Dr., #201
Beverly Hills, CA 90212
310/553-6644

California Lawyers For The Arts
247 4th St., Ste. 110
Oakland, CA 94607
Fort Mason Center
Building C, Rm. 255
San Francisco, CA 94123
415/775-7200
and 1549 11th St., Ste. 200
Santa Monica, CA 90401
310/395-8893

San Diego Lawyers for the Arts
Law Office of Peter H. Karlem, Esq.
1205 Prospect St., Ste. 400
La Jolla, CA 92037
619/454-9696

Colorado Lawyers for the Arts (CoLa)
200 Grant St., Ste. 303E
Denver, CO 80203
303/722-7994
510/444-6351 and

Connecticut Volunteer Lawyers for the Arts (CTVLA)
Conn. Commission on the Arts
and 227 Lawrence St.
Hartford, CT 06106
203/566-4770

District of Columbia Lawyers Commission For The Arts
Washington Volunteer Lawyers
918 Sixteenth St. NW, Ste. 400
Washington, DC 20006
202/429-0229

Washington Area Lawyers for the Arts
410 8th St., Ste. 601
Washington, DC 20004
202/963-2826

Volunteer Lawyers. for the Arts (Florida) Art Serve Inc.
1350 E. Sunrise Blvd.
Ft. Lauderdale, FL 33304
305/462-9191

Georgia Volunteer Lawyers for the Arts
141 Pryor St. SW, Ste., 2030
Atlanta, GA 30303
404/525-6046

Lawyers for the Creative Arts (LCA)
213 W. Institute Place, Ste. 411
Chicago, IL 60610-3125
312/944-ARTS

Mid-America Arts Resources for the Arts
c/o Susan J. Whitfield-Lungren, Esq.
P.O. Box 363
Lindsborg, KS 67456
913/227-2321

Louisiana Volunteer Lawyers for the Arts (LVLA)
c/o Arts Council of New Orleans
821 Gravier St., Ste. 600
New Orleans, LA 70112
504/523-1465

Maine Attorneys & Accountants for the Arts
25 Center St.
Yarmouth, ME 04096
207/846-0644

Maryland Lawyers for the Arts
218 W. Saratoga St.
Baltimore, MD 21201
410/752-1633

Volunteer Lawyers for the Arts of Massachusetts, Inc.
Office of Arts & Humanities
Boston City Hall, Rm. 716
Boston, MA 02201
617/523-1764

Resources & Counselling for the Arts
729 Landmark Center
75 W. 5th St.
St. Paul, MN 55102
612/292-3206

Kansas City Attorneys for the Arts
c/o Dale Wertz, Marshall Ste. 2-310
500 E. 52nd St.
Kansas City, MO 64110
816/235-5305

St. Louis Volunteer Lawyers and Accountants for the Arts (SLVAA)
3540 Washington
St. Louis, MO 63103
314/652-2410

Montana Volunteer Lawyers for the Arts
c/o Joan Jonkel, esq.
P.O. Box 8687
Missoula, MT 59807
406/721-1835

Lawyers for the Arts New Hampshire
N.H. Business Comm. for the Arts
One Granite Place
Concord, NH 03301
603/224-8300

Albany/Schenectady League of Arts (ALA)
19 Clinton Ave
Albany, NY 12207
518/449-5380

Management Assistance Program Arts Council in Buffalo and Erie County
700 Main St.
Buffalo, NY 14202-1962
716/856-7520

Volunteer Lawyers for the Arts (VLA)
1 E. 53rd St., 6th Floor
New York, NY 10019
212/319-ARTS

North Carolina Volunteer Lawyers for the Arts (NCVLA)
P.O. Box 26513
Raleigh, NC 27611-6513
919/831-6234

Volunteer Lawyers & Accountants for the Arts
c/o Cleveland Bar Association
113 St. Clair Ave., Ste. 225
Cleveland, OH 44114-1253
216/696-3525

Toledo Volunteer Lawyers for the Arts
608 Madison Ave., Ste. 1523
Toledo, OH 43604
419/255-3344

Northwest Lawyers and Arts, Inc.
520 SW Yamhill, Ste. 330
Portland, OR 97204
503/295-2787

Philadelphia Volunteer Lawyers for the Arts (PVLA)
251 S. 18th St.
Philadelphia, PA 19103
215/545-3385

Ocean State Lawyers for the Arts (OSLA)
P.O. Box 19
Saunderstown, RI 02874
401/789-5686

South Dakota Arts Council
30 S. Phillips Ave., Ste. 204
Sioux Falls, SD 57102
605/ 339-6646

Tennessee Arts Commission
320 Sixth Ave. N.
Nashville, TN 37219
615/741-1701

Artists Legal & Accounting Assistance
P.O.Box 2577
Austin, TX 78768
512/338-4458

Texas Accountants & Lawyers for the Arts
2917 Swiss Ave.
Dallas, TX 75204
214/821-1818
and 1540 Sul Ross
Houston, TX 77006
713/526-4876

Utah Lawyers for the Arts (ULA)
P.O. Box 652
Salt Lake City, UT 84110-0652
801/482-5373

appendix   b

Unions and Associations

U.S. Locals of the American Federation of Musicians (AFM)

The union is making a real effort to service today's travelling musicians, and has introduced a 24 hour 800 hotline, which offers immediate legal help to musicians who are having contractual problems with clubs or promoters. The number is **800/ROAD GIG.**

The AFM is currently consolidating some of the smaller locals of the union. Because this process is rapidly changing the jurisdiction of various locals, to find out which local services your territory look in the Yellow Pages under unions. Many of the locals have names likes the Denver Musicians Assoication, or they can be found under the heading American Federation of Musicians.

You can contact the American Federation of Musicians at:

AFM
1501 Broadway, Suite 600
New York, NY 20036,
212/869-1330.
The Internet address is www.afm.org.

The Canadian office is at:

CFM
75 The Donway West
Don Mills, ON M3C 2E9

Songwriters' Associations—U.S.

Note, these addresses often shift as officers of the organizations change. To make sure your information is current check the annual Songwriter's Market, or consult ASCAP, BMI or SESAC.

Arizona Songwriters Association
6103 N. 35th Ave.
Phoenix, 85017
602/624-8276

Los Angeles Songwriters Showcase
National Academy of Songwriters
6255 Sunset Blvd.
Hollywood, CA 90028
213/463-37178
At this writing these two organizations are combining into one group.

Songwriters Guild of America
6340 Sunset Blvd., #317
Hollywood, CA 90028
213/462-1108

Northern California Songwriters
Association
855 Oak Grove,
Menlo Park, CA 94025
415/327-8296

Santa Barbara Songwriters' Guild
Box 22
Goleta, CA 93116
805/967-8864

Rocky Mountain Music Association
Union Station
1701 Wynkoop, Ste. 210
Denver, 80222
303/623-6910

Connecticut Songwriters Association
Box 1292
Glastonbury, CT 06033
203/659-8992

Songwriters' Association of
Washington
1413 K St. NW, First Floor
Washington, DC 20005

North Florida Christian Music
P.O. Box 61113
Jacksonville, FL 33236

Atlanta Songwriters Association
Rm. 21083 Austin Ave., NE
Atlanta, GA 30307
404/522-5730

Indianapolis Songwriters Association,
Inc.
P.O. Box 44724
Indianapolis, IN 46244-0724

Midwest Christian Songwriters
Association
Dept. 2130, 1715 Marty
Kansas City, KS 66103
913/384-3891

Louisville Songwriters Cooperative
P.O. Box 16
Peewee Valley, KY 40056
503/241-1645

Louisiana Songwriters Association
P.O. Box 80425
Baton Rouge, LA 70898-0425
504/924-0804

Southern Songwriters Guild, Inc.
P.O. Box 6817
Shreveport, LA 71136
318/636-6626

Michigan Songwriters Association
28935 Flanders Dr.
Warren, MI 48093
810/771-8435

The Music Network
516 E. Front St.
Traverse City, MI 49686

Missouri Songwriters Association, Inc.
683 Green Forest Dr.
Fenton, MO 63026
314/343-6661

New Jersey & Pennsylvania Songwriters Association
226 E. Lawnside Ave.
Westmont, NJ 08108
609/854-3849

Songwriters & Lyricists Club
Box 23304
Brooklyn, NY 11202-0066

Midwest Songwriters Association
614/279/1892

Songwriters & Poets Critique
11599 Coontz Rd.
Orient, OH 43146
614/877-1727

Red River Songwriters Association
P.O. Box 412
Ft. Towson, OK 74735

Oklahoma Songwriters & Composers Association
c/o Humanities Div., Rose St. College
6420 SE 15th St.
Midwest City, OK 73110

Tulsa Songwriters Association
P.O. Box 254
Tulsa, OK 74101-0254
918/665-3334

Portland Songwriters Association
1920 N. Vancouver
Portland, OR 07227
503/281-0934

Central Oregon Songwriters Association
68978 Graham Ct.
Sisters, 99759-3107
503/549-2053

Pittsburgh Songwriters Association
408 Greenside Ave.
Canonsburg, PA 15317
412/745-9497

Rhode Island Songwriters Association
P.O. Box 301
Harmony, RI 02829-0301
401/949-4181

The Tennessee Songwriters Association
Box 2664
Hendersonville, TN 38077-2664
615/969-5967

Knoxville Songwriters.Association
P.O. Box 603
Knoxville, TN 37901
615/687-0186

Memphis Songwriters Association
1494 Prescott St.
Memphis, TN 38111
901/774/4121

Nashville Songwriters Association
International (NSAI)
15 Music Sq. W.
Nashville, TN 37203
615/256-3354

Austin Songwriters Group
P.O. Box 2578
Austin, TX 78768

Dallas Songwriters Association
7139 Azalea
Dallas, TX 75230
214/750-0916

Utah Songwriters Association
P.O. Box 751325
Salt Lake City, UT 84157
801/596-3058

Vermont Songwriters Association
RD 2, Box 277
Underhill, VT 05489
802/899-3787

The Virginia Organization of
Composers & Lyricists
P.O. Box 34606
Richmond, VA 23234
804/733-5908

Southwest Virginia Songwriter
Association
P.O. Box 698
Salem, VA 24153
703/764-7043

Pacific Northwest Songwriters
Association
Box 98564
Seattle, WA 98198
206/824-1568

Songwriters of Wisconsin
P.O.Box 2578
Neehan, WI 54956
414/725-1609

Songwriters' Organizations—Canada

Pacific Songwriters' Assoc.
Box 15453
349 W. Georgia St.
Vancouver, BC V6B 5B2
604/876-SONG

SODRAC, Inc.
Victoria Square, Ste. 420
Montreal, Quebec H2Y 2J7
Every songwriter whose work is recorded needs
to join one of the performing rights organi-
zations (*indicates main office.)

Performing Rights Organizations—U.S.

The American Society of Composers, Authors and Publishers (ASCAP)
#1 Lincoln Plaza
York, NY 10023
212/595-3050
and Suite 300, 7920 Sunset Blvd.
Los Angeles, CA 90046
213/883-1000
and 2nd Floor, 3500 W. Hubbard St.
Chicago, IL 60610
312/ 481-1194
and 2 Music Sq. W.
Nashville, TN 37203
615/742-5000

Broadcast Music, Inc. (BMI)
320 W. 57th St.
New York, NY 10019
212/586-2000
and 8730 Sunset Blvd.
Los Angeles, CA 90069
310/659-9109
and 10 Music Sq. E.
Nashville, TN 37203
615/291-6700

SESAC Inc.
421 W. 54th St.
New York, NY 10019
212/586-5430
800/826-9996
and 55 Music Sq. E.
Nashville, TN 37203
615/320-0055

Performing Rights Organizations—Canada

Society of Composers, Authors & Music Publishers of Canada (SOCAN)
41 Valleybrook Dr.
Don Mills, ONT M3B 2S6
416/445-8700

Other Music Business Organizations

American Association for Music Therapy
P.O.Box 800112
Valley Forge, PA 19484
610/265-4006
Publishes a journal and newsletter, approves college music therapy programs,
offers job referrals and a list of colleges offering music therapy programs.

American Federation of Radio & Television Artists (AFTRA)
260 Madison Ave.
New York, NY 10016
212/532-0800
A union for radio and television performers, particularly important for singers who do radio or television commercials; regional offices in Atlanta, Boston, Chicago, Cleveland, Dallas-

Fort Worth, Denver, Detroit, Fresno, Honolulu, Houston, Kansas City, Los Angeles, Miami, Milwaukee, Nashville, New Orleans, Omaha, Peoria, Philadelphia, Phoenix, Pittsburgh, Portland OR, Rochester, Sacramento, San Diego, San Francisco, Schnectady-Albany, Seattle, St. Louis, Stamford, Tri-State Indiana-Ohio-Kentucky, Minneapolis-St. Paul, Washington-Baltimore

American Guild of Musical Artists-(AGMA)
1927 Broadway
New York, NY 10019
212/265-3687

Music Critics Association (MCA)
7 Pine Ct.
Westfield, NJ 07090
908/BEETHOVEN

American Symphony Ochestra League ASOL
777 14th St. NW, Washington DC
202/628-0099

Associated Council of the Arts
570 5th Ave.
New York, NY 10018
212/345-6655

Association of Independent Music Publishers
P.O. Box 1561
Burbank CA 91507
818/842-6257
and 120 E. 56th St.
New York, NY 10022
212/758-6157

Black Music Association
1500 Locust St
Philadelphia, PA 19002
215/345-6655

California Copyright Conference
P.O. Box 1291
Burbank, CA 91507-1291
818/848-6783

Canadian Academy of Recording Art (CARAS)
Toronto, ON M4S 2Z2
416/485-3135
and 747 Cardero St.
Vancouver, BC V6G 2G3

Canadian Association for Music Therapy
P.O. Box 2132
Samia, ON N7T 7L1

Canadian Recording Industry
89 Bloor St. E.
Toronto, ON M4W 1A9

Country Music Association (CMA)
Music Circle N.
Nashville, TN 37203
615/244-2820

Gospel Music Association
7 Music Circle N.
Nashville, TN 37203
615/242-0303

Music Educators National Conference
1902 Association Dr.,
Reston, VA 22091
703/860-4000

National Academy of Recording Arts & Sciences (NARAS)
3402 Pico Blvd.
Santa Monica, CA 90405
310/392-3777
There are local chapters of NARAS in Atlanta, Austin, Chicago, Los Angeles, Memphis, Nashville, New York, San

Francisco and Seattle. Others are currently being organized. For detailed information, consult the national office listed above.

National Association for Campus Activities (NACA)
P.O. Box 6828
Columbia, SC 29260
800/732-6222

National Association of Independent Record Distributors (NAIRD)
P.O. Box 988
147 E. Main St., Ste. #2
Whitesburg, KY 41858
606/633-0946

National Association of Music Merchants (NAMM)
5140 Avenida Ensinas
Carlsbad, CA 92008
619/438-8001

National Association of Record Merchandisers (NARM)
11 Eves Dr. Ste. 140
Marlton, NJ 08053
609/596-2221

National Music Publishers Association
711 Third Ave.
New York, NY 10017
212/370-5330

Recording Industry Association (RIAA)
1020 Nineteenth St. NW,
Washington DC 20036
202/775-0101

Society of Audio Professionals (SPARS)
4300 Tenth Ave. N., #2
Lake Worth, FL 33461
SPARS sets up criteria for the profession of audio engineering, and is active in college engineering programs.

Songwriters Guild of America (SGA)
1500 Harbor Blvd.
Weehawken, NJ 07087
201/867-7535

Women in Music National Network
312121 Mission Blvd., Ste. 123
Hayward, CA 94544
510/471-1752
Consult this group for similar organizations in other cities. Members include all music retail chains and most record labels.

appendix C

Education

Degree Programs

For colleges offering two and four year programs in music industry, music merchandising and audio engineering in the United States and Canada, we suggest that you consult the following:

Music Business Programs
MEIEA Guide To Music Business Programs, by Harmon Greenblatt
Available from Dr. Scott Frederickson, Music Business Program, College of Fine Arts, University of Massachusetts-Lowell, Lowell, MA 01854 508/934-3882. This guide is published by The Music and Entertainment Industry Association, the professional organization of the people who teach in music business programs.

Music Engineering Programs
Consult the annual *Mix Directory*, published by MIX, 6400 Hollis St., #12, Emoryville, CA 94608, 510/653-3307. More detailed descriptions of individual programs can be found in Mark Drews' book *New Ears: A Guide to Education in Audio and the Recording Services.* The book is available from New Ears Productions, 1033 Euclid Ave., Syrcause, NY 13210.

Music Merchandising Programs

A free listing is available from the National Association of Music Merchants, (NAMM), 5140 Avenida Encinas, Carlsbad, CA 92008 619/438-8001

Schools Offering Musical Instrument Repair Courses

Trinidad State Junior College
Trinidad, CO 71082
306/846-5011

Western Iowa Technical Community College
Sioux City, IA 51002
712/274-6400

Red Wing Vocational & Technical Institute
Red Wing, MN 55066
612/388-8271

State University of New York Agricultural. & Technical College at Morrisville
Morrisville, NY 13048
315/684-6046

Five Towns College
2165 Seaford Ave., Seaford, NY 11783
516/424-7000

Renton Vocational & Technical Institute
3000 NE, Renton, WA 98056
206/783-8800

Spokane Falls Community College
3140 Fort George Wright Dr.
Spokane, WA 99204
509/459-3500

Publications and Bibliography

Billboard
1515 Broadway
New York, NY 10036

Cashbox
6464 Sunset Blvd., #605
Los Angeles, CA 90028

National Weekly Variety
Cahnors Publishing Company
249 W. 17th St.
New York, NY 10011

Daily Variety
5700 Wilshire Blvd., Ste. 120
Los Angeles, CA 90036
Mostly film and television, but occasional music
coverage and want ads.

Hits
14958 Ventura Blvd.
Sherman Oaks, CA 91403
Hollywood Reporter
5055 Wilshire Blvd., 6th Fl.
Los Angeles, CA 94105

Music City News
50 Music Sq. W., #601
Nashville, TN 37203

Music Row
1231 17th Ave. S.
Nashville, TN 37212
Both *Music City News and Music Row* focus
on country music.

Performance
1110 University Dr., #108
Fort Worth, TX 86107

Pollstar
4333 N. West Ave.
Fresno, CA 93705
Both *Performance* and *Pollstar* focus on live
performances.

Radio and Records
1930 Century Park, W.
Los Angeles, CA 90067

RPM
6 Brentcliff Rd.
Toronto, Ontario M3B2S6 Canada

Songwriter Tip Sheets

Gordon's Flash
1155 N. La Cienaga Blvd., Ste. 1105
Los Angeles, CA 90069

Songcasting
15445 Ventura Blvd.
Sherman Oaks, CA 91403

Music Supervisor 411
SRS Publishing
8491 Sunset Blvd., #771
Los Angeles, CA 90069-1911
For TV and motion pictures.

Song Publisher
P.O. Box 409
East Meadow, NY 11554-0409

Song Placement Guide
885 Vale View Dr.
Vista, CA 92083-6726

Magazines for Songwriters

American Songwriter
121 17th Ave.
Nashville, TN 37203

Singer Songwriter
P.O. Box 257
Wynnewood, PA 19096

Music Publisher 411
SRS Publishing
8491 Sunset Blvd., #771
Los Angeles, CA 90069-1911

Songwriter's Monthly
332 Eastwood Ave.
Feasterville, PA 19053

Performing Songwriter
P.O. Box 158159
Nashville, TN 37215-9998

Words And Music
41 Valleybrook Dr.
Don Mills, ONT M3B 2S6 Canada

Radio Tip Sheets

Album Network
120 N. Victory Blvd.
Burbank, CA 91502

Broadcasting
1735 De Salle St.
Washington, DC 20018

Chart Magazine
PO Box 332, Willowdale Station A
N. York, ONT M2N 5S9, Canada

CMJ New Music Report
11 Middle Neck Rd., Ste. 400
Great Neck, NY 11021-2301

Gavin Report
140 Second St.
San Francisco, CA 94105

Trax Dance Music Guide
111 N. La Cienaga Blvd.
Beverly Hills, CA 10113

Turok's Choice
P.O. Box 202, Old Chelsea Station
New York, NY 10113

Regional Publications

Every local music market has publications that cover the local and regional scenes. Many cities have weekly publications that cover local news and devote a good deal of their coverage to entertainment. Many of these are free and are available at local record and music stores. A comprehensive listing would be longer than the Appendix of this book. A few important ones are listed.

BAM North
3470 Buskirk Ave.
Pleasant Hill, CA 94523

BAM South
6767 Forest Lawn Dr., #110
Los Angeles, CA 90068

Music Connection
6640 Sunset Blvd., #201
Hollywood, CA 90028
This magazine publishes up-dated listings of A&R personnel, managers, agents, and music publishers. It also has frank interviews with various people. (My favorite music trade paper.)

Rocket
2028 5th Ave.
Seattle, WA 98121
Covers Portland as well as Seattle.

Magazines: The Best and Most Interesting

Absolute Sound
2 Glen Ave.
Sea Cliff, NY 11579
Sound reproduction, records, etc.

Acoustic Guitar
412 Red Hill Rd.
San Anselmo, CA 94960

Acoustic Musician
P.O. Box 1349
New Market, VA 22844-1349

American Choral Review
215 Kent Place
Summit, NJ 07091

American Harp Journal
P.O. Box 39334
Los Angeles, CA 90038-0334

American Recorder (the instrument)
P.O. Box 1067
Jackson, NJ 08527

Arts Management
408 W. 57th St.
New York, NY 10019

Audio
P.O. Box 52548
Boulder, CO 80322

Banjo Newsletter
P.O. Box 3418
Annapolis, MD 21403

Bass Player
411 Borel Ave., Ste. 100
San Mateo, CA 94402

Black Music Research Newsletter
c/o Columbia College
600 S. Michigan Ave.
Chicago, IL 60605

Bluegrass Unlimited
P.O. Box 111
Broad Run, VA 22014

Cadence
Cadence Bldg.
Redwood, NY 13769
Modern jazz.

Canadian Compose
41 Valleybrook Dr.
Don Mills, ONT M3B 2S6 Canada

Canadian Musician
23 Hannover Dr., #4
St. Catherines, ONT Z2W 1A3 Canada

Chamber Music America
545 8th Ave.
New York, NY 10018

Coda (modern jazz)
Box 1002, Station 0
Toronto, ONT M4A 2N4 Canada

Dirty Linen
P.O. Box 66600
Baltimore, MD 21239
Folk music

Electronic Musician
6400 Hollis St., #12
Emeryville, CA 94608

Downbeat
190 W. Park Ave.
Elmhurst IL 60126

Ethnomusicology
Morrison Hall, Rm. 005
University of Indiana
Bloomington, IN 47905-2501

Flutist Quarterly
P.O. Box 800597
Santa Monica, CA 91380

Goldmine
Krause Publications
600 E. State St.
Iola, WI 54990

Grammy
c/o NARAS
3402 Pico Blvd., Ste. 903
Santa Monica, CA 90405

Guitar
6 E. 32nd Street, 11th Floor
New York, NY 10016

Guitar One
6 E. 32nd Street, 11th Floor
New York, NY 10016

Guitar Player
411 Borel Ave., Ste. 100
San Mateo, CA 94402

Guitar World
1115 Broadway, 8th Floor
New York, NY 10010

Heartsong Review
P.O. Box 1084
Cottage Grove, OR 97424
New age music

High Performance Review
P. O. Box 2989
Stanford, CA 94305
Performance art.

Instrumentalist
200 Northfield Rd.
Northfield, IL 60093

International Musician
1501 Broadway
New York, NY 10036
Journal of the Musicians Union, includes
want ads for symphony jobs.

Jazz Educators Journal
Box 724
Manhattan, KS 66502

Journal of Country Music
4 Music Sq. E.
Nashville, TN 37203

Journal of Jazz Studies
Rutgers University
135 Bradley Hall
Newark, NJ 07102

Journal of Music Therapy
505 11 St., SE
Washington, DC 20003

Keyboard
411 Borel Ave., Ste. 100
San Mateo, CA 94402

Living Blues
Center for the Study of Southern Culture
University of Mississippi,
University MS 38677

Maximum Rock'n' Roll
P.O. Box 460760
San Francisco, CA 941146
Punk and alternative music.

Millimeter
P.O. Box 95759
Cleveland, OH 44104
Motion picture and TV production.

Mix
6400 Hollis St., #12
Emeryville, CA 94608
Recording studions and recording.

MMR (Music Merchandise Review)
100Wells Ave. P.O. Box 9103
Newton, MA 02159

Modern Liturgy
7921 Coronado Dr.
San Jose, CA 95129

Modern Drummer
P.O. Box 480
Mt. Morris, IL 61054-0480

Musical America
424 W. 33rd St.
New York, NY 10001

Musician
31 Commercial St.
Gloucester, MA 01930

Music Educators Journal
1904 Association Dr.
Reston,VA, 22091

Music Trades
P.O. Box 432
Englewood, NJ 07631

New York Times (Sunday Arts section)
229 W. 43rd St.
New York, NY 10036

No Depression
P.O. Box 31332
Seattle, WA 98103
The alternative country quarterly.

Opera News
Dept. 70, Lincoln Center Plaza
New York, NY 10023-6593

Option
1522 B Cloverfield Bldg.
Santa Monica, CA 90404

Popular Music
Cambridge University Press
Edinburgh Bldg. Shaftesbury Rd.
Cambridge, CB22RV, U.K.

Popular Music & Society
Bowling Green State U.
P.O. Box M
Bowling Green, OH 43043

Pro Sound News
2 Park Ave.
New York, NY 10016

Pulse
2500 Del Monte St., Bldg. C
W. Sacramento, CA 95691
Tower Records monthly guide.

Recording Magazine
5412 Idylwild Trail, Suite 100
Boulder, CO 80301-3523
Musico Pro is the Spanish edition.

Rejoice
Center for the Study of Southern Culture
University of Mississippi
University, MI 38677
Gospel music.

Rolling Stone
745 5th Ave.
New York, NY 10151

Sheet Music
P.O. Box 933
Paramus, NJ 07653

Sing Out: The Folk Song Magazine
P.O. Box 5253
Bethlehem, PA 18015-0253

Stereo Review
P.O. Box 55627
Boulder, CO 80322-5627

Up Beat
190 W. Park Ave.
Elmhurst IL 60126
For music retailers.

Washington International Arts Letter
P.O. Box 12010
Des Moines, IA 50312

Windplayer
P.O. Box 2666
Malibu, CA 90265

Books: The Top Eight

The "Top Eight" books will give you a good general picture of the music business. The bibliography that follows them consists of other music books with useful information.

Braheny, John. *The Craft and Business of Songwriting*. Cincinnati: Writer's Digest Books, 1987. John Braheny probably knows as much as anyone abut how songs are created and merchandised.

Flanagan, Bill. *Written In My Soul: Conversations With Rock's Greatest Songwriters*. Chicago: Contemporary Books, 1987. Flanagan interviewed a number of important songwriters and examines their creative processes.

Laufenberg, Cindy, Ed. *1996 Songwriter's Market*. Cincinnati: Writer's Digest, 1996. An essential guide for songwriters.

Rapaport, Diane Sward. *How To Make and Sell Your Own Record*. 4th ed. New York: Prentice Hall, 1994, An important resource for anyone who contemplates producing and/or market-ing his own record or tape.

Shemel, Sidney and Krasilovsky, Wm. *This Business of Music, and More About This Business of Music*. 7th ed. New York: Billboard Publications, 1995 Hard to read, but you need it on your bookshelf.

Small, Christopher. *Music .Society. Education*. New York: Schirmer Books, 1977. A wonderful book about music, education and society.

Wallis, Roger and Malm, Krister. *Big Sounds From Small Peoples: The Music Industry In Small Countries*. New York: Pendragon Press, 1984. A superb and thought-provoking book.

Weissman, Dick. *The Music Business: Career Opportunities and Self-Defense.* 2nd rev. ed. New York: Crown Publishers, 1977. Mix Bookshelf, 6400 Hollis St., #12, Emoryville, CA 94608, 800-223-9604 or in California

800-641-3349 has a detailed catalog of books on this subject. It also includes audio and video tapes, music software and books on the music business.

Audio Engineering

Bigelow, Steven. *Making Music With Personal Computers.* La Jolla, CA: Park Row Press, 1988.

Computers

Yelton, Geary. *Music and the Macintosh.* Decatur, GA: Midi Amer., 1990.
Bennett, H. Stith. *On Becoming a Rock Musician.* Amherst: University of

Massachusetts Press, 1980. Difficult reading, but worth it.

Cultural Study of Music

Chapple, Steve and Garafalo, Reebee. *Rock 'n' Roll Is Here to Pay.* Chicago: Nelson-Hall, 1977. Dated but useful.

Ewbank, Alison J. and papageorgiou, Fouli T. *Whose Master's Voice: The Development of Popular Music in Thirteen Cultures.* Westport, CT: Greenwood Press, 1997. It's a global music business, remember.

Frith, Simon. *Sound Effects: Youth, Leisure and the Politics of Rock 'n' Roll.* New York: Pantheon Books, 1981.

Garfield, Simon. *Money for Nothing: Greed and Exploitation in the Music Industry.* Boston, Faber & Faber, 1986.

Hebdige, Dick. *Cut 'n' Mix: Culture, Identity and Caribbean Music.* New York, Methuen & Co., 1986.
Rahn, Jay. *A Theory for all Music: Problems and Solutions in the Analysis of Non-Western Forms.* Toronto: University of Toronto Press, 1982.

Street, John. *Rebel Rock: The Politics of Popular Music.* London: Basil Blackwell, 1986.

Taylor, Timothy D. *Global Pop: World Music World Markets.* New York: Routledge, 1997. This book studies specific pop artists from around the world. *Note:* Routledge Press publishes many books on cultural studies that touch on music and media.

Film

There are many useful books on the technique of writing film scores. Business aspects are detailed in the following books.

Faulkner, Robert A. *Music on Demand: Composers and Careers in the Hollywood Film Industry.* New Brunswick, NJ: Transaction Books, 1982.

Rona, Jeff. *Synchronization from Reel to Reel.* Milwaukee, WI: Hal Leonard, 1995.

Legal and Economic Matters

Biederman, Donald and Berry, Pierson, Silfer and Glasser. *Law and Business in the Entertainment Industries.* Dover, MA: Auburn House Publishing Co., 1987. Informative and very "lawyerish."

Muller, Peter. *Music Business, a Legal Perspective.* New York: Greenwood Press, 1993.

Vogel, Harold L. *Entertainment Industry Economics.* Rev. ed. Cambridge, England: Cambridge University Press, 1995.

Copyright

Chickering, Robert B. and Hartman, Susan. *How to Register a Copyright and Protect Your Creative Work.* New York: Charles Scribner's Sons, 1987.

Nimmer, Melville B., et. al. *Entertainment Litigation including Unfair Competition, Defamation, Privacy.* 4th ed. St. Paul: West, 1991.

Weinstein, David A. *How to Protect Your Creative Work.* New York: John Wiley & Sons, 1987.

Wilson, Lee. *The Copyright Guide.* New York: Allworth Press, 1996.

Commercials

Karmen, Steve. *Through the Jingle.* New York: Billboard Books, 1989.

Also see Resources, Chapter 7.

State Arts Councils

Azerad, Michael. *Screaming Life: A Chronicle of the Seattle Music Scene.* San Francisco: Harper Collins West, 1995. Contains a CD and many photographs by Charles Peterson.

Berry, Jason, Foose & Jones. *Up from The Cradle of Jazz: New Orleans Music Since World War II.* Athens, Ga: University of Georgia Press, 1986. A superb book.

Bowman, Rob. *Soulsville USA: The Story of Stax Records.* New York: Schirmer Books, 1997. A detailed study of Stax and the Memphis music scene.

Endres, Clifford. *Austin City Limits.* Austin: University of Texas Press, 1987. The story of the television show, plus information on the local music scene.

McDonough, Jack. *San Francisco Rock: The Illustrated History of San Francisco Rock.* San Francisco: Chronicle Books, 1985.

Morrell, Brad. *Nirvana and the Sound of Seattle.* New York: Omnibus Press, 1996.

Reid, Jan. *The Improbable Rise of Redneck Rock.* New York: De Capo, 1977. A useful if subjective exploration of the roots of the Austin scene.

Willoughby, Larry. *Texas Rhyme.* Austin: Texas Monthly Press, 1984.

Also see Resources, Chapter 15.

Music Business in Canada

Coxson, Mona. *Some Straight Talk about the Music Business.* 2nd ed. Toronto: CM Books, 1989 Strong opinions, generally worthy of your consideration. One of the few available books about the Canadian music business.

Jennings, Nicholas. B*efore the Gold Rush: Flashbacks to the Dawn of the Canadian Sound.* Toronto: Viking Press, 1997.

Also see Resources, Chapter 16 for the invaluable Music Directory, Canada.

Music Business in General

Barrow, Tony and Newby, Julius. *Inside the Music Business.* London: Routledge, 1995. The best book I have found about the music business in England.

Baskerville, David. *Music Business Handbook & Career Guide.* Thousand Oaks, CA: Sage Publications, 1995. Dr. Baskerville was a pioneer in the field of music business education.

Burlingame, Jon. *For the Record*. Hollywood: Recording Musicians Association, 1997. A history of the RMA, an organization of recording musicians within the Musicians' Union.

Davison, Marc. *All Area Access: Personal Management for Unsigned Musicians*. Milwaukee, Hal Leonard Corp., 1997. This is really a book on self management for musicians. It is extremely detailed and should convince 98% of musicians why they need a personal manager and an agent if they plan to pursue a national career.

Dearing, James, W. *Making Money Making Music (No Matter Where You Live)*. Cincinnati: Writer's Digest, 1990. Some useful tips, but a bit too much detail for most musicians.

Eskelin, Gerald. *Lied My Music Teacher Told Me*. Woodland Hills, CA: Stage 3 Publishing, 1994. Deals with the disparity between the way music is usually taught and how it is actually performed.

Gibson, James. *How You Can Make $30,000 a Year without a Record Contract*. Cincinnati: Writer's Digest Books, 1986. Good if you are a well-organized person willing and able to book yourself; offers some useful options for local employment.

Hall, Charles W. and Taylor, Frederick J. *Marketing in the Music Industry*. Needham Heights, MA: Simon & Schuster Custom Publishing, 1996.

Hull, Geoffrey P. *The Recording Industry*. Needham Heights, MA: Allyn and Bacon, 1998. Some useful charts and numbers, but quite dry.

Johnson, Jeff. *Careers For Music Lovers & Other Tuneful Types*. Lincoln Wood, IL: VGM Career Horizons, 1997. Interviews with professionals.

Kashif. *Everything You'd Better Know about the Music Industry*. Venice, CA: Brooklyn Boy, 1995. Very oriented towards commercial music.

Monaco, Bob & Riordan, James. *The Platinum Rainbow: How to Succeed in the Music Business without Selling Your Soul*. Rev. ed. Sherman Oaks, CA: Swordsman Press, 1988.

Nagger, David and Brandstetter, Jeffrey D., Esqs. *The Music Business Explained in Plain English*. San Francisco: Daje Publishing, 1995. If you've never read anything about the music business, this book packs a surprising amount of information in one skinny volume.

Passman, Donald S. *All You Need to Know about the Music Business*. 2nd rev. ed. New York: Simon & Schuster, 1997. Passman is a top entertainment attorney in Hollywood, and his book, though written in a somewhat irritating wise-guy style, contains a lot of useful information.

Wacholtz, Larry. *Star Tracks: Principles for Success in the Music and Entertainment Business.*. Nashville: Thumbs Up Publishing, 1995.

Music Industry Careers

Field, Shelly. *Career Opportunities in the Music Industry.* New York: Facts On File Publications, 1986.

Kaplan, G. Ann. *Music Video Rocking Around the Clock: Music Television, Postmodernism & Consumer Culture.* New York: Methugn, 1987. A cultural study of music video.

Millard, Andre. *America on Record: A History of Recorded Sound.* Cambridge: Cambridge University Press, 1995.

Personal Management

Dumler, Egon & Cushman, Robert F. *Entertainers & Their Professional Advisers.* Hollywood, IL: Dow Jones-Irwin, 1987. Covers many topics dealing with other areas of entertainment, such as the movie business. There is an excellent fifteen page chapter on personal management by long-time manager Dee Anthony.

Eliot, Marc. *Down Thunder Road: The Making of Bruce Springsteen.* New York. Simon & Schuster, 1992. This book was written with the participation of Mike Appel, Springsteen's former manager. Its primary value is to see the perspective of a hard-working and frankly, greedy starmaker.

Frascogna, Xavier M. Jr., & Hetherington, H. Lee. *Successful Artist Management.* 3rd rev. ed. New York: Billboard Publications, 1997.

Kragen, Ken with Jefferson, Graham. *Life Is a Contact Sport: Ten Great Career Strategies That Work.* New York: William Morrow & Co., 1994. Kragen is an incurable optimist, and these are his shrewd guidelines for success.

Rose, Frank. *The Agency: William Morris and the Hidden History of Show Business.* New York: Harper Business, 1995. A very detailed and useful book.

Promotion—Concerts and Records

Stein, Howard & Zallkind, Ron. *Promoting Rock Concerts.* New York: Schirmer Books, 1979. A systemactic and sensible presentation.

O'Shea, Shad. *Just for the Record.* Cincinnati: Positive Feedback Press, 1986. Amusing and rather longwinded on many aspects of the music business. The section on promoting records in local and regional markets is useful and coherent.

Publicity

Gibson, James. *Getting Noticed: A Musician's Guide to Publicity & Self-Promotion.* Cincinnati: Writer's Digest Books, 1987. There are many useful ideas in this book, sometimes overwhelmed by its sheer mass of detailed suggestions.

Pinsky, Raleigh. *101 Ways to Promote Yourself.* New York: Avon Books, 1997.

See Resources, Chapter 3.

Radio

Hall, Claude & Barbara. *This Business of Radio Programming.* New York: Billboard Publications, 1977. An excellent book-needs updating to follow the changes in radio formats and programming.

Halper, Donna L. *Radio Music Directing.* Boston: Focal Press, 1991.

Note: There are many books by former disc jockeys about their lives in the business. Although most of these books are amusing, they rarely offer much in the way of hard facts.

Recording (History and Discussion, not Technical Audio)

Eisenberg, Even. *Explorations in Phonography.* New York: McGraw-Hill Books, 1987. Thoughtful and opinionated esssays about various aspects of recording.

Gelatt, Roland. *The Fabulous Phonograph.* New York: Collier Books, 1977.

Read, Oliver & Welch, Walter C. *From Tin Foil to Stereo.* 2nd ed. Indianapolis: Howard W. Sams, 1976.

Record Production

Burgess, Richard James. *The Art of Record Production.* London: Omnibus Press, 1997. A good guide to current techniques and producers.

Cunningham, Mark. *Good Vibrations: A History of Record Production.* Surrey, UK: Castle Communications, 1996. This book is very focused on English Music.

Lambert, Denny & Zalkind, Ron. *Producing Hit Records.* New York: Schirmer Books, 1980.

Stokes, Geoffrey. *Star-Making Machinery.* Indianapolis: Bobbs-Merrill, 1976. A detailed description of how Commander Cody recorded an album, plus a lot of informative details on how a record deal is negotiated with a major company.

Tobler, John & Grundy, Stuart. *The Record Producers*. New York: St. Martin's Press. Another book of interviews.

White, Paul. *Recording and Production Techniques for the Recording Musician*. London: Sanctuary Publishing Corp., undated.

See Resources, Chapter 9.

Songwriting and Music Publishing

Citron, Stephen. *Songwriting*. New York: William Morrow & Co., 1985. A good general guide.

Davis, Sheila. *The Craft of Lyric Writing*. Cincinnati: Writer's Digest Books, 1985.

Davis, Sheila. *Successful Lyric Writing: A Step by Step Course & Workbook*. Cincinnati: Writer's Digest Books, 1988. Davis' books are excellent resources for serious students of the song lyric. They include many detailed examples, and thoughts about how the revision process works.

Hall, Tom T. *The Songwriter's Handbook*. Nashville: Rutledge Hill Press, 1987. Hall is one of the masters of story songs; he explains how he writes songs, and why you can too.

Kasha, Al and Hirschorn, Joel. *If They Ask You, You Can Write a Song*. New York: Simon & Schuster, 1979. A good general guide to the craft of songwriting.

Kosser, Michael. *How to Become a Successful Nashville Songwriter*. Nashville: Porch Swing Press, 1981. Contains good, practical information, especially about the process of collaboration.

Mahonin, Valerie. *Market Your Songs*. Calgary: Songsmith Publications, 1986. A guide to marketing songs in Canada.

Pattison, Pat. *Writing Better Lyrics*. Cincinnati: Writer's Digest, 1995. You may not agree with everything here, but it should give you plenty of ideas to think about.

Pickow, Peter & Appleby, Amy. *The Billboard Book of Songwriting*. New York: Billboard Publications, 1988. Excellent, with many references to current songs.

Whitsett, *Tim. Music Publishing: The Real Road to Music Business Success*. Emeryville, CA: Mix Books, 1997. A very detailed and useful guide.

See Resources, Chapter 11.

Studio Work

Faulkner, Robert A. *Hollywood Studio Musicians: Their Work and Careers in the Recording Industry*. Chicago: Aldine-Atherton, 1971. A superb study of the nature and evolution of careers in the world of the recording studio.

Women in Music

Drinker, Sophie. *Music and Women.* New York: Coward McCann, 1948. The essential book on the role of women in music and music making.

Placksin, Sally. *Women in Jazz, 1900 to the Present.* Distributed by Putnum, Wideview Books, 1982.

Whitly, Sheila, Ed. *Sexing the Groove: Popular Music and Gender.* London: Routledge, 1997. 16 articles by various writers.

Zaimont, Judith Lang, Ed. *Women in Music: An International Perspective.* Vols. I and II. New York: Greenwood Press, 1983, 1986.

Musical Styles

Classical Music

Epstein, Helen. *Music Talks: Conversations with Working Musicians.* New York: McGraw Hill, 1987. A revealing book about famous and lesser known classical musicians and teachers.

Furlong, William Barry. *Season with Solti.* New York: Macmillan, 1974. A fascinating study of the interactions of players in the Chicago Symphony.

Hart, Philip. *Orpheus in the New World.* New York: Norton, 1973. A detailed and informative study of the symphony orchestra in the United States.

Country Music

Hemphill, Paul. *The Nashville Sound: Bright Lights & Country Music.* New York: Pocket Books, 1971. Contains many valuable insights.

Willis, Barry R. *America's Music: Bluegrass.* Franktown, Colorado: Pine Valley Music, distributed by Mel Bay, 1997. An encyclopedic work.

Jazz

Spellman, A.B. *Four Lives in the Bebop Business.* New York: Schoken Books, 1970. Some editions of this book are called *Black Music, Four Lives.* A sobering book on the difficulties of making a living as a jazz artist.

Rock And Roll

Friedlander, Paul. *Rock and Roll: A Social History.* Boulder, Colorado: Westview Press, 1996. Particularly good for 1950s and '60s rock.

Garofalo, Reebee. *Rockin' Out: Popular Music in the USA.* Boston: Allyn and Bacon, 1997. Garofalo is an excellent commentator on the relationship between music and culture.

Gillette, Charlie. *The Sound of the City.* New York: Dutton, 1970. Still the best overall history of rock.

Rap

Rose, Tricia. *Black Noise: Rap Music and Black Culture in Contemporary America.* Hanover, NH: Wesleyan University Press, 1994. The best book to date.

There are many interesting autobiographical works by rappers, including Ice T, Chuck D, and L.L. Cool J.

Blues & Soul

Peter Guralnick is a superb, sympathetic writer with fine musical sensibilities. The first two books also include some material on country music.

Guralnick Peter. *Feel Like Goin' Home: Portraits in Blues & Rock 'n' Roll.* New York: Random House, 1981.

Guralnick Peter. *Lost Highway: Journeys & Arrivals of American Musicians.* Boston: David Godine, 1979.

Guralnick Peter. *Sweet Soul Music: Rhythm & Blues and the Southern Dream of Freedom.* New York: Harper & Row, 1986.

The Chicago Public Library has an excellent bibliography of books, periodicals and directories on the business of music, which they actually stock. Write to Music Information Center, Visual & Performing Arts, Chicago Public Library, 78 E. Washington, Chicago, IL 60602, 312/269-2886.

MIDI, Sampling, Drum Machines, etc.

Boom, Michael. *Music Through MIDI: Using MIDI to Create Your Own Electronic Music System.* Belleview, Washington: Microsoft Press, 1987.

Edited by Editors of Guitar Player Magazine. *Guitar Synth & MIDI.* Steven Creek, CA, 1988.

Dominic Milano, Ed. *Mind over MIDI.* Steven Creek, CA: GPI, 1988.

Rona, Jerffrey C. *MIDI: The Ins Outs & Thrus.* Milwaukee: Hal Leonard Books, 1987/1989, Easy to follow and entertaining.

Tomlyn, Bo and Leonard, Steve. *Electronic Music Dictionary.* Hal Leonard, 1988.

Etc...

Kaye, Deena and Le Brecht, James. *Sound and Music for the Theatre.* New York: Back Stage Books, 1992.

Mandell, Jim. *The Studio Business Book.* 2nd rev.ed., Emeryville, CA: Mix Books, 1995.

Schuyler, Nina. *The Business of Multimedia.* New York: Allworth Press, 1995.

Shagen, Rena. *Booking and Tour Management for the Performing Arts.* New York: Allworth Press, 1996. A practical guide to touring.

Sievert, Jon. *Concert Photography.* San Francisco: Humble Press, 1997. A unique guide.

Directories and Other Publications

Billboard, Musical America, Performance and *Pollstar* all publish annual guides that variously list venues, agents, managers and all sorts of information about recording. Two other useful guides are the *Recording Industry Sourcebook,* available from Sourcebook, 3301 Barham Blvd., Suite 300, Los Angeles, CA 90068, and *The Yellow Pages of Rock,* available from The Album Network, 120 N. Victory Blvd., Burbank, CA 91502.

Miscellaneous Books for Musicians

Buttwinick, Marty. *How to Make a Living as a Musician.* Glendale, CA: Sonata Publishing, 1993. Career Strategies for the Working Musician.

Halloran, Mark, Ed. *The Musician's Business & Legal Guide.* Englewood Cliffs, NJ: Prentice Hall, 1991. A collection of articles of varying value.

Hustwit, Gary. *Releasing an Independent Record.* San Diego, CA: Rock Press, 1995, Fifth Edition. Strategies, directories, etc.

Kohn, Al and Bob. *The Art of Music Licensing.* Englewood Cliffs, NJ: Prentice Hall, 2nd ed. 1997. Describes every conceivable music license. Not for the novice.

Stanfield, Jana. A *Musician's Guide to Outrageous Successs: Making and Selling CDs and Cassettes.* Nashville: Jana Stans Tunes Music, 1996. Includes a section on cyberspace marketing.

Instructional Audio and Videotapes

Jamey Abersold
P.O. Box 1244
New Albany, IN 47150
Many jazz instructional tapes and CDs.

Homespun Tapes
Box 694 F
Woodstock, NY 12498
Audio and video instructional tapes for folk,bluegrass, country music and jazz.

Music Minus One Records
50 Executive Blvd.
Elmsford, NY 10523
A pioneering company in this field.

Alfred Music, Mel Bay Publications, Hal Leonard, Music Sales Corp. and Warner Bros. Publications all produce taped instructional materials. For addresses see the list of music print publishers following.

Promotional Tools

ABRACADABRA, c/o Rick Abramson, 1010 Palm Avenue, West Hollywood, CA 90069 supplies a catalog of T-shirts, mugs and other such giveaways that a band can use to promote itself or to sell to fans. Look for similar companies in your city or region.

Alternative Radio Lists

Lists are available in various styles of music from Icebird Record Company, P.O. Box 216, Lakebay, WA 98349, 206/884-9705. The lists are available on disk or in printed form.

Music Print Publishers

Most music publishers no longer print music. They exist for the purpose of getting artists to record songs that the publishers own. These publishers then receive revenue from record sales, performances on radio and television, and other uses of their songs.

The publishers listed below print sheet music collections and instructional folios.

Alexander Publishing
3537 Old Conejo Rd., Ste. 101,
Newbury Park, CA 91320
Specializes in high-tech oriented music.

Alfred Music Publishing, Inc.
16380 Roscoe Blvd., P.O. Box 10003,
Van Nuys, CA 91406
School band, choral and instructional books.

Mel Bay Publications
4 Industrial Dr.
Pacific, MO 63069
Guitar, instrumental methods and collections.

Cherry Lane Music Co.
6 E. 32nd St., 11th Floor
New York, NY 10016
Heavy metal and rock and pop material.

Hal Leonard Corp.
7777 W. Bluemound Rd.
Milwaukee, WI 53213
Pop, standards, rock, band and choral music. Distributes other publishers.

Music Sales Corp.
257 Park Ave. S.
New York, NY 10003
A strong catalog in folk-related instructional materials. Also includes jazz and rock publications.

Theodore Presser
Presser Bldg.
Bryn Mawr, PA 19010
Classical collections and methods. Distributes much European music.

Warner Brothers Publications
15800 NW 48th Ave.
Miami , FL 33014
Pop, classical, rock and music for school bands and choral groups.

A great resource for books about the music business is the Music Books Plus catalog. Call 1-800-265-8481 to get one.

Biography:

Richard Weissman

Education:

Goddard College	B.A. Black Studies
	Thesis: *Leadbelly, His Life and Music*
University of Colorado at Denver	B.A. Music, Theory & Composition
University of Oklahoma	M.L.S. Sociology of Music
	Thesis: *Performing Original Music in Public:*
	A Study of Thirty Full and Part-Time
	Musicians

Professional Experience

1998 -	Chair, Professional Studies Dept., UCD College of Arts and Media
1996 -	Associate Professor of Music (tenured) University of Colorado at Denver
1991-1997	Wrote music for three Oil, Coke, Chemical and Atomic Workers national conventions; a play about Karen Silkwood; wrote ten songs for OCAW cassette
1990-1996	Assistant Professor of Music, University of Colorado at Denver
1988-1990	Instructor, Music Management, Colorado Institute of Art

1987-1988   National Education Coordinator, NARAS (National Academy of Recording Arts & Sciences)

1987-1992   Half-time Instructor of Music, Colorado Women's College

1977-1987   Coordinator and teacher, Musicians & Songwriters' Workshop, Colorado Mountain College, Breckenridge, CO

1960-   Author, record producer, recording musician, songwriter (over 60 recorded songs and instrumental pieces). Songs recorded by Judy Collins, Every Mother's Son, Merv Griffin, Kingston Trio, Peter, Paul and Mary, Carly Simon, etc; composed two feature film scores

Books

1999   Weissman, R. *Making a Living in Your Local Music Market.* Rev. ed. Hal Leonard Corp.

1997   Weissman, R. *The Music Business, Career Opportunities & Self Defense.* 2nd rev. ed. Crown Publications

1997   Ed. *Bluegrass, America's Music.* By Barry Willis. Dist. Mel Bay

1994   Weissman, R. *Creating Melodies.* Writer's Digest

1990   Weissman, R. *Making a Living in Your Local Music Market.* Hal Leonard Corp.

1989   Sandberg, L. & Weissman, R. *The Folk Music Sourcebook.* Da Capo Press. Rev. ed. Book originally published by Alfred Knopf, 1976.

1983   Weissman, R. *Making Music in America.* Frederick Ungar

During the past few years have published numerous articles in *Acoustic Guitar, Come All Ye, International Musician* and *Recording Magazine.*

Recordings Performed or Produced

1998   *Reflections.* A CD of original compositions. Folk Era

1998   *Ron Brentano: A Pilgrim in Life & Music*

1995   *American Dreams.* Folk Era CD 1419

1992   *New Traditions.* Folk Era CD 1400

1995-1997   Played on over 1,000 recording sessions, produced over 80 albums for Capitol, Warner Brothers and many smaller labels.

Recognitions, Honors, Etc.

1999   *Crossroads Magazine* Alternate winner, Acoustic Music Recording of the year *(Reflections)*

1998:   UCD College of Arts & Media Outstanding Research/Creative Prof.

1998	University of Colorado, $3,500 grant for Peggy Seeger, lecture-performance
1997	University of Colorado $750 mini-grant for visiting lecturer on the blues
1997	UCD Urban University grant to start a music program at the Denver Children's Home
1994-1995	UCD Faculty Fellowship to research a book on 20th century American multicultural vernacular music
1993	Outstanding Research/Creative Professor, UCD School of the Arts
1991	Parent's Choice Award for a children's recording produced for David and Helene Van Manen
1990	Grant from Boulder Arts Commission for a performance art piece
1984-1987	Artist, Colorado Council on the Arts & Humanities Artist in Residence Program
1983	NEH College Teacher's Fellowship
1977	Deems Taylor ASCAP Music Critic's Award for *The Folk Music Sourcebook*

Other Recent Professional Activities

1997	Did a one week residence at the Liverpool Institute for Performing Arts in England, an inter-disciplinary arts program that includes students from all over the world
1997	Wrote and arranged three songs and twenty instrumental cues for a performance at the national convention of the Oil, Coke, Chemical & Atomic Workers Union in Las Vegas for the Study of Popular Music (IASPM) at UCD
1996-1998	Executive Board, Neighborhood Arts Council of Denver

Index